RADICALS AND CONSERVATIVES

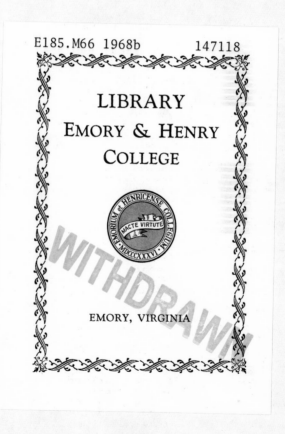

Sourcebooks in Negro History

RADICALS AND CONSERVATIVES

And Other Essays on the Negro in America

Kelly Miller

Introduction by Philip Rieff

SCHOCKEN BOOKS · NEW YORK

CONTENTS

INTRODUCTION

BY PHILIP RIEFF

KELLY MILLER was one of the dominant intel-
lects of black America from the turn of the century
to the nineteen thirties. In 1934, Miller retired
from his alma mater, Howard University, after
long and distinguished membership in that institution, first in mathematics and then as Professor
of Sociology—and, from 1907 to 1918, as Dean of
the College. He died in 1939.

Miller was born in South Carolina, in 1863, the
son of a free Negro tenant farmer and his slave
wife. A paternal uncle served in the state legislature during Reconstruction. The young Kelly
Miller was lucky, in a classical way: the bright,
doomed peasant boy was given a chance to raise
himself by a churchman, who, correctly reading
the signs of intellectual promise, helped him into a
better school. By 1886, Kelly Miller had worked
his way through Howard, meanwhile saving
enough money from his outside job in the United
States Pension Office to buy his parents a farm
as *his* graduation gift to them. Miller thus inverted
the customary ritual exchange between parents
and children of higher social strata; here, upon the
occasion of the graduation gift, the child gave to
the parents. Further details of Miller's life and
career are easily accessible in the article on him,
in the *Dictionary of American Biography* (Supplement 2), pp. 456–457, by his even more distinguished successor to the Chair of sociology at

Howard, E. Franklin Frazier; I refer the reader
to that article.

The essays in this volume were written by
Miller for various magazines or as polemical pam-
phlets published separately and first collected by
him in 1908 under the main title, *Race Adjustment*.
This book has been out of print for more than a
generation.

As Miller himself realized, I think, W. E. B.
DuBois was the supreme intellect of black America
during his own time. DuBois was Miller's superior
both as writer and scholar. In the leading (and
now titular) essay of this book, Miller acknowledges DuBois' "extraordinary scientific and literary talent." However, part of Miller's analysis of
DuBois' early career should be read against the
history of rivalry between men equally passionate
in their devotion to that justice and welfare which
they knew, with equal subtlety, their people
would have to acquire for themselves, through
continuing struggle with the American experience.
In the first years of the twentieth century, the
leadership of the new militants, gathering around
that fascinating Harvard contemporary of DuBois,
William Monroe Trotter, editor of the *Boston
Guardian*, might have fallen to Miller. But Miller
was no 'radical'; the mantle of militancy passed
swiftly from Trotter to a figure no less angular
and aristocratic, DuBois.

The earliest excellence to appear in this book
is Miller's own reflection on radicals and conservatives, as types, among the leaders of black America
in Miller's own time. I shall concentrate the main
part of this introductory essay upon a brief analysis of what radicalism and conservatism may
mean, when drawn along the color line, then and

now. In Part II, as a coda, I shall draw some implications for the rise of black militancy within the context of the larger and deeper revolutionary crisis of western culture. After the titular essay, many other pieces of wisdom remain here to be found by the reader: Miller's reflections on "Surplus Negro Women"; the iron courtesy with which he frames his irrefutable denunciation of a white racist literary gent, Thomas Dixon, Jr., who was the author of that *Birth of a Nation* upon which D. W. Griffith based his great and vicious film; Miller's passionate reading of Whitman; his "Brief for Higher Education." In fact, all the essays following "Radicals and Conservatives" remain usable sources for the contemporary reader's knowledge of the inner history of black America.

I

As Miller tells us, it is nonsense to imagine that any reflective Negro can be satisfied with the condition of his existence in American society. In this sense, there are no conservative blacks. Precisely in the face of white caste defensiveness and racial ambivalence, how could any self-respecting Negro be conservative? "Every consideration of enlightened self-respect impels him to unremitting protest." The latent thought behind this manifest truth is constantly present in this volume: protest is itself, in the oppressive condition of Negro life, a function of self-respect. Yet there remain two major questions: first, the *form* of protest, whether lawful or unlawful (Miller is straightforwardly for lawful protest); second, the *ubiquity* of the oppressive condition. Miller and his generation of black leaders were quite clear about the terrible condition of the Negro people. Yet none adopted some apocalyptic fantasy-theory of a deeper disorder, in which Negroes, as the prisoners of a racist social structure, rattle their chains also against high culture, oppressive somehow even in its most sublime expressions. There was no disagreement in *theory* among the Negro leaders of Miller's time: all must protest and seek a fundamental change in the order of black and white America. But such protest had nothing whatever to do with apocalyptic theories of a saving disorder or a liberating chaos of destruction. The black leaders were deeply committed, in their own persons, to high culture, and to its ideas of law and order. Their disagreements were mainly, then, about the *tactics* of orderly change.

About the tactics of orderly change, based, as all tactics must be, upon estimates of one's own weaknesses as compared with the enemy's particular strengths, there were, in Miller's time as in our own, continuing disagreements. Miller refused to take a dogmatically rigid position, militant or moderate. Tactics have to be adjusted, as he rightly said, "to the dictates of prudence." The radicals of the Trotter-DuBois school were embarked, with the second manifesto of the "Niagara Movement" (called into being by DuBois in 1905), on a course of "verbal vehemence void of practical power to enforce demands" against the strongholds of racism. On the other hand, the dominant conservatives, led by Booker T. Washington, were not vehement enough, too prudent before the structured impulse cruelties of white society, too accommodating before racist fantasies passed off as recondite science or common knowledge about the permanent (because inherent) inferiority of blacks in a high culture that was never to be their own. To the radicals, these Negro conservatives looked like sycophants, court jesters without courage and wit enough to goad the ruling race in the right direction—toward a society freed from racist grotesquerie.

In Miller's long view, the tactical range of opposition to white racism must include both radicals and conservatives. There was no doubt in his mind that the "Niagara Movement" would grow out of its "declamatory stage" and become "tempered by dealing with the actualities of the situation." Miller's expectation was justified by historical developments. To be truly creative, militant movements must institutionalize the newly released energies. By 1909, the "Niagara Movement" invested its new energies as the NAACP. Thus the militants contributed something vital, as Miller thought they would, to the "many agencies working together for the general cause."

Miller did what he could to push Washington and the conservatives, beyond their programs of racial self-strengthening, toward the necessary risks of anti-racist demands and programs. He rightly judged and accepted Washington as a "practical opportunist, accepting the best terms which he thinks it possible to secure." But there was a tactical trap into which a conservative leader such as Washington might fall all too easily: a permanent acceptance of the best terms of one encounter with racism as necessarily the best terms of subsequent encounters. Miller took it upon himself publicly to urge Washington, who was vulnerable from the black side of the color line because of his obvious usefulness on the white side,[1] not to be content with the constricting "practical" achievements which, even if they succeeded, would cut off the Negro from his just chances of leading the life of the mind. At a banquet, in proposing a toast to the greatness of Booker T. Washington, in the very face of the great man himself, Miller included an implicit threat that Washington's leadership was far from unconditionally acceptable. On the contrary, it was important for Washington not to take too seriously the "sycophantic adulation" with which he liked to be surrounded. In some phrases hard with Miller's usual iron courtesy in criticism, Washington was advised that he would do better to "invite candid criticism." Nor did Miller spare the great black father the central criticism. Wrapped inside the velvet tributes of the banquet toast, there was an unyielding demand for more militant action. "Pursue policies," he urged Washington, "that are commensurate with the entire circle of our needs, and which are broad-based upon the people's will, and advocate the fullest opportunity of Negro youth to expand and exploit their faculties." This was certainly the radical line, couched in terms that Washington could not rebut.

Throughout Miller's career, and practically until our own time, radical and conservative Negro leaders agreed on anti-racist theory, the end in view; but, specially in view of the historical remoteness of that end, they differed mainly on

[1] Washington established his national pre-eminence with his famous separate-but-equal metaphors of the hand and fingers, in his Atlanta Exposition address of September 18, 1895.

race tactics. The Generals of opposing tactics were
DuBois and Washington. It was true that Washington could be interpreted as a monumental
time-server to the white racist establishment. This
interpretation of Washington did not alarm Miller.
As a sophisticated participant-observer of all the
internecine struggles that accompanied the struggle with the real enemy, white racism, Miller knew
the universal rules of the political game and tells
us, flatly, that there is something of the time-
server in "all truly useful men." At the same time,
militancy was equally necessary and practical,
despite the self-indulgent passion of militants for
'verbal vehemence' and the dangers of raising the
ideological temperature of the white racists. Such
risks were worth taking in order to raise the
ideological temperature of the blacks—to make
them more active on their own behalf.

What was the theory agreed among the black
leadership of Miller's era, radicals and conservatives alike, even as they disagreed about tactics?
That theory referred to an eventual reality upon
which all students of the race problem must agree,
in reason, although the reality to which the theory
referred was not yet fact. On the contrary, far
from being accomplished fact, the trouble with the
theory was that it pointed to a tragically remote
eventuality, a future fact toward which present
fact would continue to work itself—but with painful reluctance. In the following passage, Miller
summarizes the theory that framed all tactics,
radical and conservative, up to the most recent
period: he held the *"intellectual conviction that two
races cannot live indefinitely side by side, under the
same general regime, without ultimately fusing."*
(My italics.)

Now, there is an important sense in which a theory can be a hypothetical prediction. Since a 'fusing' or amalgamation of the races, as a social phenomenon, must, like other social phenomena, take its real existence from the subjective meaning attached to such an eventuality by the social actors themselves, Miller understood perfectly that his hypothetical prediction was no prediction at all. There were necessary conditions without the operation of which such an outcome as an ultimate 'fusing' was not assured. Patently, the necessary conditions were not present and the prediction remains, for our time as for Miller's, merely hypothetical.

Massive fusing had taken place, of course. It was the most visible sign of the degradation, the concubinage, to which black Americans had been subjected—and in that forced amalgam, a new racial type, the Negro American, unknown elsewhere, was being created. However, under the present and foreseeable conditions of race relations in America, Miller's theory, as a hypothetical prediction, carried neither "the utterance of a preference nor the formulation of a policy." He could safely say that he knew of no Negro "who advocates amalgamation as a feasible policy of solution." White racists are mistaken. "The Negro does not 'hope and dream of amalgamation'. This would be self-stultification with a vengeance."

The validity of a theory may be distinguished from its practical applicability; it may, indeed, explain tactical limits and also, in its validity, be so different from the observed facts as to stand in transformative judgment over them. In their historical situation, black radicals and conservatives held to the theory, as Miller phrased it, that the "amalgamation of the races is an ultimate possibility, though not an immediate probability." The theory remains true. It is imperative, I think, that anti-racist theory be held fast, nowadays; only by holding onto it can blacks and whites rightly assert their common humanity. Here is the ultimate question answering itself: rightly asserted by the directive theory, all racial tactics will remain subordinate to it.

"But what have you and I to do with ultimate questions, anyway?" Miller asks, in careful irony, of the white racist to whom were addressed the passages from which I have been quoting.[2] What, indeed! Without keeping the ultimate theoretical questions in mind, as Miller did in the courageous act of insisting upon their validity—and, moreover, precisely in view of the fact that the main racist frenzy is about just this theory—immediate tactical answers lose all sense of direction. Through all the tactical struggles between radicals and conservatives, Miller kept his sense of direction, of what tactics we may and may not use—which *is* the theoretical sense. He rejected color line and caste, constantly breaking anyway under the historic arrangements of racial life in America, as principles of social organization. The Negro must organize his own corporate identity in both tactical moods, radical and conservative, precisely in order to break beyond racial forms of social organization. Beyond all tactics, then, there was no conflict of principles, of ultimate questions, of theory. Miller kept clearly in mind, I suggest, the difference between theory and tactics. He did not

[2] See "As to the Leopard's Spots," pp. 42–70.

allow anti-racist theory to become confused in his mind with racial tactics. Precisely this confusion of theory and tactics—and, moreover, a conflict of theories—is now occurring, with a vengeance for the failure of anti-racist theory to overtake and transform more swiftly the facts of racial life in America.

There appears to be developing within our contemporary Negro leadership a split in theory as well as tactics. Proudly, and without the slightest trace of anxiety in the acceptance of it, Miller did accept the great truth that there were neither 'white' nor 'black' values, neither white nor black properties in cultures. A culture, Miller proclaimed, is "the equal inheritance of anyone who can appropriate and apply it." Shakespeare and Whitman belonged to him; they were part of his inalienable life; they did not belong to butchers in London or slobs in Camden simply because they happen to be white men. Race is the most terrible cultural simplification of all; in his wisdom and learning, Miller rejected the fatal simplicity that the provenance of a value determined membership in it. "The Negro enters into the inheritance of all the ages on equal terms with the rest." Here, I think, is another truth of which we are reminded by a reading of these essays. That there have been modes of African cultural genius is also true, and urgently needs teaching. But this is only to amplify the basic theoretical point: that "the white man has no exclusive proprietorship of civilization." There are no values for whites only and none are black, whatever their origins. Our moral demands stand or fall on the proposition that they belong to those who enact those demands in their own lives.

Nevertheless, it appears to me that a new generation of Negro radicals has all but abandoned
anti-racist theory, as, under the accelerating force
of its failures, they pursue racial tactics. Although
they are still intended, mainly, I think, to raise
the ideological temperature of Negro communal
life, to motivate movements of self-help, militant
declamations on 'black values', if they are offered
as expressions of racist theory, can only damage
the dignity and restrict the range of the Negro's
own infinitely human capacities. What are 'black
values' anyway? A culture has no color; it belongs,
as Miller insisted, to him who lives and enacts it.
A high culture is a living and active faith. Blood
cannot civilize. Even vague as they are at present,
'black values' sound suspiciously like an inversion
of that kind of racist theory which even asserted
Shakespeare for WASPS only, once used to keep
Jews from teaching in English departments. Will
black militants insist on artistic parity for LeRoi
Jones, in English departments, alongside Shakespeare, with black teachers for Jones and white for
Shakespeare? And what of all the Jewish literary
dancers who, opposing the historic faith of Israel,
make their protests in the name of the new Baal
of Sex-Revolution? Are they to be constrained
to the Song of Solomon? Will Pushkin become
required reading in the original Russian, as a
'black' writer? Or will he have to be translated,
first, into the language of the slave-traders, Swa-
hili? There is something phony about the present
talking up of 'black values'. I hear in this talk the
characteristic hysterical tones of racist theory,
except this time, in counterpoint to Miller's, the
racist hysteria is also black.

II

Perhaps the current radical Negro turn to racist theory—at least to racist declamations that imply a theory—represents a desperate adaptation of the ideological movement by which our common culture is destroying itself from within. Black racist theory may be a desperate kicking at the old white womb of Negro consciousness. But the white womb has felt these self-same kicks before, from earlier children of its own making. Morally revolutionary whites have been kicking inside that same womb for more than a century. I suspect that, its ancestry traced back far enough, revolutionary black racist theory includes some great white fathers—Marx, Nietzsche, and D. H. Lawrence, for example—all those persuasive white haters of 'ideals' who wrote and acted in opposition to a culture high precisely in the creative discontent of its identification with ideals. In the racist context of modernity, ideals are easily associated with inhibition of the black power of impulse and self-gratification. "Away with ideals!" Lawrence declaimed. Who does not now know that 'white' is uptight? But this also implies that 'black' is slack. In the symbolic of western cultural modernity, dependent as it is upon racist prejudices shared by some blacks, 'black' is associated with those efforts to reject the faltering interdictory motifs that must dominate this (or any other) culture, by asserting its remissive motifs—more direct sexuality; spontaneity; the impulse life; personality as the flash point of will; gaiety; playfulness; arrogance. These are the kicks of the therapeutic through the womb of repressive, idealizing (but not white) culture in order to reassert the remissive part of that very same interdictory-remissive culture under an inverse order. The spreading collective violence of western life is explainable, I think, as a massive and long-prepared experiment in a remissive culture of play and self-gratification. We are witnessing a socio-logical freak of western cultural development, what might be called 'Revolution as therapy'. Revolt may be treated as an end in itself, the therapeutic heightening of a sense of personal well-being.

In this theoretical perspective, here briefly in-dicated,[3] the racist declamations of our contem-porary black militants become understandable as one aspect of the remissive motifs integral to our culture; into the thrust toward interdictory domi-nance of these remissive motifs, the archetypal threatening figure of the black is welcomed, with a shiver of *Schadenfreude*, as an all-purpose sub-versive of culture itself. This expressive side of our inherited cultural ambivalence is quite as dangerous to the humanity of Negroes as the repressive side was in Miller's period of race psycho-history. The racist structure of modern cultural ambivalence can never be adapted, by an inversion of the established but failing interdic-tory-remissive contents, to serve the cause of racial justice.

Why not "chaos and disorderliness"? that moral revolutionary, Lev Chestov, once asked.

[3] For a more extended perspective, see the main theoretical chapters beginning and ending *The Triumph of the Thera-peutic* by Philip Rieff (New York, 1968), Harper Torchbook edition, pp. 1–27 and pp. 232–261.

The black has long served as a figure of chaos and disorderliness. By their willing loan of the archetypal violent black to revolutionary (as well as defensively hostile) whites, as a counter-ideal of themselves, the new Negro militants have been sucked into a white revolutionary movement that cuts across the path of their own, diverting them from their anti-racist normative theory. That white revolutionary movement has made nonsense of the old political distinctions between Left and Right. Hitler's armed bohemians made serious, anti-establishment noises even more loudly than the students of the New Left nowadays. On the one hand, the most radical voices of the nineteenth and twentieth centuries have shouted for a destructiveness that goes far beyond politics. On the other hand, in the perspective suggested here, merely political Marxism appears now as a conservative cultural force, quite at odds with the deeper current of moral revolution in the West. Caught now in this deeper current, the militant black leaders, in their declamations of violence and free-floating racial hostility, have become archetypal Americans; I suspect that many whites secretly envy them their American freedom from the constraints of civility. All men long for this freedom. As their frontier culture was so much a form of escape from the constraints of civility, Americans have learned to enjoy living on the brink of that flash point of will we like to call 'personality'; just this flash point threatens our compensatorily rigid collectivities, from within, with chaos.

The culture of economic man is a jungle of barely suppressed hostilities anyway. Perhaps its putative inheritor, the remissive culture of psychological man,[4] will not be much worse. But successive evaginations of the American moral order, raising to the superficies of thought and behavior what were once more deeply installed inhibitions of impulse and hostility, promise a terrible harvest of free-floating hostility in our future even within a more and more manipulable technological culture. Blacks have ample reason to be doubly hostile. For centuries they were constrained to be uniquely and universally subject to the flash points of white will. With blacks one could do what was otherwise not done. Thus enhanced, white Americans could falsely celebrate their racial submissions to interdictory civilities and restraints.

The opening up of possibility, the liquidation of that which is 'not done', represents the long revolution of modernity at its most basic level. Our revolution cannot be described in the received terms—Left or Right, Red or Black. As I have said, the moral revolutionaries of white modernity have been, often enough, fascist. Some variety of black fascism cannot break the racist structure of that modernity. Any effort to harden that structure with a racist theory derived from the black side of the color line is an evil to be fought in the name of all God's children. A victory for black racism would be tantamount to a defeat for black humanity. The counter-ideal of the moral revolutionaries is to make 'niggers' of us all—and this would be the deepest defeat of all to the real blacks, of America or Africa, past or present, different as they are from white racist-libertarian fantasies of them. I consider the implicit use of

[4] On 'psychological man,' see Rieff, *Freud: The Mind of the Moralist* (New York, 1961), revised ed., pp. 361–392.

the black as the new storm-trooper of the white revolutionary movement against its own failing interdicts as another grave threat to the dignity, self-respect, and ultimate triumph of black men over all racist theories. Under this latest and most subtle inversion of white racist theory, not the black man but chaos will triumph.

I think it is possible that, in the complex internecine warfare of modern western culture against itself, chaos and destruction will emerge as the real victors. The most militant black dream, of a racial state carved out of America, can only lead to full-scale racist wars of extermination, for racist theory is always and everywhere an instrument for the release of that sadistic impulse by which one self or a corporate self can demonstrate its existence only by over-powering another. In the heart of darkness, a Kurtz or a Hitler can only assert himself through his power to destroy others.

In their own peculiar version of racist tactics, preempting the anti-racist theory of Kelly Miller and his generation of Negro leaders, the new radicals of black America are repeating a revolutionary call to the worship of Chaos that has enchanted the modern white mind. That terrible enchantment has now spread to the militant black leadership. On your knees before the New Disorder: bourgeois, old folks, men of taste and women of refinement—white and black! The modern worship of Chaos has had its successes, drawing to itself the naïve and sophisticated alike. Our black revolutionaries are captives of the white revolutionaries. Being black, they are assigned the horrific role of negating white history with black values; they are to supply the myth and madness by which the logic of the past is to be cut short.

The success that would come out of such chaos certainly has the power to draw new worshippers. After all, success is the longest-lived of the gods. Perhaps white history has this chaos coming to it. The white establishment has itself worshipped none other than that self-same god, Success, but always in the name of order. At once thus enchanted and disenchanted with Success-Chaos in its two faces of power, black and white, the new radicalism is very different from the old radicalism that Miller reviews for us in this volume. The new Adam that the black racists seek is really the son and heir of the old Adam of white racism. Away with all thought of new, innocent Adams; they will grow up to be even more evil than their guilty fathers.

As a special type of modern revolutionary, psychological men are trying to teach themselves how to be honest enough to enjoy the experience of self overpowering some other self, how to take pleasure straightforwardly in the experience of smashing the face of authority. But this is a pleasure and an honesty no culture can afford to admit openly. Violence cannot become a way of life. A violent culture is a dying one. In order to survive, a culture must endure the guilt it necessarily produces, for it is a structure by which certain possibilities are closed off, made impossible to conceive, repressed—but not eliminated. No culture can long endure massive and open violence, because violence is the principal means by which the impossible is made possible and nothing is 'not done'. In order to break the fatal modern symbolic of therapeutic violence that has overtaken the historic effort to cope with racism, anti-racist theory must be maintained superior to, and judge of, all racial tactics. Here is a humane book, to help preserve us to the necessary anti-racist theory, in control over the welter of racial tactics—however tragically necessary those tactics may be. Only under the name of right theory can we preserve our saving sense of what is not to be done.

University of Pennsylvania
Philadelphia
May, 1968

RADICALS AND CONSERVATIVES

WHEN a distinguished Russian was informed that some American Negroes are radical and some conservative, he could not restrain his laughter. The idea of conservative Negroes was more than the Cossack's risibilities could endure. " What on earth," he exclaimed with astonishment, " have they to conserve? "

According to a strict use of terms, a " conservative " is one who is satisfied with existing conditions and advocates their continuance; while a " radical " clamors for amelioration of conditions through change. No thoughtful Negro is satisfied with the present status of his race, whether viewed in its political, its civil or general aspect. He labors under an unfriendly public opinion, one which is being rapidly crystallized into a rigid caste system and enacted into unrighteous law. How can he be expected to contemplate such oppressive conditions with satisfaction and composure? Circumstances render it imperative that his attitude should be dissentient rather than conformatory. Every consideration of enlightened self-respect impels him to unremitting protest, albeit the manner of protestation may be mild or pronounced, according to the dictates of prudence. Radical and conservative Negroes agree as to the end in view, but differ as to the

most effective means of attaining it. The difference
is not essentially one of principle or purpose, but
point of view. All anti-slavery advocates desired
the downfall of the iniquitous institution, but some
were more violent than others in the expression of
this desire. Disagreement as to method led to personal estrangement, impugnment of motive, and unseemly factional wrangle. And so, colored men who
are alike zealous for the betterment of their race,
lose half their strength in internal strife, because of
variant methods of attack upon the citadel of prejudice. Mr. Booker T. Washington is, or has been,
the storm-center about which the controversy rages,
and contending forces have aligned themselves in
hostile array as to the wisdom or folly of the doctrine of which he is the chief exponent. The unseemly " Boston Riot," in which he was threatened
with bodily violence, served to accentuate the antagonism and to deepen the line of cleavage.

Several years ago a number of New England colored men, " exotics," as some would say, of the New
England colleges, having grown restive under what
they deemed the damaging doctrine of the famous
Tuskegeean, founded the *Boston Guardian* as a
journal of protest. These men declared that the
teachings of Mr. Washington were destructive of
the guaranteed rights and privileges of the Negro
race, especially in the Northern States, and pledged
themselves to spare no effort to combat his political
and social heresies.

Mr. William Monroe Trotter, a Harvard graduate, who is said to have maintained a higher scholastic average than any other colored student of that
famous institution, was head and front of the new
movement. As promoter of the " Boston Riot " he
was convicted and sentenced to the common jail.

His incarceration but served to intensify his animosity.

Mr. Trotter is well suited to play the rôle of a martyr. He delights in a reputation for vicarious heroics. Being possessed of considerable independent means, he willingly makes sacrifices for the cause, and is as uncompromising as William Lloyd Garrison. Mr. Trotter, however, lacks the moral sanity and poise of the great emancipator. With him agitation is not so much the outgrowth of an intellectual or moral comprehension of right and reprehension of wrong, as it is a temperamental necessity. Endowed with a narrow, intolerant intensity of spirit, he pursues his ends with a Jesuitical justification of untoward means. Without clear concrete objective, such as the anti-slavery promoters had in view, he strikes wildly at whatever or whoever he imagines obscures the rights of the Negro race. He has the traditional irreverence of the reformer, an irreverence which delights to shatter popular idols. President Eliot of Harvard University, Theodore Roosevelt, and Booker T. Washington are shining marks for his blunt and bitter denunciation. He sets himself up as the moral monitor of the Negro race. This Negro Puritan is of spotless and austere personal character, and yet he does not scruple to use the weapons of unrighteousness to promote his cherished hopes. He is equally indifferent to the allurements of culture and the blandishments of business; he has sacrificed a business career which was opening up with large prospects, in order to fight the Washington heresy. A Harvard graduate, with a class-standing that puts him easily in touch with the intellectual élite of his alma mater, he has thrown away all the restraints of culture, spurned the allurements of refined association, and conducts

The Guardian with as little regard to literary form and style as if he were a back-woodsman.

By his blunt, persistent assault on Booker T. Washington he has focalized the more radical elements of the Negro race, and has made himself the most forceful personality that the Negroes in the free States have produced in a generation. He is irreconciled to his great foe. This intrepid editor saw clearly that the so-called radical Negroes were wholly wanting in organization and leadership. He chafed under the chide of having no concrete achievement or commanding personality as basis and background of his propaganda. His enemies sought to silence the loudsome pretensions of those of radical persuasion by the cry that they had founded no institutions and projected no practical projects. That the same might have been said of Garrison and Phillips was regarded as a barren rejoinder. It is difficult to found an effective organization on a protest. There is little constructive possibility in negation. Through the influence of *The Guardian*, Mr. Trotter has held together and inspired the opposition to Mr. Washington. His every utterance leads to the Cato-like refrain: " Booker Washington must be destroyed." Conscious of his own lack of attractive personality and felicity of utterance requisite to ostensible popular leadership, Trotter began to cast about for a man of showy faculties who could stand before the people as leader of his cause. He wove a subtle net about W. E. B. DuBois, the brilliant writer and scholar, and gradually weaned him from his erstwhile friendship for Mr. Washington, so as to exploit his prominence and splendid powers in behalf of the hostile forces.

The author of the " Souls of Black Folk " is also a Harvard man, and possesses extraordinary scientific and literary talent. Few men now writing the English language can equal him in linguistic felicity. He is a man of remarkable amplitude and contrariety of qualities, an exact interrogator and a lucid expositor of social reality, but withal a dreamer with a fantasy of mind that verges on " the fine frenzy."

Dr. DuBois began his career, not as an agitator, nor as a carping critic of another's achievements, but as a painstaking investigator and a writer of remarkable lucidity and keenness. The men who are now extolling him as the peerless leader of the radicals were a few years ago denouncing him bitterly for his restrained and reasoned conclusions. It is almost impossible to conceive how the author of " The Philadelphia Negro " could have penned the " Second Niagara Movement Manifesto," without mental and moral metamorphosis. When DuBois essays the rôle of the agitator, and attempts to focus the varied energies of his mind upon a concrete social emergency, it is apt to result, as did his " Atlanta Tragedy," in an extravaganza of feeling and a fiasco of thought. His mind being cast in a weird and fantastic mold, his place is the cloister of the reflective scholar. He lives behind the veil; and whenever he emerges to mingle with the grosser affairs of life we may expect to hear, ever and anon, that sad and bitter wail. Dr. DuBois is passionately devoted to the welfare of his race, but he is allowing himself to be exploited in a function for which he is by nature unfit. His highest service will consist in interpreting to the white people the needs and feeling of his race in terms of exact knowledge and nice language, rather than as an agitator or promoter of concrete achievement. Trotter is the real guiding power of the " Niagara Movement," for he, almost by his single hand, created the growth that made it possible. Although we may hear the voice of Jacob, we feel the hand of Esau. DuBois ostensibly manages the new movement, but when he dares to deviate from the inflexible intentions of Trotter, there will be war within, and victory will rest with the intrepid editor.

We need not feel surprised, therefore, that such picturesque points as Niagara Falls and Harper's Ferry figured in the " Niagara Movement," under the guiding mind of DuBois. They were planned by a poetic mind. It is a poet's attempt to dramatize the ills of a race with picturesque stage setting and spectacular scenic effect.

At the call of DuBois a number of men met at Niagara Falls, in August, 1905, and launched the " Niagara Movement " amid the torrential downpour of the mighty waters. In this gathering were some of the ablest and most earnest men of the Negro race. The call appealed mainly to those of vehement temperament, every one of whom was an avowed opponent of Booker T. Washington. An address was issued to the country setting forth in manly, pointed terms the rights of the colored race. The platform of the movement contained nothing new, and its dynamic was derived from dissent. It was merely a protest against American color discrimination, based upon Mr. Washington's alleged acquiescence. Many of the subscribers to the new movement had not, up to that time, been known for their activity in behalf of the race, and espoused the cause as " a cult " with all the wonted zeal and intolerance of new converts.

The second manifesto of this body, issued from Harper's Ferry, the scene of John Brown's martyrdom, is scarcely distinguishable from a wild and frantic shriek. The lachrymal wail befits the child, which

has "no language but a cry." Verbal vehemence
void of practical power to enforce demands in an inef-
fectual missive to be hurled against the stronghold of
prejudice

Another meeting has been called at Oberlin, Ohio,
because of its stirring anti-slavery suggestiveness.
We may expect a future session at Appomattox, so
prone is the poetic temperament to avail itself of epi-
sodal and dramatic situations.

When the "Niagara Movement" grows out of
the declamatory stage and becomes tempered by
dealing with the actualities of the situation it will
find its place among the many agencies working together for the general cause.

The radical and conservative tendencies of the
Negro race cannot be better described than by com-
paring, or rather contrasting, the two superlative
colored men in whom we find their highest embodiment—Frederick Douglass and Booker Washington,
who were both picked out and exploited by white
men as the mouthpiece and intermediaries of the black
race. The two men are in part products of their
times, but are also natural antipodes. Douglass
lived in the day of moral giants; Washington lives
in the era of merchant princes. The contemporaries
of Douglass emphasized the rights of man; those
of Washington, his productive capacity. The age
of Douglass acknowledged the sanction of the Golden
Rule; that of Washington worships the Rule of *Gold*.
The equality of men was constantly dinned into
Douglass's ears; Washington hears nothing but the
inferiority of the Negro and the dominance of the
Saxon. Douglass could hardly receive a hearing to-
day; Washington would have been hooted off the
stage a generation ago. Thus all truly useful men
must be, in a measure, time-servers; for unless they

serve their time, they can scarcely serve at all. But great as was the diversity of formative influences that shaped these two great lives, there is no less opposability in their innate bias of character. Douglass was like a lion, bold and fearless; Washington is lamblike, meek and submissive. Douglass escaped from personal bondage, which his soul abhorred; but for Lincoln's proclamation, Washington would probably have arisen to esteem and favor in the eyes of his master as a good and faithful servant. Douglass insisted upon rights; Washington insists upon duty. Douglass held up to public scorn the sins of the white man; Washington portrays the faults of his own race. Douglass spoke what he thought the world should hear; Washington speaks only what he feels it is disposed to listen to. Douglass's conduct was actuated by principle; Washington's by prudence. Douglass had no limited, copyrighted programme for his race, but appealed to the Decalogue, the Golden Rule, the Declaration of Independence, the Constitution of the United States; Washington, holding these great principles in the shadowy background, presents a practical expedient applicable to present needs. Douglass was a moralist, insisting upon the application of righteousness to public affairs; Washington is a practical opportunist, accepting the best terms which he thinks it possible to secure.

Booker T. Washington came upon the public stage at the time when the policies which Douglass embodied had seemed to fail. Reconstruction measures had proved abortive; Negro politicians, like Othello, had lost their occupation, and had sought asylum in the Government departments at Washington; the erstwhile advocates of the Negro's cause had grown indifferent or apologetic, and the plain intent of the Constitution had been overborne in the South with the connivance of the North. The idea of lifting the Negro to the plane of equality with the white race, once so fondly cherished, found few remaining advocates. Mr. Washington sized up the situation with the certainty and celerity of a genius. He based his policy upon the ruins of the policy that had been exploited. He avoided controverted issues, and moved, not along the line of least resistance, but of no resistance at all. He founded his creed upon construction rather than upon criticism. He urged his race to do the things possible rather than whine and pine over things prohibited. According to his philosophy, it is better to build even upon the shifting sands of expediency than not to build at all simply because you cannot secure a granite foundation. He thus hoped to utilize for the betterment of the Negro whatever residue of good feeling there might be in the white race. Tuskegee Institute, which is in itself a marvelous achievement, is only the pulpit from which Mr. Washington proclaims his doctrine. Industrial education has become so intricately interwoven into his policy that his critics are forced into the ridiculous attitude of opposing a form of training essential to the welfare of any people. For reasons of policy, Mr. Washington has been provokingly silent as to the claim of higher education, although his personal actions proclaim loudly enough the belief that is in his heart. The subject of industrial and higher education is merely one of ratio and proportion, and not one of fundamental controversy.

Mr. Washington's bitterest opponents cannot gainsay his sincerity or doubt that the welfare of his race is the chief burden of his soul. He follows the leading of his own light. Few men of this genera-

tion have shown such signal devotion, self-abnega-
tion and strenuous endeavor for an altruistic cause.

One of the chief complaints against the Tuskegeean is lack of definite statement upon questions of
vital concern. Mr. Washington is a diplomat, and
a great one. He sinks into sphinxlike silence when
the demands of the situation seem to require emphatic
utterance. His carefully studied deliverances upon
disputed issues often possess the equivocalness of a
Delphic oracle. While he does not openly avow, yet
he would not disclaim, in distinct terms, a single plank
in the platform of Douglass. The white race saddles
its own notions and feelings upon him, and yet he
opens not his mouth. His sagacious silence and
shrewdly measured assertions must be taken, if not
with the traditional grain of salt, at least with a
goodly lump of diplomatic allowance. We do not
usually associate deep moral conviction with the
guileful arts of diplomacy, but we must remember
that the delicate rôle of race statesmanship cannot
be played without rare caution and tactful prudence.

Mr. Washington's popularity and prominence depend largely upon the fact that his putative policy
is acceptable to the Southern whites, because he allows them to believe that he accepts their estimate
of the Negro's inferior place in the social scheme.
He is quiescent, if not acquiescent, as to the white
man's superior claims. He shuts his eyes to many
of the wrongs and outrages heaped upon the Negro
race. He never runs against the Southerner's traditional prejudices, and even when he protests against
his practices the protestation is so palliatory that,
like a good conscience, it is void of offence. Equality
between the races, whether social, political, or civil, is
an unsavory term to the white man's palate, and,
therefore, Mr. Washington obliterates it from his

vocabulary. The higher education of the Negro is in general disfavor, so Mr. Washington gives the approval of his silence to the charge that such pure and devoted philanthropists as President Ware of Atlanta, Patton of Howard, Tupper of Shaw, and Cravath of Fisk, who did more than all others to quicken and inspire the Negro race, have lived, loved, labored, and died in vain. Nor is Washington objectionable to the white man by reason of his self-assertive personality. He is an exact modern counterpart of Chaucer's knight: "Curteys he was, lowly, and servysable." Even when he violates the sacred code of the whites by dining with the President or mingling on easy terms with ultra-fashionable circles, they lash themselves into momentary fury, but straightway proceed to laud and glorify his policy. The North applauds and sustains his propagandism because he strives to be at peace with all men. He appeals to the amity and not the enmity of both races. We are in the midst of an era of good feeling, and must have peace at any price. It is interesting to witness how many of the erstwhile loud-voiced advocates of the Negro's rights have seized upon Mr. Washington's pacific policy as a graceful recession from the former position. The whites have set up Booker Washington as in a former day they set up Frederick Douglass, as the divinely appointed and anointed leader of his race, and regard as sacrilege all criticism and even candid discussion on the part of those whom he has been sent to guide. They demand for him an exemption which they have never accorded their own leaders, from George Washington to Theodore Roosevelt. Nothing could be further from Mr. Washington's thoughts than the assumption of divine commission which the whites seek to impose upon him. He makes no claim to have received a revelation, either from burning bush or mountain top. He is a simple, sincere, unsophisticated colaborer with his brethren; a single, though signal, agency for the betterment of his race.

Mr. Washington did not start out as a leader of his people's own choosing; he did not command an enthusiastic and spontaneous following. He lacks that magnetic personality that would cause men to love him and women to adore him. His method is rather that of a missionary seeking the material and moral betterment of an unfortunate people, than of a spontaneous leader voicing their highest self-expression. He is deficient in the fearlessness, the self-assertion, the aggressive and heroic spirit necessary to quicken and inspire. Such a leader must not hold up for painful contemplation or emphasize to the outside world the repugnant, grotesque and ludicrous faults and foibles of his own people, but he must constantly direct their attention to higher and better ideals. His dominant note must be pitched in the major key. He must not be of the earth earthy, with range of vision limited to the ugliness of untoward conditions, but must have the power of idealization and spiritual vista. Exaggerated self-importance is deemed an individual fault, but a racial virtue. It has been the chief incentive of every race or nation that has ever gained prominence in the world's affairs. The triumphant, God-sent leader of any people must be the exponent and expounder of their highest aspirations and feelings, and must evoke their manhood and self-esteem, yea, even their vanity and pride.

Mr. Washington's following was at first very largely prudential and constrained; it lacked spontaneousness and joyance. He was not hailed with glad acclaim as the deliverer of his people. He

brought good gifts rather than glad tidings. Many
believed in him for his work's sake; some acquiesced
rather than antagonize one who had gained so
large a measure of public confidence; others were
willing to co-operate in the accomplishment of good
deeds, though they inwardly detested his doctrine;
while those of political instinct sought his favor as
a pass-key to prestige and place. Few thoughtful
colored men espoused what passed as Mr. Washington's " policy " without apology or reserve. Many
of the more dispassionate and thoughtful are disposed to yield to his primacy because he has such a
hold on the sentiment and imagination of the white
race that, if for any reason the spell should be broken,
no other colored man could ever hope for like consideration and esteem.

Mr. Washington's critics assert that his leadership
has been barren of good results to the Negro race,
unmindful of the magnitude of the contract he has
promised the American people that he would solve
the race problem. Under his regnancy it is claimed
that the last vestige of political power has been swept
away. Civil privileges have been restricted, educational opportunities, in some States at least, have
been curtailed; the industrial situation, the keystone
of his policy, has become more ominous and uncertain, while the feeling between the races is constantly
growing more acute and threatening. In answer to
this it is averred that no human power could stay
the wave of race hatred now sweeping over the country, but that the Tuskegeean's pacific policy will
serve to relieve the severity of the blow. All of the
leaders before him essayed the task in vain, and gave
up in despair.

The majority of thoughtful men range between
these wide-apart views, appreciating the good and

the limitations of both.   They believe in neither surrender nor revolution, and that both forces have
their place and function in the solution of the race
problem.   They are joint factors of a common
product, whose relative strength and importance may
increase or diminish with the shifting exigencies of
conditions.   While it would be unseemly for those
who breathe the free air of New England to remain
silent concerning the heavy burden borne by their
brethren in the South, yet we must not forget that
Frederick Douglass himself could not to-day build up
an institution in Alabama, nor do the imperative constructive work in that section.   The progress of all
peoples is marked by alternations of combat and contention on the one hand, and compromise and
concession on the other, and progress is the result
of the play and counterplay of these forces.   Colored
men should have a larger tolerance for the widest
latitude of opinion and method.   Too frequently
what passes as " an irrepressible conflict " is merely
difference in point of view.

The Negro's lot would be sad indeed if, under al-
lurement of material advantage and temporary easement, he should sink into pliant yieldance to
unrighteous oppression; but it would be sadder still
if intemperate insistence should engender ill will and
strife, when the race is not yet ready to be "battered
with the shocks of doom." The words of Guizot
never found a more pertinent application than to the
present circumstances and situation of the Negro
race:

We continually oscillate between an inclination to complain
without sufficient cause and to be too easily satisfied.   We have
extreme susceptibility of mind, an inordinate craving, an ambition in our thoughts, in our desires, and in the movements of
our imagination; yet when we come to practical life, when

trouble, when sacrifices, when efforts are required for the attainment of our object, we sink into lassitude and inactivity. Let us not, however, suffer ourselves to be invaded by either of these vices. Let us estimate fairly what our abilities, our knowledge, our power enable us to do lawfully, and let us aim at nothing that we cannot lawfully, justly and prudently—with a proper respect for the great principles upon which our social system, our civilization, is based—attain.

Mr. Booker T. Washington's later career is exemplifying more and more the philosophy of this sentiment.

Under the spur of adverse criticism and the growing sense of responsibility which his expanding opportunities impose, Mr. Washington has become so enlarged that his leadership is universally conceded, and well-nigh universally accepted. Few men have shown such power of enlargement. Even those who continue to challenge his primacy confess that they are opposing the Washington of long ago rather than the Washington of to-day. He rises triumphantly on stepping-stones of his dead self to higher things. He began his career with a narrow educational bias and a one-sided championship of industrial training, as offset to the claims of literary culture which had hitherto absorbed the substance of Northern philanthropy. But he has grown so far in grasp and in breadth of view that he advocates all modes of education in their proper place and proportion. He at first deprecated the Negro's active participation in politics, but with broadening vision and increasing courage he now serves as consulting statesman touching all political interests of the race.

Washington's equability of temper is most remarkable. He receives a bequest of a million dollars, dines with the President, listens to the adulation of half the world or the bitter abuse of those whom he strives to serve, with the same modest and unruffled

demeanor.   His sanity and poise are unsurpassed.
In a toast at a banquet given in honor of Mr. Washington in the city of Washington, the present writer
proclaimed his conditional leadership, which the
Negro race is now accepting with lessening reserve:

"We have as our guest to-night one who has
come up from slavery, up from the coal caverns of
West Virginia, struggling up against narrow theories, lack of early education and bias of environment, tactfully expanding the prudential restraints
of a delicate and critical situation, rising upon successive stepping-stones of past achievements and past
mistakes, but ever planting his feet upon higher and
higher ground.   Sir, you enjoy a degree of concrete
achievement and personal distinction excelled by few
men now living on this planet.   You are not only
the foremost man of the Negro race, but one of the
foremost men of all the world.   We did not give
you that 'glad eminence' and we cannot take it
away, but we would utilize and appropriate it to
the good of the race.   You have the attention
of the white world; you hold the pass-key to the
heart of the great white race.   Your commanding position, your personal prestige, and the
magic influence of your illustrious name entail
upon you the responsibility to become the leader of
the people, to stand as daysman between us and the
great white God, and lay a propitiating hand upon
us both.   Some have criticised in the past, and reserve the right to do so in the future.   A noble soul
is big enough to invite candid criticism, and eschew
sycophantic adulation.

"Sir, if you will stand upon the granite pedestal
of truth and righteousness, and pursue policies that
are commensurate with the entire circle of our needs,
and which are broad-based upon the people's will,

and advocate the fullest opportunity of Negro youth to expand and exploit their faculties, if you will stand as the fearless champion of the Negro's political rights before the law and behind the law, then a united race will rise up and join in gladsome chorus:

> "'Only thou our leader be,
> And we still will follow thee.'"

AS TO THE LEOPARD'S SPOTS

An Open Letter to Thomas Dixon, Jr.

As to the Leopard's Spots—"I regard it as the ablest, soundest, and most important document that has appeared on this subject in many years.

"Geo. W. Cable."

September, 1905.

Mr. Thomas Dixon, Jr.

Dear Sir: I am writing you this letter to express the attitude and feeling of ten million of your fellow-citizens toward the evil propagandism of race animosity to which you have lent your great literary powers. Through the widespread influence of your writings you have become the chief priest of those who worship at the shrine of race hatred and wrath. This one spirit runs through all your books and published utterances, like the recurrent theme of an opera. As the general trend of your doctrine is clearly epitomized and put forth in your contribution to the *Saturday Evening Post* of August 19, I beg to consider chiefly the issues therein raised. You are a white man born in the midst of the Civil War; I am a Negro born during the same stirring epoch. You were born with a silver spoon in your mouth; I was born with an iron hoe in my hand. Your race has afflicted accumulated injury and wrong upon mine; mine has borne yours only service and good will. You express your views with the most scathing frankness; I am sure you will welcome an equally candid expression from me.

Permit me to acknowledge the personal consideration which you have shown me. You will doubtless recall that when I addressed the Congregational ministers of New York City, a year or more ago, you asked permission to be present and listened attentively to what I had to say, although, as might have been expected, you beat a precipitous retreat when luncheon was announced. In your article in the *Post* you make several references to me and to other colored men with entire personal courtesy. So far as I know you have never varied from this rule in your personal dealings with members of my race. You are merciless, however, in excoriating the race as a whole, thus keenly wounding the sensibilities of every individual of that blood. I assure you that this courtesy of personal treatment will be reciprocated in this letter, however sharply I may be compelled to take issue with the views you set forth and to deplore your attitude. I shall endeavor to indulge in no bitter word against your race or against the South, whose exponent and special pleader you assume to be.

I fear that you have mistaken personal manners, the inevitable varnish of any gentleman of your antecedents and rearing, for friendship to a race which you hold in despite. You tell us that you are kind and considerate to your personal servants. It is somewhat strange that you should deem such assurance necessary, any more than it is necessary for you to assure us that you are kind to your horse or your dog and fond of them. But when you write yourself down as " one of their best friends," you need not be surprised if we retort the refrain of the

ritual, " From all such proffers of friendship, good
Lord deliver us." An astronomer once tried to convince a layman, unlearned in astronomical lore, that
the North Star was bigger than the moon. The
unsophisticated reply was, " It might be so, but it
has a mighty poor way of showing it." The reconciliation of your apparently violent attitude with
your profession of friendship is, I confess, too subtle
a process for the African intellect.

I beg to call your attention to a fault of temper
which may be unconscious on your part. The traditional method of your class in dealing with adverse
opinion was " a word and a blow "; with you it is a
word and an epithet. Your opponents in the field
of opinion are set down as " pot-house politicians,"
" the ostrich man," " the pooh-pooh man," and " the
benevolent old maid." Of course, Theodore Roosevelt, Andrew Carnegie, J. L. M. Curry, Lyman Abbott, Chancellor Hill, John D. Rockefeller and E.
Gardner Murphy would fall under the one or the
other of your sonorous designations. Your choicest
assortment of epithets, I presume, is reserved for
Robert C. Ogden and the General Education Board,
whom you seem to regard with especial repugnance.
For these, doubtless, you intended such appellatives as
" weak-minded optimists " and " female men." The
most illustrious names in America, living and dead,
would fall under the ban of your opprobrium. According to your standard, the only Americans who
could be accounted safe, sane and judicious on the
race issue would be the author of " The Leopard's
Spots," Senator Tillman, and Governor Vardaman.

Your fundamental thesis is that " no amount of
education of any kind, industrious, classical or religious, can make a Negro a white man or bridge the
chasm of the centuries which separates him from

the white man in the evolution of human history."
This doctrine is as old as human oppression. Calhoun made it the arch-stone in the defense of Negro
slavery—and lost.

This is but a recrudescence of the doctrine which
was exploited and exploded during the anti-slavery
struggle. Do you recall the school of pro-slavery
scientists who demonstrated beyond doubt that the
Negro's skull was too thick to comprehend the
substance of Aryan knowledge? Have you not
read in the now discredited scientific books of
that period with what triumphant acclaim it was
shown that the shape and size of the Negro's skull,
facial angle, and cephalic configuration rendered
him forever impervious to the white man's civilization? But all enlightened minds are now as ashamed
of that doctrine as they are of the one-time dogma
that the Negro had no soul. We become aware of
mind through its manifestations. Within forty years
of only partial opportunity, while playing, as it
were, in the back yard of civilization, the American
Negro has cut down his illiteracy by over fifty per
cent.; has produced a professional class, some fifty
thousand strong, including ministers, teachers, doctors, editors, authors, architects, engineers, and is
found in all higher lines of listed pursuits in which
white men are engaged; some three thousand Negroes
have taken collegiate degrees, over three hundred
being from the best institutions in the North and
West established for the most favored white youth;
there is scarcely a first-class institution in America,
excepting some three or four in the South, that is
without colored students, who pursue their studies
generally with success, and sometimes with distinction; Negro inventors have taken out four hundred
patents as a contribution to the mechanical genius of

America; there are scores of Negroes who, for conceded ability and achievements, take respectable rank
in the company of distinguished Americans.

It devolves upon you, Mr. Dixon, to point out
some standard, either of intelligence, character, or
conduct, to which the Negro cannot conform. Will
you please tell a waiting world just what is the
psychological difference between the races? No reputable authority, either of the old or of the new school
of psychology, has yet pointed out any sharp psychic
discriminant. There is not a single intellectual,
moral, or spiritual excellence attained by the white
race to which the Negro does not yield an apprecia-
tive response. If you could show that the Negro is
incapable of mastering the intricacies of Aryan
speech; that he could not comprehend the intellectual
basis of European culture, or apply the apparatus
of practical knowledge; that he could not be made
amenable to the white man's ethical code or appreciate his spiritual motive—then your case would be
proved. But in default of such demonstration we
must relegate your eloquent pronouncement to the
realm of generalization and prophecy, an easy and
agreeable exercise of the mind in which the romancer
is ever prone to indulge.

The inherent, essential and unchangeable inferiority of the Negro to the white man lies at the basis
of your social philosophy. You disdain to examine
the validity of your fondly cherished hope. You
follow closely in the wake of Tom Watson, in the
June number of his homonymous magazine. You
both hurl your thesis of innate racial inferiority at
the head of Booker T. Washington. You use the
same illustrations, the same arguments, and you set
them forth in the same order of recital, and for the
most part in identical language. This seems to be

an instance of great minds, or at least of minds of the same grade, running in the same channel.

These are your words: "What contribution to human progress have the millions of Africans, who inhabit this planet, made during the past four thousand years? Absolutely nothing." These are the words of Thomas Watson spoken some two months previous: "What does civilization owe to the Negro race? Nothing! Nothing!! Nothing!!!" You answer the query with the most emphatic negative noun and the strongest qualifying adjective in the language. Mr. Watson, of a more ecstatic temperament, replies with the same noun and six exclamation points. One rarely meets, outside of yellow journalism, with such lavishness of language wasted upon a hoary dogma. A discredited doctrine that has been bandied about the world from the time of Canaan to Calhoun, is revamped and set forth with as much ardor and fervency of feeling as if revealed for the first time and proclaimed for the enlightenment of a waiting world. But neither boastful asseveration on your part nor indignant denial on mine will affect the facts of the case. That Negroes in the average are not equal in developed capacity to the white race, is a proposition which it would be as simple to affirm as it is silly to deny. The Negro represents a belated race which has not yet taken a commanding part in the progressive movement of the world. In the great cosmic scheme of things, some races reach the lime-light of civilization ahead of others. But that temporary forwardness does not argue inherent superiority is as evident as any fact of history. An unfriendly environment may hinder and impede the one, while fortunate circumstances may quicken and spur the other. Relative superiority is only a transient phase of human development. You tell us

that " The Jew had achieved a civilization—had his
poets, prophets, priests and kings, when our Germanic ancestors were still in the woods cracking
cocoanuts and hickory nuts with the monkeys."
Fancy some learned Jew at that day citing your
query about the contribution of the Germanic races
to the culture of the human spirit, during the thousands of years of their existence! Does the progress
of history not prove that races may lie dormant and
fallow for ages and then break suddenly into prestige
and power? Fifty years ago you doubtless would
have ranked Japan among the benighted nations and
hurled at their heathen heads some derogatory query
as to their contribution to civilization. But since
the happenings at Mukden and Port Arthur and
Portsmouth, I suppose that you are ready to change
your mind on the subject. Or maybe, since the Jap
has proved himself a " first-class fighting man," able
to cope on equal terms with the best breeds of
Europe, you will claim him as belonging to the white
race, notwithstanding his pig eye and yellow pigment.

In the course of history the ascendency of the
various races and nations of men is subject to strange
variability. The Egyptian, the Jew, the Indian, the
Greek, the Roman, the Arab, has each had his turn
at domination. When the earlier nations were in
their zenith of art and thought and song, Franks and
Britons and Germans were roaming through dense
forests, groveling in subterranean caves, practicing
barbarous rites, and chanting horrid incantations
to graven gods. In the proud days of Aristotle the
ancestors of Newton and Shakespeare and Bacon
could not count beyond the ten fingers. As compared
with the developed civilization of the period, they
were a backward race, though, as subsequent development has shown, by no means an inferior one.

There were hasty philosophers in that day who branded these people with the everlasting stamp of inferiority. The brand of philosophy portrayed in " The Leopard's Spots " and in *Tom Watson's Magazine* has flourished in all ages of the world.

The individuals of a backward race are not, as such, necessarily inferior to those of a more advanced people. The vast majority of any race is composed of ordinary and inferior folk. To use President Roosevelt's expression, they cannot pull their own weight. It is only the few choice individuals, reinforced by a high standard of social efficiency, that are capable of adding to the civilization of the world.

There is no hard and fast line dividing the two races on the scale of capacity. There is the widest possible range of variation within the limits of each. A philosopher and a fool may not only be members of the same race but of the same family. No scheme of classification is possible which will include all white men and shut out all Negroes. According to any test of excellence that your and Mr. Watson's ingenuity can devise, some Negroes will be superior to most white men; no stretch of ingenuity or strain of conscience has yet devised a plan of franchise which includes all of the members of one race and excludes all those of the other.

Learned opinion on the other side ought, at least, to weigh as much against your thesis as your own fulminations count in favor of it. You surely have high respect for the authority of Thomas Jefferson. In a letter to Benjamin Banneker, the Negro astronomer, the author of the great Declaration wrote: " Nobody wishes more than I do to see such proofs as you exhibit that Nature has given to our black brethren talents equal to those of the other colors of men, and that the apparent want of them is owing merely to the degraded condition of their existence, both in Africa and America."

Mr. William Mathews, a noted author, writing some time ago in the *North American Review*, asserts: "We affirm that the inferiority of the Negro has never been proven, nor is there any good ground to suppose that he is forever to maintain his relative position, or that he is inferior to the white man in any other sense than some white races are inferior to each other."

Prof. N. F. Shaler, a native of the South, and Professor in Harvard University, writes in the *Arena:* "There are hundreds and thousands of black men who in capacity are to be ranked with the superior persons of the dominant race, and it is hard to say that in any evident feature of mind they characteristically differ from their white fellow-citizens."

Benjamin Kidd, in his work on Social Evolution, declares that the Negro child shows no inferiority, and that the deficiency which he seems to manifest in after life is due to his dwarfing and benumbing environment. Prof. John Spencer Bassett, of Trinity College, North Carolina, has had the courage to state the belief that the Negro would gain equality some day. He also tells us that Dr. Booker Washington, whom Mr. Watson takes so sharply to task for hinting that the Negro may be superior to some white men, is the greatest man, with a single exception, that the South has produced in a hundred years. This is indeed a suggestion of Negro superiority with a vengeance. In the judgment of this distinguished Southerner, one Negro, at least, is superior to millions of his white fellow-citizens, including the editor of *Tom Watson's Magazine* and the author of "The Leopard's Spots."

" But," rejoins the objector, " if the Negro possesses this inherent capacity, why has he not given the world the benefit of it during the course of history? " Capacity is potential rather than a dynamic mode of energy. Whatever native capacity the mind may possess, it must be stimulated and reinforced by social accomplishment before it can show great achievement. In arithmetic a number has an inherent and local value, the latter being by far the more powerful function in numerical calculation. The individual may count for much, but the social efficiency counts for most. It is absolutely impossible for a Francis Bacon to thrive among the Bushmen, or a Herbert Spencer among the Hottentots. The great names of the world always arise among the people who, for the time being, are in the forefront of the world's movements. We do not expect names of the first degree of lustre to arise among suppressed and submerged classes.

In confirmation of this view let us turn for a moment to the pages of history. Mr. Lecky tells us in his " History of European Morals ":

" I regard it as one of the anomalies of history that within the narrow limits and scanty population of the Greek states should have arisen men who in almost every conceivable form of genius, in philosophy, in ethics, in dramatic and lyric poetry, in written and spoken eloquence, in statesmanship, in sculpture, in painting, and probably also in music, should have attained almost or altogether the highest limits of human perfection."

Mr. Galton in his " Hereditary Genius " tells us: " We have no men to put beside Socrates and Phidias. The millions of Europe breeding as they have done for the subsequent two thousand years have never produced their equals. It follows from all this that the average ability of the Athenian race is, on the lowest estimate, very nearly two grades higher than our own; that is, about as much as our race is above that of the African Negro." And yet this intellectual race, this race of Phidias and Homer, of Plato and Socrates, has continued for two thousand years in a state of complete intellectual stagnation. When they lost their political nationality and became submerged beneath the heavy weight of oppression, to use the language of Macaulay, " their people have degenerated into timid slaves and their language into a barbarous jargon." Can there be any stronger proof of the fact that great achievements depend upon environment and social stimulus rather than innate capacity?

Where now is the boasted glory of Egypt and Babylon, of Nineveh and Tyre? Expeditions from distant continents are sent to unearth the achievements of renowned ancestors beneath the very feet of their degenerate descendants, as a mute reminder to the world of the transiency of human greatness.

The Jews seem to form an exception to this rule, but the exception is seeming rather than real. While they have lost their political integrity, they have preserved their spiritual nationality. The race of Moses and Paul and Jesus still produces great names, though not of the same grade of glory as their prototypes of old.

Our own country has not escaped the odium of intellectual inferiority. The generation has scarcely passed away in whose ears used to ring the standing sneer, " Who reads an American book?" It was in the day of Thomas Jefferson that a learned European declared: "America has not produced one good poet, one able mathematician, one man of genius in a single art or science." In response to this charge Jefferson enters an eloquent special plea. He says: "When we shall have existed as a people as long as the Greeks did before they produced a Homer, the Romans, a Virgil, the French, a Racine, the English, a Shakespeare and Milton, should this reproach be still true, we will inquire from what unfriendly cause it has proceeded." How analogous to this is the reproach which you and Mr. Watson, treading the track of Thomas Nelson Page, and those of his school of thought, now hurl against the Negro race? The response of Jefferson defending the American colonies from the reproach of innate inferiority will apply with augmented emphasis to ward off similar charges against the despised and rejected Negro. A learned authority tells us: "Hardly two centuries have passed since Russia was covered with a horde of barbarians among whom it would have been as difficult to find any example of intellectual cultivation and refinement as at this day to find the same phenomenon at Timbuctoo or among the Negroes of Georgia or Alabama." It is well for the good fame of the Russian people that *Tom Watson's Magazine* did not exist in those days.

According to a study of the distribution of ability in the United States, a study made by Hon. Henry Cabot Lodge, the little State of Massachusetts has produced more men of distinction and achievement than all the South combined. " In architecture, agriculture, manufacture, finance, legislation, sculpture, religion, organization, painting, music, literature, science, the wedding of the fine arts of religion," the South is relatively backward as compared with other sections of the country. But this lack of comparative achievement is not due at all to innate inferiority of Southern white men to their brethren in higher latitudes. Mr. Thomas Nelson Page, in his famous

book on the Old South, accepts this derogatory fact
and explains its cause with much ingenuity. The
white people of the South claim, or rather boast of,
a race prepotency and inheritance as great as that
of any breed of men in the world. But they clearly
fail to show like attainment.

It would evidently be unfair to conclude that the
white race in Georgia is inherently inferior to the
people of New England because it has failed to produce names of like renown. The difference in wealth,
culture and bracing tone of environments are quite
sufficient to account for the difference in results. I
think that you and Mr. Watson will be generous
enough to concede to the Negro the benefit of the
same argument which the defenders of the South
resort to in justification of its own relative back-
wardness. The Negro has never, during the whole
course of history, been surrounded by those influences which tend to strengthen and develop the mind.
To expect the Negroes of Georgia to produce a
great general like Napoleon when they are not even
allowed to carry arms, or to deride them for not pro-
ducing scholars like those of the Renaissance when
a few years ago they were forbidden the use of letters, verges closely upon the outer rim of absurdity.
Do you look for great Negro statesmen in States
where black men are not allowed to vote? Mr. Watson can tell something about the difficulty of being
a statesman in Georgia, against the protest of the
ruling political ring. He tried it. Above all, for
Southern white men to berate the Negro for failing
to gain the highest rounds of distinction reaches the
climax of cruel inconsistency. One is reminded of
the barbarous Teutons in " Titus Andronicus," who,
after cutting out the tongue and hacking off the
hands of the lovely Lavinia, ghoulishly chided her

for not calling for sweet water with which to wash her delicate hands.

Here is another specimen of the grade of reasoning to which the readers of *Tom Watson's Magazine* are treated:

" Let me repeat to you, Doctor, the unvarnished truth, for it may do you good. The advance made by your race in America is the reflection of the white man's civilization. Just that and nothing more. The Negro lives in the light of the white man's civilization and reflects a part of that light."

Here again we come across the threadbare argument of the advocates of suppression and subordination of the Negro. The aptitude of any people for progress is tested by the readiness with which they absorb and assimilate the environment of which they form a part. I wonder if Mr. Watson would contend that the red Indian shows capacity for civilization because he neither borrows nor imitates. Civilization is not a spontaneous generation with any race or nation known to history, but the torch is handed down from race to race and from age to age, and gains in brilliancy as it goes. The progress made by the Negro has been natural and inevitable. Does Mr. Watson expect the American Negro to invent an alphabet before he learns to read? The Negro has advanced in exactly the same fashion that the white race has advanced, by taking advantage of all that has gone before. Other men have labored and we have entered into their labors. The Japanese did not invent the battleship, modern artillery, or the modern manual of arms, but they use them pretty effectively. The young race, like the individual, must first appropriate and apply what has already gone before. The white man has no exclusive proprietorship of civilization. White man's civilization is as much a misnomer as the white man's multiplication table. It is the equal inheritance of any one who can appropriate and apply it. This is the only practicable test of a people's capacity. I have no doubt that Mr. Watson would say that the million white people of Georgia are a very capable folk. And yet how many of them have added anything to the processes of civilization? They have simply entered into, and carried on the processes already established. When Mr. Watson concedes the Negro's ability to do this much he negatives the whole argument of inferiority.

You and Mr. Watson, by common, unaccountable parallelism, make the same quotation from Buckle's " History of Civilization," and in some mysterious manner endeavor to turn his words to the detriment of the Negro:

> The discoveries of great men never leave us; they are immortal, they contain those eternal truths which survive the shock of empires, outlive the struggle of rival creeds and witness the decay of successive religions. The discoveries of genius alone remain; it is to them we owe all that we now have; they are for all ages and all times; never young and never old, they bear the seeds of their own life, they flow on in perennial, undying stream; they are essentially cumulative, and giving birth to additions which they subsequently receive, they thus influence the most distant posterity, and after lapse of centuries produce more effect than they were able to do even at the moment of their promulgation.

Genius has no age, no country, no race; it belongs to mankind—who cares whether Sir Isaac Newton or Watts or Fulton was red, or white, or brown? Shakespeare means no more to you than he does to me, except in so far as you may have greater capacity of appreciation and enjoyment. Bacon and Darwin appeal to the world. Do you think that

when the candle of genius has been lighted by fire
from above it can be hid under a bushel of racial
exclusiveness?   Nay; rather, it is set on a candle-
stick and gives light unto all who grope in darkness.   The Negro enters into the inheritance of all the
ages on equal terms with the rest, and who can say
that he will not contribute his quota of genius to
enrich the blood of the world?

The line of argument of every writer who under-
takes to belittle the Negro is a well-beaten path.
Liberia and Hayti are bound to come in for their
share of ridicule and contemptuous handling.   Mr.
Watson calls these experiments freshly to mind, " lest
we forget, lest we forget."   We are told all about
the incapacity of the black race for self-government,
the relapse into barbarism, and much more, all of
which we have heard before; and yet when we take
all the circumstances into account, Hayti presents to
the world one of the most remarkable achievements
in the annals of human history.   The panegyric of
Wendell Phillips on Toussaint L'Ouverture is more
than an outburst of rhetorical fancy; it is a just
measure of his achievements in terms of his humble
environment and the limited instrumentalities at his
command.   Where else in the course of history has
a slave, with the aid of slaves, expelled a powerfully
intrenched master-class and set up a government
patterned after civilized models, which without
external assistance or reinforcement from a par-
ent civilization has endured for a hundred years
in face of a frowning world?   When we consider the
difficulties that confront a weak government, without
military or naval means to cope with its more powerful rivals, and where commercial adventurers are ever
and anon stirring up internal strife, thus provoking

the intervention of stronger governments, the marvel is that the republic of Hayti still endures, the only self-governing State of the Antilles. To expect as effective and proficient government to prevail in Hayti as at Washington would be expecting more of the black men in Hayti than we find in the white men of South America. And yet, I suspect that the million of Negroes in Hayti are as well governed as the corresponding number of blacks in Georgia, where, only yesterday, eight men were taken from the custody of the law and lynched without judge or jury. It is often charged that these people have not maintained the pace set by the old master-class, that the plantations are in ruins and that the whole island wears the aspect of dilapidation. Wherever a lower people overrun the civilization of a higher there is an inevitable lapse toward the level of the lower. When barbarians and semi-civilized hordes of northern Europe overran the southern peninsulas the civilization of the world was wrapped in a thousand years of darkness. Relapse inevitably precedes the rebound. Is there anything in the history of Hayti contrary to the law of human development?

You ask: "Can you change the color of the Negro's skin, the kink of his hair, the bulge of his lip, or the beat of his heart with a spelling-book or a machine?" This rhetorical outburst does great credit to your literary skill, and is calculated to delight the simple; but analysis fails to reveal in it any pregnant meaning. Since civilization is not an attribute of the color of skin, or curl of hair, or curve of lip, there is no necessity for changing such physical peculiarities, and if there were, the spelling-book and the machine would be very unlikely instruments for its accomplishment. But why, may I ask, would you desire to change the Negro's heart-throb,

which already beats at a normal human pace? You
need not be so frantic about the superiority of your
race. Whatever superiority it may possess, inherent
or acquired, will take care of itself without such
rabid support. Has it ever occurred to you that the
people of New England blood, who have done and
are doing most to make the white race great and
glorious in this land, are the most reticent about
extravagant claims to everlasting superiority? You
protest too much. Your loud pretensions, backed
up by such exclamatory outburst of passion, make
upon the reflecting mind the impression that you
entertain a sneaking suspicion of their validity.

Your position as to the work and worth of Booker
T. Washington is pitiably anomalous. You recite the
story of his upward struggle with uncontrolled admiration: " The story of this little ragged, bare-
footed pickaninny, who lifted his eyes from a cabin
in the hills of Virginia, saw a vision and followed
it, until at last he presides over the richest and most
powerful institution in the South, and sits down
with crowned heads and presidents, has no parallel
even in the ' Tales of the Arabian Nights.' " You
say that this story appeals to the universal heart of
humanity. And yet in a recent letter to the *Columbia State*, you say you regard it as an unspeakable
outrage that Mr. Robert C. Ogden should walk arm
in arm with this wonderful man who "appeals to
the heart of universal humanity," and introduce him
to the lady clerks in a dry goods store. Your passionate devotion to a narrow dogma has seriously
impaired your sense of humor. The subject of your
next great novel has been announced as " The Fall
of Tuskegee." In one breath you commend the work
of this great institution, while in another you condemn it because it does not fit into your precon-

ceived scheme in the solution of the race problem.
The Tuskegee ideal—" to make Negroes producers,
lovers of labor, independent, honest, and good "—is
one which you say that only a fool or a knave can
find fault with, because, in your own words, " it rests
squarely upon the eternal verities." Over against
this you add with all the condemnatory emphasis of
italics and exclamation point: " Tuskegee is not a
servant training-school!" And further: " Mr.
Washington is not training Negroes to take their
places in the industries of the South in which white
men direct and control them. He is not training
students to be servants and come at the beck and
call of any man. He is training them to be masters
of men, to be independent, to own and operate their
own industries, plant their own fields, buy and sell
their own goods." All of which you condemn by
imperative inference ten times stronger than your
faint and forced verbal approval. It is a heedless
man who wilfully flaunts his little philosophy in face
of the " eternal verities." When the wise man finds
that his prejudices are running against fixed principles in God's cosmic plan he speedily readjusts
them in harmony therewith. Has it never occurred
to you to re-examine the foundation of the faith,
as well as the feeling that is in you, since you admit
that it runs afoul of the " eternal verities "?

Mr. Washington's motto, in his own words, is that
" The Negro has been worked; but now he must
learn to work." The man who works for himself is
of more service to any community than the man
whose labor is exploited by others. You bring forward the traditional bias of the slave regime to modern conditions, viz., that the Negro did not exist
in his own right and for his own sake, but for the
benefit of the white man. This principle is as false

in nature as it is in morals. The naturalists tell us that throughout all the range of animal creation there is found no creature which exists for the sake of any other, but each is striving after its own best welfare. Do you fear that the Negro's welfare is incompatible with that of the white man? I commend to you a careful perusal of the words of Mr. E. Gardner Murphy, who, like yourself, is a devoted Southerner, and is equally zealous to promote the highest interest of that section: "Have prosperity, peace, and happiness ever been successfully or permanently based upon indolence, inefficiency, and hopelessness? Since time began, has any human thing that God has made taken damage to itself or brought damage to the world through knowledge, truth, hope, and honest toil?" Read these words of your fellow Southerner, Mr. Dixon, and meditate upon them; they will do you good as the truth doeth the upright in heart.

You quote me as being in favor of the amalgamation of the races. A more careful reading of the article referred to would have convinced you that I was arguing against amalgamation as a probable solution of the race problem. I merely stated the intellectual conviction that two races cannot live indefinitely side by side, under the same general regime, without ultimately fusing. This was merely the expression of a belief, and not the utterance of a preference nor the formulation of a policy. I know of no colored man who advocates amalgamation as a feasible policy of solution. You are mistaken. The Negro does not "hope and dream of amalgamation." This would be self-stultification with a vengeance. If such a policy were allowed to dominate the imagination of the colored race its women would give themselves over to the unrestrained passion of white

men, in quest of tawny offspring, which would give
rise to a state of indescribable moral debauchery.
At the same time, you would hardly expect the
Negro, in derogation of his common human qualities,
to proclaim that he is so diverse from God's other
human creatures as to make the blending of the races
contrary to the law of nature. The Negro refuses
to become excited or share in your frenzy on this
subject. The amalgamation of the races is an ultimate possibility, though not an immediate probability. But what have you and I to do with ultimate
questions, anyway? Our concern is with duty, not
destiny. There are statisticians who can tell you,
to the tick of the clock, when the last ton of coal
in the bowels of the earth will be consumed; but you
will not lower the temperature of your sitting-room
one degree next winter in view of that ultimate con-
tingency. The exhaustion of solar heat is within the
purview of astronomical calculation, and yet we eat
and drink and make merry in supreme indifference
to that far-off calamitous event. Do you not suppose that the future generations will have wisdom
adequate to the problems of their day? We certainly have no surplus wisdom to advance them.
Sufficient unto the day is the ignorance thereof.
Your frantic dread of amalgamation reminds me of
those religionists who would frighten a heedless world
into the belief that the end is at hand. It is conceivable that you voluntarily unfrocked yourself as
a priest of God, where your function was to save the
individual soul from punishment in the next world, in
order that you might the more effectively warn your
race to flee from amalgamation as from the wrath
to come.

But do you know, Mr. Dixon, that you are probably the foremost promoter of amalgamation be-

tween the two oceans? Wherever you narrow the
scope of the Negro by preaching the doctrine of hate
you drive thousands of persons of lighter hue over to
the white race, carrying more or less Negro blood
in their train. The blending of the races is less
likely to take place if the self-respect and manly
opportunity of the Negro are respected and encouraged than if he is to be forever crushed beneath the
level of his faculties for dread of the fancied result.
Hundreds of the composite progeny are daily cross-
ing the color line and carrying as much of the despised blood as an albicant skin can conceal without
betrayal. I believe that it was Congressman Tillman, brother of the more famous Senator of that
name, who stated on the floor of the Constitutional
Convention of South Carolina that he knew of four
hundred white families in that State who had a taint
of Negro blood in their veins. I personally know,
or know of, fifty cases of transition in the city of
Washington. It is a momentous thing for one to
change one's caste. The man or woman who affects
to deny, ignore, or scorn the class with whom he
previously associated is usually deemed deficient in
the nobler qualities of human nature. It is not
conceivable that persons of this class would undergo
the self-degradation and humiliation of soul necessary to cross the great " social divide " unless it be
to escape for themselves and their descendants an
odious and despised status. Your oft expressed and
passionately avowed belief that the progressive development of the Negro would hasten amalgamation
is not borne out by the facts of observation. The
refined and cultivated class among colored people
are as much disinclined to such unions as the whites
themselves. I am sorry that you saw fit to charac-
terize Frederick Douglass as " a bombastic vituper-

ator." You thereby gave poignant offense to ten
millions of his race who regard him as the best embodiment of their possibilities. Besides, millions of
your race rate him among the foremost and best beloved of Americans. How would you feel if some
one should stigmatize Jefferson Davis or Robert E.
Lee in such language, these beau ideals of your
Southern heart? But I will not undertake to defend Frederick Douglass against your calumniations.
I am frank to confess that I do not feel that he
needs it. The point I have in mind to make about
Mr. Douglass is that he has a hold upon the affection
of his race, not on account of his second marriage,
but in spite of it. He seriously affected his standing
with his people by that marriage.

Degradation would soonest lead to race blending
through illicitness. Had the institution of slavery
existed for another century without fresh African
importation there would scarcely have remained an
unbleached Negro on the continent. The best possible evidence that the development of self-respect
does not lead to amalgamation is furnished by Oberlin College in Ohio and by Berea College in Kentucky. These institutions have had thousands of
students of the two races, male and female, associating on terms of personal equality, mutual respect,
and good will, and yet in all these years not a single
case of miscegenation has resulted. Contrast this
record with the concubinage of the Southern plantation and the illicit relations of the city slum, and
it is easy to see where the chief stress should be
placed by those who so frantically dread race admix-
ture.

It seems to me, Mr. Dixon, that this frantic abhorrence of amalgamation is a little late in its appearance. Whence comes this stream of white blood

which flows, with more or less spissitude, in the veins of some six out of ten million Negroes? It is due to the bleaching breath of Saxon civilization. The Afro-American is hardly a Negro at all, but a new creature. Who brought about this present approachment between the races? Do you not appreciate the inconsistency in the attitude and the action on the part of many of the loud-mouthed advocates of race purity? It is said that old Father Chronos devoured his offspring in order to forestall future complications. But we do not learn that he put a bridle upon his passion as the surest means of security. The most effective service you can render to check the evil of amalgamation is to do missionary work among the males of your own race. This strenuous advocacy of race purity in face of proved proneness for miscegenation affords a striking reminder of the lines of *Hudibras:*

> "The self-same thing they will abhor,
> One way, and long another for."

I beg now to call your attention to one or two statements of fact. You state that " only one-third of the cotton crop is to-day raised by Negro labor." I would like to ask, what is your authority for that statement? According to the twelfth census, the latest available data on the subject, out of a total cotton crop of 9,534,707 bales for 1899, Negro proprietors alone produced 3,707,881 bales, or 39 per cent. of the total crop. There were 746,715 such proprietors, against 1,418,343 Negro agricultural laborers. If we suppose that these hired laborers were as efficient as the more independent tenants, it will be seen that, instead of raising only one-third, the Negro's immediate labor produced practically all of the cotton crop of the South.

Again, you say that " we have spent about $800,-000,000 on Negro education since the war." This statement is so very wide of the mark that I was disposed to regard it as a misprint, if you had not reinforced it with an application implying a like amount. In the report of the Bureau of Education for 1901 the estimated expenditure for Negro education in all the former slave States since the Civil War is put down at $121,184,568. The amount contributed by Northern philanthropy during that interval is variously estimated from fifty to seventy-five millions. Your estimate is four times too large. It would be interesting and informing to the world if you would reveal the source of your information. These misstatements of fact are not of so much importance in themselves as that they serve to warn the reader against the accuracy and value of your general judgments. It would seem that you derive your figures of arithmetic from the same source from which you fashion your figures of speech. You will not blame the reader for not paying much heed to your sweeping generalizations when you are at such little pains as to the accuracy of easily ascertainable data.

Your proposed solution of the race problem by colonizing the Negroes in Liberia reaches the climax of absurdity. It is difficult to see how such a proposition could emanate from a man of your reputation. Did you consult Cram's Atlas about Liberia? Please do so. You will find that it has an area of 48,000 square miles and a population of 1,500,000, natives and immigrants. The area and population are about the same as those of North Carolina, which, I believe, is your native State. When you tell us that this restricted area, without commerce, without manufacture, without any system of organized in-

dustry, can support every Negro in America, in addition to its present population, I beg mildly to suggest that you recall your plan for revision before
submitting it to the judgment of a critical world.
Your absolute indifference to the facts, and your
heedlessness of the circumstances and conditions involved in the scheme of colonization, well befit the
absurdity of the general proposition.

The solution of the race problem in America is
indeed a grave and serious matter. It is one that
calls for statesmanlike breadth of view, philanthropic
tolerance of spirit, and exact social knowledge. The
whole spirit of your propaganda is to add to its
intensity and aggravation. You stir the slumbering fires of race wrath into an uncontrollable flame.
I have read somewhere that Max Nordau, on reading
"The Leopard's Spots," wrote to you suggesting
the awful responsibility you had assumed in stirring
up enmity between race and race. Your teachings
subvert the foundations of law and established order.
You are the high priest of lawlessness, the prophet
of anarchy. Rudyard Kipling places this sentiment
in the mouth of the wreckless stealer of seals in the
Northern Sea: "There's never a law of God nor
man runs north of fifty-three." This description
exactly fits the brand of literature with which you
are flooding the public. You openly urge your
fellow-citizens to override all law, human and divine.
Are you aware of the force and effect of these words?
"Could fatuity reach a sublimer height than the
idea that the white man will stand idly by and see the
performance? What will he do when put to the test?
He will do exactly what his white neighbor in the
North does when the Negro threatens his bread—
kill him!" These words breathe out hatred and
slaughter and suggest the murder of innocent men

whose only crime is quest for the God-given right
to work. You poison the mind and pollute the imagination through the subtle influence of literature.
Are you aware of the force and effect of evil suggestion when the passions of men are in a state of unstable equilibrium? A heterogeneous population,
where the elements are, on any account, easily distinguishable, is an easy prey for the promoter of
wrath. The fuse is already prepared for the spark.
The soul of the mob is stirred by suggestion of
hatred and slaughter, as a famished beast at the
smell of blood. Hatred is the ever-handy dynamic
of the demagogue. The rabble responds much more
readily to an appeal to passion than to reason. To
stir wantonly the fires of race antipathy is as execrable a deed as flaunting a red rag in the face of a
bull at a summer's picnic, or raising a false cry of
"fire" in a crowded house. Human society could
not exist one hour except on the basis of law which
holds the baser passions of men in restraint.

In our complex situation it is only the rigid observance of law reinforced by higher moral restraint
that can keep these passions in bound. You speak
about giving the Negro a "square deal." Even
among gamblers, a "square deal" means to play
according to the rules of the game. The rules which
all civilized States have set for themselves are found
in the Ten Commandments, the Golden Rule, the
Sermon on the Mount, and the organic law of the
land. You acknowledge no such restraints when the
Negro is involved, but waive them all aside with
frenzied defiance. You preside at every crossroad
lynching of a helpless victim; wherever the midnight
murderer rides with rope and torch in quest of the
blood of his black brother, you ride by his side;
wherever the cries of the crucified victim go up to

God from the crackling flame, behold, you are there;
when women and children, drunk with ghoulish glee,
dance around the funeral pyre and mock the death
groans of their fellow-man and fight for ghastly
souvenirs, you have your part in the inspiration of
it all. When guilefully guided workmen in mine and
shop and factory, goaded by a real or imaginary
sense of wrong, begin the plunder and pillage of
property and murder of rival men, your suggestion
is justifier of the dastardly doings. Lawlessness is
gnawing at the very vitals of our institutions. It is
the supreme duty of every enlightened mind to allay
rather than spur on this spirit. You are hastening
the time when there is to be a positive and emphatic
show of hands—not of white hands against black
hands, God forbid! not of Northern hands against
Southern hands, heaven forfend! but a determined
show of those who believe in law and God and constituted order, against those who would undermine
and destroy the organic basis of society, involving
all in a common ruin. No wonder Max Nordau exclaimed: "God, man, are you aware of your responsibility!"

But do not think, Mr. Dixon, that when you evoke
the evil spirit you can exorcise him at will. The
Negro in the end will be the least of his victims.
Those who become inoculated with the virus of race
hatred are more unfortunate than the victims of it.
Voltaire tells us that it is more difficult and more
meritorious to wean men of their prejudices than it
is to civilize the barbarian. Race hatred is the most
malignant poison that can afflict the mind. It freezes
up the font of inspiration and chills the higher faculties of the soul. You are a greater enemy to your
own race than you are to mine.

Permit me to close this letter with a citation from

Goldsmith's " Elegy on a Mad Dog." Please note the reference is descriptive and prophetic of the fate of the wreakers of wrath and the victims of it.

" This man and dog at first were friends,
   But when a pique began,
The dog to gain some private ends,
   Went mad and bit the man.

" Around from all the neighboring streets,
   The wondering neighbors ran,
And swore the dog had lost his wits,
   To bite so good a man.

" The wound it seemed both sore and sad
   To every Christian eye,
And while they swore the dog was mad
   They swore the man would die.

" But soon a wonder came to light,
   That show'd the rogues they lied,
The man recovered of the bite;
   The dog it was that died."

I have written you thus fully in order that you may clearly understand how the case lies in the Negro's mind. If any show of feeling or bitterness of spirit crops out in my treatment of the subject, or between the lines, my letter is, at least, wholly without vindictive intent; but is the inevitable outcome of dealing with issues that verge upon the deepest human passion.

AN APPEAL TO REASON ON THE RACE PROBLEM

AN OPEN LETTER TO JOHN TEMPLE GRAVES

SUGGESTED BY THE ATLANTA RIOT

OCTOBER, 1906.

MR. JOHN TEMPLE GRAVES,
Atlanta, Georgia.

My Dear Sir: The world has read with horror of the Atlanta massacre and of the part you played during that awful hour. The outbreak is but the fruits of the seeds of race wrath which you and others have been assiduously sowing. They who sow the wind may expect to reap the whirlwind.

Your open appeal to the passion of the American people while this riot was yet at its height was fraught with evil suggestiveness. That half the people of Atlanta were not slain is due to the fact that other counsel than yours prevailed. The rabble is ever actuated by sinister influence. It obeys the acquiescent nod of secret understanding. There is a wireless communication between the baser elements of society and the cunning instigator who provokes them to wrath. Shakespeare with inimitable faithfulness has described the inner workings of this subtle and guilty control whereby the obsequious is prone to take the humor of the mighty for a warrant " to break within the bloody house of life " on the winking of authority.

After a wide scanning of the American press, yours is the only voice which I have heard, South or North, white or black, still breathing out hatred

71

and slaughter amidst this awful carnival of blood.
You alone occupy that "bad eminence." You broke
the unanimity of appeal to reason when wild passion
had reached its whitest heat.

Your attitude contrasted with that of the foremost member of the afflicted race measures the whole
diameter of difference between cruelty and mercy.
While Negroes, innocent of any crime, were suffering
torture which would cause even the bruised worm
to turn, Booker T. Washington, with Christ-like forgiveness of spirit, counseled his people to resist not
evil.

The natural impulse of one belonging to the victim race is to indulge in indignant and bitter words.
It is almost impossible to repress this natural ebul-
lition of feeling. When human nature is so flagrantly outraged the very stones would cry out if
men should hold their peace. It requires the highest
self-repression and poise of spirit to refrain from
verbal vehemence. But the voice of wisdom counsels
only such expression as will tend to relieve rather
than to intensify the strain of a critical situation.

I wish to utilize this gruesome occasion to discuss
in an epistolary form some of the issues growing
out of race relations in this country. I shall strive
to be entirely courteous and considerate, and yet I
shall abate no whit the fullest candor and plainness
of statement demanded of one who speaks for the
best interest of his people. Even an ambassador in
bonds should speak with becoming boldness. There
is a lamentable lack of expression which is at once
candid and considerate, as respects the attitude of
one race toward the other. We are prone to indulge
in either wild, ungoverned onslaught, or diplomatic
dissimilation and prudential concealment of real opinion and feeling. Honesty of utterance is usually

accompanied with such ruthless and brutal frankness on the one hand, and resentful defiance on the other, as to render rational discussion impossible; while considerate temperament is too often given to indulgence in such fulsome flattery or unmanly yieldance as to make wholesome discussion unprofitable. Several years ago I sat on the platform of a meeting in Atlanta composed of about equal numbers of the two races. If I mistake not, you were present on that occasion. Local representatives on both sides of the race line vied with each other in vowing racial affection and ties of endearment. Words could go no further in expressing friendly relationship. But as I sat there, I divined, as I thought, a hidden spirit not revealed in the spoken words, which seemed to me to be simply verbal civilities and diplomatic platitudes. When the meeting adjourned each went to his own company with no surer knowledge of the real feeling or purpose of the other than when it convened.

Mr. Thomas Nelson Page has suggested in his recent book that the time has come for the best representatives of both races to meet together in conference on matters vitally concerning the common weal. It is needless to say that the value of such conference will depend upon the candor and frankness of spirit on both sides. The strained relation between the races calls for the temper and spirit of a statesmanship which discards wild hysterics and the heated passion of the moment, and sanely safeguards the interests of all the people. We are confronted with a problem whose factors are as intricate and whose outcome is as far-reaching as any that has ever taxed human wisdom for solution.

I am addressing this letter to you not merely because of the leading part which you played in the recent eruption, but also because you stand for a policy and a propaganda whose fatuity it fully reveals. It is a dangerous thing to arouse the evil spirit. It will turn again and rend you. The recent Atlanta outbreak fully illustrates the folly of appealing to the baser passion, especially in a parti-colored community.

Have you stopped to consider the cause and outcome of Atlanta's shame? The State of Georgia had been lashed into fury for more than a year of bitter race discussion. The atmosphere was ominous and tense. The fuse was ready for the spark. There were assaults or rumors of assaults by black or blackened fiends, upon white women, in and around Atlanta. These were eagerly seized upon and exaggerated by an inflammatory press. They became the alarum and rallying cry about which the pent-up wrath of race found vent. Red journalism ran rife. The terrorized imaginations saw a fiend incarnate in every darksome face. One paper, a little redder than the rest, boldly offered a reward for a lynching bee in the capital of the Empire State of the South. The flaring headlines fanned the fire into a furious flame. The evil passion of a people always finds lodgment in the breasts of its basest members. The half-grown, half-drunk, half-savage descendants of Oglethorpe's colonists can no longer contain themselves. Like the Indian on the war-path, they must have a savage yell. "Kill the Negro brutes!" is the tocsin. They kill and beat and bruise Negroes on sight. The air is filled with ghoulish yells, mingled with the shrieks and groans of the mangled and dying. Although the hollow cry of virtue is ever on the lip, the mob has no more conception of righteousness than a bloodhound set upon a scent cares about the guilt or innocence of his quarry.

The aroused appetite for blood must be satiated. The police sprinkle the mob with the water hose; but they laugh at this complaisant impotency and joke with the mayor over the awful deeds of death, and cry out louder for blood. The Negroes are in seclusion; the liquor dens are closed; red headlines are suppressed in the local press. The fury of the mob ceases when it has nothing further to feed on. Twenty innocent Negroes are dead. The guilty escape amid the slaughter of the innocent. Not a single criminal has been touched. No evil propensity has been eradicated. As the spasm of delirium relaxes the city's name stands tarnished before the world. The sin of it, the shame of it will abide for many a day. The Negroes emerge bleeding and torn; the whites are dumbfounded at the evil possibilities of their baser class. The race problem still remains unsolved and the remedy for evil unsuggested. No knot is untied in the tangled web. Such is the fatuity of your doctrine that the Negro must be controlled through the terror of the senses.

Atlanta may be regarded as the Athens of the South. It abounds in schools and colleges for both races. Here is the home of many of the most illustrious names in the South. Here lived the late Henry W. Grady, the oracle of the New South. Joel Chandler Harris and Clark Howell wield a journalistic and literary influence second to none of that section. Among the Negroes Atlanta is noted for its increasing class of cultivated and refined people. Bowen, DuBois, and Crogman are men of light and leading, whose influence and power for good have gone out to all the land; and yet deliberate appeal to race passion may involve this community, with so many influences of refinement and restraint, in riot and ruin in a single night.

While the Atlanta riot still raged, a hurricane was blowing up from the tropics which destroyed hundreds of lives and millions of property in several Southern cities. But there was no blood-guiltiness. These cities will bury their dead and rebuild their waste places and pursue their path of peace and progress, forgetful and unregretful of this disastrous touch of nature. But the stain of Atlanta will abide. Immigration and capital will shun a mob-ruled city as they would a place infected with pestilence and death. The evil passion of man is more to be dreaded than the terror of earthquake or storm.

You represent the ultra type of opinion and feeling which find lodgment in the breast of the lower order of your own race. You would shut the Negro out from competition on the narrow and intolerant theory that there may not be enough " for you and us." Fearful that the tree of civilization is not big enough to bear fruit for all, you would deny the black man the God-given right to stretch forth his hand and partake of its fullness.

You are a disciple of Senator Tillman, who is the guide, philosopher, and friend of those who worship at the shrine of racial narrowness and hate.

Mr. William Garrott Brown, a scion of the traditional South, tells us in his most interesting book on " The Lower South in American History " that " the triumph of the Tillmanites in South Carolina worked a change in the internal policies of that State deeper than the change in 1776 and 1860." When we study the deep significance of the Tillman movement, we find that these words convey only the sober truth. The Tillman influence is by no means limited to his own State, but is equally potent in all parts of the South. The more cautious and considerate leaders have followed in his wake, while they have not cared openly to acknowledge his regency. Rough, ready, quick-witted, of blunt and bitter speech, unschooled, unrestrained by traditional amenities, Benjamin R. Tillman has become the embodiment and expounder of the rule of the nether whites. In this scheme of government the Negro has no part or parcel, except to be ruled with a rod of iron. The old aristocratic class is accorded only such influence as it may gain by seeming to conform to the spirit of those whom it formerly regarded with scorn. The traditional society of the South was based upon belief in the Negro's complaisant subordination. The Tillman regime is based upon the fear that, after all, the Negro might not be inferior. He is deprived of his rights lest he develop suspected power. Tillman openly proclaims that he intends to keep the serpent frozen. The Devils also believe and tremble. The shifting of the seat of power from the upper to the lower stratum marks indeed a momentous transformation. The Senate seats once held by Calhoun and Jefferson Davis, and later by Hampton and Lamar, are now occupied by Tillman and Williams.

Up to the time of Tillman's advent opposition to the aristocratic regime took the form of combining the cause of the poorer whites with that of the Negroes in bonds of political union. By this means, Mahone won in Virginia, Pritchard and Butler in North Carolina, while Cobb and Watson led their following to glorious and, as they claimed, fraudulent defeat in Alabama and Georgia. Tillman was the first to pitch the poor whites against the Negro in fierce and bitter array. He understood the dynamic power of hatred. He won, and put an end to the aristocratic dynasty in the South. No longer does any faction form political alliance with the Negro. Wade Hampton threw out the olive branch, which was rejected. Now

all factions vie with each other in denunciation of
this race. Even the lily whites, a new variety of political exotics, which, like their botanical prototype,
neither toil nor spin, but array themselves in the
victory and spoils of office, have caught the contagion.

A *novus homo*, a Pharaoh, who knows not Joseph
the black, is now on the throne. The novice statesmen who are now so frantic about white supremacy
are experiencing the first delirium of power. Under
the old regime they were rigorously excluded from political authority. They never owned a slave nor anything else. But now the old line aristocrats habituated
to governmental control must obey the behests of their
new and numerous allies. They are forced to sacrifice both their statesmanlike breadth of view and
traditional chivalric spirit.

Mr. E. Gardner Murphy asks with affirmative,
though solicitous, intimation: " Is the organization
of Democracy in the South never to include the
Negro? Is he never to be a factor in the government and heir to a free and generous life?" Senator Tillman answers with a bitter and defiant negative. He declares with vehement asseveration that
the black man will ever be excluded from a participating part in the government under which he lives.
Race outbreaks in the South are but the outgrowth
of this feeling on the part of the half-enlightened
whites, but recently conscious of their political power,
against the black man, whom they regard as a natural rival and whom they hold in bitter despite.
Rumors of assaults but furnish occasions and excuse
for the exercise of this pent-up feeling. They are
no more the real cause than the gust of wind which
topples the mighty oak after the ax-man has plied
his last stroke is the dynamic cause of its downfall.

The volcanic eruption breaks through at the point where the mountain crust is thinnest.

A different excuse was found at Wilmington, N. C., where the race passion reached an atrocious climax a few years ago.

But there are two voices in the South to-day. While one preaches hatred and strife, another proclaims justice and humanity. The late Chancellor Hill, Bishop Galloway, Professor John Spencer Bassett, Joel Chandler Harris, and William H. Fleming, and a host of others represent the erstwhile silent South, which has remained tongue-tied under the threat of political and social calamity. When the advocates of a more humane and tolerant doctrine first began to make themselves heard they were regarded as incendiaries, simpletons, or harmless enthusiasts. George W. Cable was banished, Louis H. Blair ignored, J. L. M. Curry was listened to with courtesy, and Dr. Atticus G. Haygood was made a bishop.

But of late this voice has become " something louder than before " and can no longer be ignored as an important, if not a controlling factor in the Southern situation. The fundamental question to-day is which of these voices shall prevail—the voice of Tillman, which you loudly re-echo, or the voice of his vanished adversary, whose dying whisper was, " God bless all the people, white and black." The one breathing out hatred and slaughter, the other proclaiming peace and good will to all the people.

These two principles were exemplified in the Atlanta riot. It was the voice of cunning appealing to baser passion that provoked that shameful outbreak; but it was the firm, stern voice of higher quality and tone that restored peace and quiet. We are told that there was no member of the aristocratic class in that miserable rabble; neither was there any member of the baser element in that deliberate and determined body, composed of the best representatives of both races, which brought order out of chaos. If there is any indication that Providence, in this instance, has overruled the wrath of man for good, it is to be found in the working understanding reached by these two races on the common platform of mutual welfare. For they must live and work and thrive and suffer together for all time, with which you and I are concerned, despite your eloquent and fiery demand for racial separation.

In your address before the University of Chicago, several years ago, you not only justified, but extolled, the lynching of human beings. The punishment of Negroes for crimes committed against white persons furnishes the acutest phase of the race problem to-day. Lynching is apt to follow any serious offense against the person of a male member of the ruling race, and is sure to be inflicted where the complainant is of the other sex. The charge of rape is but one of the excuses for which the Negro suffers swift and summary vengeance. There is a growing understanding that the Negro must be lynched for offenses of certain nature and degree which is hedged about with as much nicety and exactness as the extinct *code duello*.

I am interrupted in the writing of this letter to read on a single page of my daily paper accounts of four lynchings in different parts of the country. In only one instance is assault on woman alleged; and even in this case, there was no judicial determination of guilt. These are fair samples of the nature of the charges upon which Judge Lynch passes sentence upon the black culprit without trial.

"Rape means rope," says the sententious Sam

Jones, and the moral sense of mankind approves the verdict. The only point of contention is whether this rope should be set apart by judicial sanction or extemporized by the bloodthirsty mob to appease ignoble race hatred.

There seems to be a deliberate propaganda on the part of those who appeal to the nether portion of the white South to place the colored race in evil repute in order to justify iniquitous practices. To make a race odious in the eyes of the world is ample excuse for all forms of outrages and cruel treatment. Such is the sinister homage that cunning pays to conscience. It always seizes upon the most sacred instincts and passionate ideals as its palliating cloak. Russia would make believe that the Jews offer up Christian babes in their horrid sacrificial rites to justify the butchery of a meek and lowly race. The lamb below the wolf is always charged with muddying the stream above him. Even among white men in the South the dead man is usually the guilty man. This propaganda has skillfully and willfully exaggerated assaults by colored men so as to give the black race an evil reputation. When all the facts in the case are calmly and carefully considered, due weight being given to all the contributing influences, it will be found that such offenses by Negroes are not greatly out of proportion to like offenses among white men. A careful student of current happenings informs me that he clipped from the newspapers fifteen cases of assaults by white men in one day in a single city. Where the Negro is involved it is the widespread circulation that inflames the popular mind.

Assault by a Negro, actual or alleged, is displayed by the press in the boldest headlines, whereas like offenses by white men are compressed within a half inch space, as part of the ordinary happenings of the day. Whenever a Negro is accused of this crime the Associated Press sends the announcement all over the land. The morning papers proclaim it in bold headlines, only to be outdone by their more reckless evening contemporaries. The weekly journals rehash the same with gruesome particularities, until the whole nation becomes inflamed against the race on account of the dastardly deed of a single wretch.

The Negroes of Atlanta, some forty thousand in number, who had hitherto sustained a good reputation for decency and order, were held up to the abhorrence of the whole civilized world by reason of two or three suspected criminals of their blood. This is as flagrantly unjust to the Negro as it would be to base the reputation of the population of London upon the deeds of Jack the Ripper, or the good name of Englishmen upon the disclosures of William T. Stead. If cases of lightning stroke were proclaimed with such horrifying publicity as heinous crimes committed by Negroes, we should all live in momentary dread of the terror of the sky.

Your chief complaint is not due so much to the heinousness of the assault itself as to the fact that the perpetrators belong to one race and the victims to another. The abhorrence of the deed is intensified by the color and degree of the evil-doer. Shakespeare has painted Caliban and Miranda, the one hideous and depraved, the other fair and pure as the rose of the morning, to illustrate how difference in degree and rank of the offender and the victim adds grievousness to the foulest offense. A nameless assassin, sprung from the scum of the earth and nurtured in a murderous cult, extending his cowardly hand in simulated greetings, struck down William McKinley, the most amiable and beloved of our rulers. This wretch in human form, whose unpronounceable name shall be anathema for evermore, aimed this deadly blow at the idol of the American people, and rolled a heavy stone on the nation's heart. Was ever deed more dastardly or better calculated to excite summary vengeance? This was all but the universal impulse. And yet the anxious solicitude of our dying chieftain was that no harm should come to his assailant not sanctioned by due process of law. Summary vengeance wreaked upon the vilest miscreant answers no worthy end. It neither wipes out the crime committed, nor prevents its repetition. A bitter and bloody experience shows too plainly that vindictive vengeance acts as a suggestive rather than a deterrent to the evilly disposed.

The prevalence of lynching in the South causes a double reaction of feeling. In the first place it causes the whites to hate the Negro, as it is a part of human nature to hate those whom we have injured. In the second place it causes the Negro to hate the whites. It is universally conceded that lynching has no deterrent effect upon the class of crimes alleged to excite its vengeance. On the contrary, it probably has the opposite effect. The criminals and outlaws of the Negro race, who care nothing for life or death, may be thus hardened into resolves of revenge, and lie waiting to strike the hated race where the blow will be most keenly felt.

You ask the Northern press to join in the work of blackening the name of the race by giving two paragraphs to every alleged assault and but scant notice to lynching. You would make it appear that " Negro," " rape " and " lynch " are connotative terms. But you seem to forget, or purposely ignore, the fact that the direst vengeance is often inflicted for other than rapeful assault. In Statesboro, a

remote village of your own State, two colored men,
intent on robbery, murdered a whole family and set
fire to the dwelling to hide their awful deed. The
accused were apprehended and sentenced to death
within two months after the horrible performance.
Race passion ran high. Threats and rumors of
lynching flew thick and fast. The bloodthirsty mob
vowed summary vengeance. The Governor dispatched State troops to quell the turbulent spirit
and vindicate the majesty of the law. But the mob
had scented blood and was not to be foiled of its
prey by an empty show of force. It snatched the
prisoner from the hands of the law, mocked the trial
judge, ignored the sheriff, and overpowered the militia, which, like tin soldiers, yielded without inflicting or receiving a wound. Cries of crucifixion filled
the air. The sovereign State of Georgia lies pros-
trate under the feet of the maddened mob, infuriated
at the aroused instinct for blood. The culprits are
dragged tremblingly through the streets, their bodies
saturated with oil, and chained to a decaying tree
trunk. The inflammable fagots are piled high, the
torch is applied while men, women, and children dance
with ghoulish glee at the death groans issuing from
the flames. In another instance a woman was burned
alive on a gruesome funeral pyre. Such fiendish
procedure outrages human nature and hurts the
heart of the world. All of this you would palliate
and excuse and ask the Northern press to pass over
with a scant and hasty paragraph.

I am disposed to hope that you will not be indifferent to the wrongs and injustice inflicted upon a
helpless, and, on the whole, rightly inclined people.

The woes and miseries of the Negro race are made
to culminate upon the subject of crime and its summary punishment. The black man's political rights,

civil privileges, educational opportunities, and the advantage of sympathetic and helpful contact with the white race will be conditioned upon the evil reputation foisted upon him by mob violence, inflicted on account of alleged execrable crimes. No people will tolerate a race of potential rapists in their midst. If this lecherous brand can be fixed upon the Negro's forehead it will be more loathsome than the murderous mark of Cain. The race would be shunned as a colony of moral lepers. No individual of this blood, however upright his personal life, could escape the taint of racial reputation.

This propaganda of evil has so far succeeded as to cool the ardor of those who are disposed to defend the Negro's cause. There is scarcely a single voice in all this land that dares, with undisguised boldness, to defend the rights of human nature for fear of the reproach of encouraging an unworthy people. There has been a sharp change in public sentiment during the last quarter century, which marks the period during which the Negro's alleged evil propensities have been proclaimed to the world with shrewd and unholy design. In 1881 Dr. Atticus G. Haygood, a courtly, pious son of Georgia, wrote a book and styled it "Our Brother in Black." Twenty years later we were startled at the title, "The Negro a Beast." These contrasted titles fairly gauge the drift of sentiment during that interval. So powerful for evil has been the attempt to convince the world that the black man is imbued with a low and evil nature, so despiteful has become the estimate in which the Negro is held, that at the slightest charge against him, the cry, "Lynch the Negro!" leaps spontaneously from the lips of the gathering multitude in the streets of our most populous and peaceful cities. We are so accustomed to the startling headlines in the daily press, "Negro Lynched" or "Negro Burned at the Stake," that the whole American people would become one national nervous wreck were it not that frequently repeated shocks of the same nature render the system insensible to further impressions. There is danger that the national feeling will become numb and the national conscience sear. Clippings from the columns of any leading daily on this subject for the past three months would be sufficient to form a mammoth Sunday edition, with a blood-red supplement of atrocious horrors. The intelligent Negro bears heavily the brunt of this load. The sins of his race, actual and alleged, weigh heavily upon him. Almost every reflecting Negro of my acquaintance is growing prematurely gray.

The Negro complains because of the insistent statement that lynching is resorted to only as punishment for rape, when the plain facts of record show that not more than one case in four can plead the allegement of rape in extenuation. The causes run the whole gamut of offenses, from the most serious crimes to the most trifling misdemeanors. Indeed, lynching is coming to be looked upon as the proper mode of punishment for any offense which the Negro commits against a white person; and yet every time a Negro is lynched or burned at the stake the race is held up to the world as responsible for the execrable crimes.

Mr. George P. Upton, associate editor of the *Chicago Tribune*, has kept records of lynchings in the United States, in itemized form, since 1885. The accuracy of his figures has never been questioned. The following facts are taken from an article contributed by him to the *Independent*, September 29, 1904:

" Between 1885 and 1904 there were 2875 lynchings in the United States. Of these, 2499 were
attributed to the South, 302 to the West, 63 to the
Pacific Slope, and 11 to the East. The alleged causes
were as follows:

For alleged and attempted criminal assault............	564
For complicity and for the double charge of assault and murder	138
For murder	1277
For theft, burglary and robbery.......................	326
For arson	106
For race prejudice....................................	94
For unknown reason...................................	134
For simple assault....................................	18
For insulting whites..................................	18
For making threats...................................	16

The remaining cases were inflicted for such offenses as " slander, miscegenation, informing, drunk-
enness, fraud, voodooism, violation of contract, re-
sisting arrest, elopement, train-wrecking, poisoning
stock, refusing to give evidence, political animosity,
disobedience of quarantine regulations, passing
counterfeit money, introducing smallpox, concealing
criminals, cutting levees, kidnapping, gambling riots,
testifying against whites, seduction, incest, and forcing a child to steal." The causes include well-nigh
every offense in the catalogue of human transgression.

In view of these undisputed facts, can you, with
clear conscience, continue to mislead the world into
the belief that the Negro is lynched only for " the
usual crime "? If words are used in their usual sense,
the " usual crime " for which Negroes are lynched
would be other than assault on women.

Again, the Negro suffers injustice in that the mild-
est protest against such red-handed procedure is con-

strued as sympathy for criminals and condonation of crime of the most abominable nature. The Negro race is the gainer by every miscreant that meets his merited doom at the end of a rope. Nor is it particularly concerned as to the manner of his death, nor "the deep damnation of his taking off." If swift, summary vengeance followed as personal punishment for personal transgression, no Negro, as such, would open his lips, albeit he might plead for law and order on the broad basis of humanity. But the vengeance of the mob is not confined to the guilty, if indeed it is aimed at him. Its leading purpose, as you advise, is to strike terror in the whole Negro population. To this end there is little pains to identify the victim or to establish his guilt. The innocent and the guilty are alike objects of its vengeance. Governor Candler of Georgia stated in a public utterance some years ago: "I can say of a verity that I have, within the last month, saved the lives of half a dozen innocent Negroes, who were pursued by the mob, and brought them to trial in a court of law in which they were acquitted." The mob has neither the temper nor the disposition carefully to determine the guilt of the accused. We must not place too much reliance upon the alleged identification of the culprit by the delirious victim, nor upon alleged confession of guilt wrung from the accused by indescribable torture. Although the newspapers glibly tell us of the confession, the courts have never yet been able to determine the identity of the confessor. In many cases it is known that innocent men have suffered death and torture at the hands of the mob. Of the two thousand Negro victims of violence, who can tell how many guiltless souls have been hurled into eternity with the protestation of innocence on their lips? But the innocent equally with the guilty serve to impair the Negro's good name. Several years ago the whole Italian nation was aroused at the lynching of a dozen of its subjects in Louisiana. It was not because of sympathy for or regret at the loss of a few worthless individuals, but because such high-handed procedure served to insult, humiliate, and degrade the entire race and nation to which the unfortunate victims belonged. It is for such reasons that the Negro pleads for the supremacy of law, and not because he has any sympathy for a crime that always excites the wildest passions of human nature.

It is not denied that depraved and vicious Negroes, as of other races, do at times commit these heinous crimes; but it cannot be said that sexual infirmity is an especial failing of the colored race. It is well known that rapeful assault has always been, and is still, a more or less common practice among all races and peoples. Students of the Bible know full well that this practice was not unknown among the Hebrews. Jupiter, father of gods and men, who embodied the vices as well as the virtues of the Greek race, to his numerous epithets might properly have had added the cognomen " ravisher of women." The practice is quite common among all European races to-day. England and Wales, in 1887, furnished 878 prisoners convicted on this charge. From 1871 to 1880 there were in the same country 758 persons convicted for assaults upon girls under thirteen years of age. The eleventh census returns 814 white prisoners in the United States convicted on the charge of rape. And yet to listen to your scathing denunciations of the black man one would be led to believe that a crime as old as human frailty was invented by the American Negro as a new mode of human atrocity.

We must not overlook the fact that where a col-

ored man and white woman are concerned, rape has
a larger definition than is set down in the diction-
aries. Relations are often punished under this head
which, if sustained among members of the same race,
would receive a less abominable, though perhaps an
equally unhallowed name.

There are certain delicate phases of question whose
discussion the seriousness of the situation alone jus-
tifies. The womanhood of the Negro race has been
the immemorial victim of the white man's lascivious-
ness and lust. The black woman has yielded to
higher authority and superior guile. A lower will
is overborne by a higher as easily as a weaker by a
stronger physical force. While breathing out
slaughter against the Negro man, does the white
lord and master ever stop to reflect upon the un-
numbered assaults which he for centuries has made
upon black and bleached womanhood? The Negro
domestic who must fight daily to preserve her integrity from the subtle guile or forceful compulsion of
her white employer, and who yields only when her
strength of body or will is not sufficient to hold out
longer, is a victim who commands the deepest sympathy. While the white man is beholding the mote in
his black brother's eye, he should not fail to consider the beam within his own. This point cannot
be better enforced than by the lines of the poet
Burns:

> "You see your state wi' theirs compared,
>   And shudder at the niffer;
> But cast a moment's fair regard,
>   What makes the mighty differ:
> Discount what scant occasion gave,
>   That purity ye pride in,
> And (what's oft mair than a' the lave),
>   Your better art o' hidin'."

In the refutation of the charge brought against

him the Negro is entitled to every argument that can
be brought forward in his behalf.

1. In Africa, the fatherland, or rather the mother-
land, of this race, rape is almost unknown, and when
it does occur, is visited with the severest punishment.

2. We have heard nothing of this abnormal tendency during the days of slavery.   When the care
and safety of white women of the South were entrusted to the keeping of slaves they returned in-
violate all that had been entrusted to them.

3. Some are so careless with facts and reason as
to attribute this alleged tendency to the last two
amendments of the Federal Constitution.   They seem
to forget that during the days of reconstruction,
when these amendments were in force, such charges
were never preferred.   It cannot be then, as you affirm, due to the outgrowth of the spirit of equality
on the part of the Negro.

4. Of the hundreds of lady missionaries from the
North who have and do still entrust their safety to
the colored race, not a single case of violation, up
to this last day of Christian grace, has been reported
to their friends in the North.

5. In South America and the West Indian archipelago, where the Negroes live in largest numbers,
" rape and rope " has never become a subject for popular agitation.

What evil spirit then has come upon the present
day Afro-American that a people who, from the days
of Homer until this generation, have borne the
epithet of " blameless Ethiopians," should now be
accused as the scourge of mankind?   Why has this
demoniacal possession held itself in restraint until
now, and why does it not manifest itself in peoples of
like blood in different parts of the globe?

The self-respecting Negro is upbraided because he

does not exercise a restraining influence over the
vicious and criminal members of his own race. As a
matter of fact, he has little or no contact with or
control over them. He is sought to be made his
brother's keeper with no coercive or corrective influence over his brother's conduct. Responsibility
implies authority. The Negro is rigorously excluded
from governmental power and divested of every
semblance of official prerogative. The depraved and
criminal Negroes, as of other races, do not go to
school, they belong to no church or fraternal order,
they are no more influenced by moral agencies than
if they were located on another continent. All attempts to interfere on the part of his self-respecting
brother would lead to the ancient response, "Who
made thee a prince and a judge over us?" Those
who occupy places of governmental authority and
power are responsible to the world for the punishment of the guilty and protection of the innocent.
Moral suasion has little or no influence with hardened
criminals—they are answerable to the law alone.
The white race, clothed with full authority and
power, is confessedly unable to restrain its own vicious
classes. It is an extravagant compliment to the
Negro to expect him to do by moral suasion alone
that which the white man cannot accomplish with
moral suasion backed by public power.

The stockades and chain-gangs maintained by the
State of Georgia are training schools of crime.
Those who enter must leave all hope behind. They
are hardened into hatred of society. Have you
ever stopped to think that the State may be responsible for the criminal class which you so loudly
reprobate?

The Negroes are charged with shielding criminals
of their own race. In so far as this charge may have

the semblance of truth, it is due to the fact that the
black culprit, guilty or innocent, is likely to meet
with mob violence, and to assist in the apprehension
of the accused is equivalent to joining in a man-hunt
for blood. Whenever a Negro is pursued by a posse,
charged with a serious offense against a white person,
the newspaper headlines usually foreshadow his doom
with unerring accuracy: " Will be lynched if caught."
The conscientious citizen of the North a generation
ago refused to aid the man-hunter in quest of run-
aways from a cruel bondage, although he was clothed
with full authority by an iniquitous law. Every good
citizen will uphold and defend the authority and dignity of the law, but he will not aid the mob in quest
of vengeance upon a man of unproved guilt. You did
not restrain that Atlanta mob of murderers, and yet
you censured the Negroes of that city for not suppressing a few suspected criminals, whom even the
microscopic eye of the law could not detect. The
Negro feels that he cannot expect justice from
Southern courts where white and black are involved. In his mind accusation is equivalent to condemnation. For this suspicion the jury rather than
the judge is responsible. The very spirit in which,
he feels, the law is administered makes it difficult for
the colored citizen to exercise cheerful co-operation
and acquiescence.

I think I ought to say that after diligent inquiry
from colored men in all parts of the South, I am
advised that Southern courts are usually fair and
often generous to the Negro in cases which do not
involve race feeling, but where this issue arises the
outcome, in the Negro's mind, is a foregone conclusion. Herein lies the greatest condemnation of existing rule. It fails to make the humble citizen feel
safe and secure under the protecting ægis of the law.

In the British Indies, where there is a race situation more complicated than in America, we are told
that the behavior toward the whites is exemplary, and
the type of crimes so bitterly deplored in this country
is unknown. This desirable state of things is due,
in my judgment, to the fact that the British Government administers justice with absolute equality as
between man and man, without regard to race. Where
the Negro sees the white man made amenable to the
requirements of the law he is apt to regard it with
reverence and respect. On the contrary, in the South
a white man is rarely punished for offense against
his black brother. Of the thousands of cases of murder of blacks by whites since emancipation there has
been scarcely a legal execution, and comparatively
few prison sentences. The offender usually escapes
with the stereotyped verdict, " Justifiable homicide,"
or at best with a nominal fine. If the relations were
reversed, whatever the provocative circumstances, the
Negro would almost certainly be sentenced to death
or to life imprisonment, if indeed the mob allowed
the case to reach a judicial hearing. To say that
these flagrant discrepancies have not their influence
upon the black man's attitude toward the law, would
be to deny that he is controlled by ordinary human
motives. The best example that the South can set
for the Negro would be punishment of white men for
their crimes according to the requirement of the law.
Mean white men will continue to mistreat Negroes
just so long as they can do so with impunity by hiding
themselves behind the cloak of racial arrogance.
Mobs will continue to wreak their wrath on Negro
culprits, innocent or guilty, until they are deterred
by effective bayonets and bullets at the hands of a
firm and unrelenting law. When the Negro sees that
the white man can override the law with impunity it

begets in him the spirit of desperation, vindictiveness and reprisal. This is the elemental law of human passion. It is firmly lodged in the breast of the ignorant and untutored. The intelligent Negro will be restrained by reason and prudence, but the depraved and the base will follow his wild, untutored human impulse. Good policy requires the placing of the stress of emphasis upon the white offender as upon the black wrongdoer. Judgment in this instance should begin at the house of God. The Negro will follow the pace set by the white man. Reverence and respect for law and order on his part will beget like sentiment in his black brother. Equality before the law is the South's only salvation.

The Negro is by no means the only sufferer from these outrageous practices—the white people are also victims of their own wrath. According to the law of retribution, the perpetrators of wrong must suffer equally with the victims of it. The spirit of violence and lawlessness permeates the atmosphere and is breathed in every breath of air. It has been claimed that the Spanish incurred their blood-thirsty disposition by their fierce struggle in subduing the Moors. The acquired disposition passed into heredity and became a permanent trait of the race.

Is the white South not in danger of such a fate? Some time ago Rev. Sam Jones, with a self-gratulatory spirit, claimed that not one Southerner in ten had ever participated in a lynching. Supposing that these figures approximate the truth. It will be seen that more persons have been engaged in lynching Negroes than there were soldiers in the Confederate army. Every such person has blood on his conscience which cannot be washed away by high-sounding declamation about Anglo-Saxon supremacy.

" Nor florid prose, honeyed lies of rhyme
    Can blazon evil deeds or consecrate a crime."

The evil has reached such alarming proportions as to become of national importance. While lynching is confined mainly to the South, it is not wholly so. Negroes have been lynched in Ohio, Indiana, Illinois, Colorado, and even in bleeding Kansas, the State of brave old John Brown, whose soul must for once have halted in its onward march at such dreadful news. The " ape and tiger " slumber all too lightly beneath the thin veil of civilization, whose chief concern is to keep them subdued under the beneficent sway of reason and law. If they are allowed to break forth and rave at will in the State of Georgia, will not this savage triumph embolden like spirit throughout the land? Does not the unrestrained fury of a wild animal that escapes from a menagerie encourage his encaged fellows to break forth, too, and vent their pent-up rage? There is no contagion so swift and sure of diffusion as the baser passion of man. The nation puts forth a strenuous endeavor to stamp out cholera or yellow fever, however remote the plague spot where it first breaks forth. The baleful effect of the burning and lynching of human beings cannot be limited to any locality, State or section, but is as widespread as the nation whose dormant evil passion it tends to encourage, and whose good name it serves to tarnish. The question is truly a national one, and as such should appeal to every man, woman and child who loves his country, and is pledged to uphold its good name and high ideals.

The infectious germ has inoculated almost every State in the Union. The list for States and Territories, from 1885 to 1904, is as follows:

Mississippi	298	Indiana	38
Texas	272	Kansas	38
Louisiana	261	California	33
Georgia	253	Nebraska	33
		Michigan	6
Alabama	232	North Dakota	5
Arkansas	207	Nevada	5
		Minnesota	4
Tennessee	191	Wisconsin	4
Kentucky	148	Wyoming	33
		Colorado	31
Florida	128	Montana	29
South Carolina	100	Idaho	21
		Illinois	19
Virginia	84	Washington	16
Missouri	79	Ohio	13
		Iowa	12
North Carolina	58	South Dakota	11
Indian Territory	54	Oregon	10
		Alaska	4
West Virginia	43	Maine	3
Oklahoma	38	Pennsylvania	3
		New York	2
Maryland	20	New Jersey	1
Arizona	18	Connecticut	1
		Delaware	1
New Mexico	15	Massachusetts	0
		New Hampshire	0
		Vermont	0
		Rhode Island	0
Total for South	2,499	Utah	0
		Total for North	376
Total for Nation			2,875

You proclaim the doctrine of State sovereignty and reprobate federal interference. But every man lynched or burned in the South furnishes the nation an invitation to step in and vindicate the national honor.

What a blot upon our civilization these figures disclose to the foreigner who may still be skeptical as to the boasts of our free institutions! What will Russia and Turkey and Cuba say? How long will Theodore Roosevelt, bent on setting the world to rights, keep his hands off?

A large majority of these victims are of the colored race, but a goodly proportion of them are white men. The evil practice cannot be limited to any race or section. A distinguished citizen of Georgia, during the heated anti-slavery discussion, boasted that he would yet call the roll of his slaves under the shadow of Bunker Hill Monument. His boasted prediction would doubtless have been fulfilled had not the institution of slavery been destroyed altogether. Unless the American people stamp out lynching its baleful influence will become as widespread as the national domain. Either the law must destroy lynching or lynching will destroy the law, involving the whole nation in anarchy and red ruin.

You appeal to the North to help separate the races. In this you are speaking in an unknown tongue. The absurdity of the suggestion places it beyond the sphere of practical discussion. I may agree with you that if the Negroes were removed from the South, whether sent to Africa or to some hotter place, there would be no Negro problem left, as such; but I am by no means certain that an equally serious human problem would not spring up in its place. If you should advocate transporting ten million Negroes to the moon your language would be equally intelligible. Even if the races were separated by interstellar space, such separation would last only until some enterprising white man contrived some means of communication. Three hundred years ago the races were absolutely separated. The Negro basked in the sunshine of savage bliss, and was happy, but the white man sought him amid his " sunny clime and palmy wine " and dragged him to the western world. Since then he has become an inseparable part of the two continents, and of the adjacent archipelagos. There are more Negroes in the western world than members of any other race. He is rooted and grounded in the soil; he is here to stay; he is in the South to stay; we need a brand of statesmanship which will adjust itself to this great determining fact.

I beg to suggest that in dealing with the Southern situation you look upon the task as a race problem, rather than as a human problem. The human aspect is ignored and the racial feature over emphasized. We have before us a dual problem of the perfectibility of the people, and of racial peace and harmony.

The South is freighted with an awful load of ignorance and poverty, and resultant degradation. Much of this attaches to the white race, but more to the Negro. There are no nostrums or miracles that will roll away this reproach. It requires the united effort of all the nation to enlighten, upbuild and adjust these neglected people. A wise and far-seeing statesmanship would not seek to isolate and perpetuate these incapacities in one race, but would banish them entirely. Unless ignorance and poverty are destroyed, they will rise up ever and anon to perplex and to trouble. Ignorance and vice are not racial attributes; knowledge and virtue are not racial endowments: they are the outcome of condition. Crime has no color; the criminal no race; he is the common enemy of society. He should be isolated and dealt with according to the desert of his evil deed. It is folly to punish a race for the wrong doings of an individual. The enlightened elements of both races should make common cause with knowledge against ignorance, with virtue against vice, and with law against the lawless.

I must not close this letter without expressing the firm conviction that Negroes of light and leading have grave and serious responsibility. Their race is the victim in every conflict. While they cannot restrain the hardened criminal without governmental authority, yet they are in duty bound to put forth strenuous efforts to reach and to influence for good the weak, helpless and neglected elements of their own race, and to keep them from falling into evil ways. There is a subtle sympathy of race which renders individuals more easily amenable to the moral control of those of their own blood. The Negro school teacher and minister of the gospel stand in the high place of moral authority. They should utilize all the power which they are permitted to wield, and by example, precept and persuasion sustain their weaker brethren in all right directions. They must bridge over the widening chasm between the educated and the more unfortunate by a practical sympathy and a more vital and brotherly touch. In this great work of human development we ask and should receive the hearty good will and co-operation of all those who believe in the perfectibility of man. The Negro is impressionable and responsive to kind treatment. If given the necessary encouragement he will become a safe, conservative factor, and not the economic or moral menace which you so vociferously proclaim him to be. It will not be necessary to ruthlessly override all human and divine order at the behest of the narrow racial arrogance. All far-seeing and conservative Americans believe that in the final outcome peace and good will, friendship and amity will prevail, and that " Ephraim shall not envy Judah, and Judah shall not vex Ephraim."

Mr. Harry Stillman Edwards, your distinguished fellow Georgian, in a recent article contributed to the *Century Magazine*, expresses the hopeful belief that the two races can live together in righteous peace. These are his words: " Neither can settle the questions involved in their lives, but both may, and despite political riders, I believe both will. I must either believe this or prepare my descendants for anarchy."

Compared with your doctrine of dread and terror, subversive of established order and public peace, few patriotic Americans will fail to feel that Mr. Edwards has chosen the better part.

THE NEGRO'S PART IN THE NEGRO PROBLEM

THE presence of the African element in the United States gives rise to a tripartite problem. The white man of the North, the white man of the South, and the Negro are the parties in interest. The only possible satisfactory solution of this problem must depend upon the united wisdom and conciliatory spirit of this triple alliance, and must be just and honorable to all.

For more than a generation the North alone has directed and controlled our national policies, against the incessant antagonism of the South. This antagonism has been most sharply accentuated over measures intended to promote the black man's welfare. Northern philanthropy and statesmanship have persisted in busying themselves with this problem, despite the resentful hue and cry against meddlesome interference. On the other hand, the South has regarded the Negro question very much as a distinguished politician once characterized the tariff—as a local issue. It has stubbornly and sullenly insisted that it alone possessed the requisite knowledge and experience to deal with its own problems, without the gratuitous assistance of outside busybodies. Nevertheless, the South has not yet put forth any positive, progressive measure toward this end, but has pursued an unbroken policy of negation, protest, and retrogression.

The oft-repeated asseveration of the Southern white man that he understands the Negro better than his Northern brother is not borne out by experience, nor

does it manifest itself in enlightened action. As Mr.
Carl Schurz has so forcibly pointed out, every essential prediction which the South has based upon its
assumed superior wisdom has proved to be erroneous
in the light of subsequent development. It declared
that the black man would die out under freedom; but
the census shows that the four million slaves of 1860
has given rise to eight million freemen in 1900. It asserted that the Negro would not work except by
physical compulsion; but the material progress of
that section, based largely upon Negro labor, renders
the assertion beneath refutation. It once affirmed
that the Negro was uneducationable, but the North
showed the absurdity of the statement by educating
him. The reputation of the prophet is discredited
by the too frequent failure of his predictions.

The Southern white man bases his claim to superior
knowledge upon long association and intimacy of
contact. Long habituation with an environment is
rather apt to deaden than sharpen the critical sense.
Near-sightedness, no less than far-sightedness, is a
serious ocular defect. The three treatises on American institutions which are admitted to show the most
insight and critical acumen were written by a French-
man, an Englishman, and a German, as a result of
their temporary sojourn among us.

The North has shown superior wisdom on every
phase of our national life, and the most enlightened
minds of the South are now openly avowing that the
salvation of that section depends upon the adoption
of the more enlightened Northern spirit and methods.
Northern knowledge has discovered the industrial possibilities of the South and furnished the means and
directive skill for exploiting them, has demonstrated
the folly of suicidal governmental theories once so
fondly cherished by the South, and has led the way

in every feature of intellectual, material, and social progress. Is it reasonable, then, to suppose that omniscience, so manifestly withheld in every other domain of knowledge, has been vouchsafed to the white man of the South on the race problem alone?

Hitherto little attention has been given to the Negro as a factor whose sensibilities should be regarded and whose voice should be heeded upon questions which affect his own destiny. This race has been looked upon as an inanimate mass to be exploited and controlled according to the interest or caprice of the white lord of creation. But the growing self-knowledge and self-assertion on the part of the awakening race adds a new element to the problem that can no longer be ignored. The wise physician, however great he may deem his diagnostic knowledge and therapeutic skill, always encourages the cheerful co-operation of the patient under treatment. Even though the patient is not supposed to have any wisdom to contribute, he is at least always accorded the privilege of saying how he feels. The South and the North, as attendant and consulting physicians, are now planning a common line of action; but they will not wisely leave out the intelligent Negro, whose inside view might at least be supposed to assist external wisdom.

The fact that the colored race has followed the guidance of the white man of the North has given rise to deep and bitter complaint. Ever since the Negro has begun to animadvert upon his own condition, the North and South have seemed to him to be as wide apart as the poles on questions touching his welfare. In the momentous conflict of thought and conscience which preceded the arbitrament of arms, the North stood for liberty, the South for slavery. At countless cost of blood and treasure the North broke his chains, against the equally strenuous endeavor of the South to rivet them more tightly. The North wrote the last three amendments in our Federal Constitution, while the South protested with all the power at its command. Northern statesmanship placed legislation upon the statute-books recognizing the equality of all men before the law, every line of which met with strenuous opposition and obstruction on the part of the South. Northern philanthropists have given their substance and their service for the intellectual and moral betterment of the black man, while the South, for the most part, has looked on with icy indifference, and often with ill-concealed disapproval. At the present day the North is rather disposed to uphold the doctrine of " a government of laws and not of men," while the South insists on dealing with the Negro as a subject-class.

The law of human passion requites friendship with affection. The black man, perhaps, has not been critical of the motive that has actuated this benefaction toward him. The conduct of the North may indeed have been actuated by economic motive and political policy, as well as by an abstract love of the principles involved. But gratitude is oblivious of motive. The Emancipation Proclamation does not fail to evoke the black man's grateful emotions because he is told that it was merely an incident of a larger policy. It is sufficient for him to know that the slave has been transformed into a freeman, the chattel into a citizen, and that the North has been the chief instrument in effecting this marvelous transformation. It should not occasion surprise or resentment that the black man has given his allegiance to the policies of the North rather than the South, especially when we remember that the African is very largely a creature of affection and is controlled mainly by emotion.

When the Negro aligns himself, on public questions, with the people of the North, he is accused of spiteful antagonism to his white neighbors. But he is merely following the impulse that ordinarily governs human motive. He has put human rights before economic interest, and righteous public policy before the blandishments of personal kindliness and individual favor.

It must be conceded, on the other hand, that the Southern white man frequently displays commendable personal good-will toward individual Negroes who come within the circle of his acquaintance or control. In general, there is the widest margin between his avowed public policy and his personal demeanor. No reputable Southerner is half as bad as Senator Tillman talks. The South seizes upon every act of prejudice or proscription practised against the Negro in the North, and holds it up as proof positive of the insincerity of its righteous pretensions. The *tu quoque* argument is never resorted to except in palliation of conduct that is intrinsically indefensible. The universality of an act does not improve its moral quality.

Surprise has often been expressed that the Negro does not move in mass from the South, against whose public policy he so bitterly complains, to those sections where political and civil conditions are more liberal and generous. The Negro has an attachment for locality that almost amounts to instinct. He is not of a nomadic nature, and lacks the restlessness and daring spirit of the pioneer. The climatic conditions of the North are not congenial to his tropical nature, and the strenuous social and economic regime does not accord with his industrial experience and aptitude. Six millions of white people from the South, with their wonted industrial habits and eco-

nomic notions, would find themselves as much dis-
qualified for Northern competition as their less
favored brother in black. The Negro also confronts
industrial intolerance in the North which shuts him
out from the higher forms of endeavor.

Between the relative advantages and discouragements of each section he stands curiously bewildered.
The bulk of the race is destined to remain where it
was most thickly planted by the institution of slavery.
Notwithstanding a continuous stream of immigration
toward the North and West for the past forty years,
the mass centre of Negro population is moving
steadily toward the Gulf of Mexico. The Negro and
the Southern white man must live together, in intimate
neighborhood, for all time which we are able to foresee. It is essential to the welfare of both that their
relations should be characterized by amity and good-
will. But the Negro ought not to be expected to
accept with satisfaction any condition that is not
honorable and just, and that does not accord with
the spirit and genius of American institutions.

The part which the Negro has played in American
history has contributed in no small degree to the welfare of the nation. The African was brought to this
country for the purpose of performing manual and
menial labor. There was no more thought of incor-
porating him in the body-politic than of thus ennobling the lower animals. His function was intended
to be as purely mechanical as that of the ox which
pulls the plough. For more than two hundred years
he performed this manual mission. He cleared the
forests, and planted the fields, and made the wilderness
to blossom as the rose. The whole economic and
social fabric of the South was built upon his muscular
energy under the guidance of the white man's intelligence. Through the discipline of slavery he gained

the English language, the Christian religion, a notion of political and civil institutions, and settled industrial habits and methods. His grasp upon these principles is still imperfect and uncertain, and needs to be confirmed and strengthened by the discipline of knowledge and freedom. The institution of slavery exploited the physical capacities of the Negro for the aggrandizement of the white race. Whatever incidental benefit may have accrued to the slave cannot be ascribed to the moral credit of that regime which possessed not the slightest semblance of altruistic intent.

The Negro was transformed from a chattel into a citizen, as it were, in a moment, in the twinkling of an eye. He was thrust into the body-politic with such suddenness and shock as if shot from the cannon's mouth. At the time of reconstruction the race was solidly illiterate, excited with the first excesses of freedom, and without the least experience in governmental affairs. And so the Negro became the natural and inevitable prey of the self-seeker and the adventurer. Grossness and grotesqueness are the inevitable outcome of good-natured ignorance under the control of calculating villainy. The negro merely played the part of bouffe politics. The native Southerner and the carpetbag adventurer vied with each other for public plunder and spoil. It cannot be shown, however, that the Negro ever supported any measure against human liberty or in conflict with the Federal Constitution. The reconstruction constitutions display a higher degree of patriotism and public righteousness than the fraudulently conceived, though cunningly contrived, instruments which have succeeded them.

As an industrial worker the Negro is docile and productive. He does not join in the ranks of the restless and discontented. He is loyal to the institutions of the country, and strives to become as good an American as his fellow-citizens will permit him to be.

The criminal propensity of the Negro is the charge that is being most widely exploited in current discussion. By fragments of fact and jugglery of argument he is made to appear a beast in human form whose vicious tendency constitutes a new social plague. The Negro is held in moral disesteem because he is being searched and sifted mercilessly for ugly and uninviting information. All his faults are being conned and set down by rote. If as diligent search were made for unseemly and forbidden data concerning any other class, the disclosure might be equally darksome and damaging. A mental and moral morbidity is acquired by dwelling upon the pathological side of society. If we listen to the pessimistic wail of the social purist we would be convinced that the human race is doomed to speedy destruction through innumerable physical and social sins. Intemperance, sexual impurity, and civic corruption are sure to effect our national destruction. And yet society moves on, like a mighty river, and, despite polluted streams that flow into it, purifies itself as it goes. Although the Negro is hampered by an initial weight of social and moral degradation, yet his upward struggle from corruption to purity has been marked and unmistakable. Those who are most prone to indulge in wholesale tirade about his moral turpitude do not seek knowledge from the more progressive and ambitious element, but preserve a studious ignorance concerning their higher aims and nobler modes of life. Generalization based upon the study of the most degraded part is not fair to the whole. This mode of procedure would blacken the reputation of any people. We do not judge a society by the misfortune of its submerged members, but by the ideals toward which it strives and by the potency and promise which it displays.

Several years ago a colored man of glib rhetorical facility wrote a book entitled " The American Negro," which received the imprint of a leading publishing house. The Negro author excoriated his race in the most merciless manner. He held it up to the scorn of mankind as a breed of moral vipers. These scathing denunciations were supported by no data and upheld by no verifiable reference, but rested solely upon the pessimistic utterances of a defamer of his own race. Indeed, the innuendoes were indignantly denied by white and black alike, who had opportunity for knowledge and judgment for generalization. These statements gained plausibility and credence from the fact that the author was of the same color as the class which is reprobated; and the book has been widely appealed to as a buttress to blacken the moral reputation of the Negro race and to damn a struggling people to everlasting infamy.

Damaging charges against the Negro's social character are usually based upon the following facts and assumptions:

1. That the Negro shows an overwhelming criminal record as compared with the white race.

2. That the percentage of crime has increased under freedom and education.

3. That the Negro of the North shows a much higher criminal average than his more benighted brother in the South.

4. That the colored man is especially addicted to crime of an execrable and nameless character.*

* This subject is discussed in open letter to John Temple Graves.

According to the census of 1890, the Negro constituted only 12 per cent. of the population of the United States and contributed 30 per cent. of the criminals. In Mississippi there were 1,425 colored and 219 white prisoners out of each million of the respective races; while in Massachusetts the numbers were 6,864 colored and 2,262 whites. Such are the facts which, uninterpreted, can be quoted in support of any damaging doctrine that might be advanced. No person of knowledge and candor will deny that the Negro in the South is more readily apprehended and convicted on any charge than the white offender. The Negro constitutes the lower stratum of society, where the bulk of actionable crime is committed the world over. Social degradation is the great contributing factor to his high criminal record. If the lower element of the white race should be segregated and brought under the microscope of sociological investigation, the proscribed class would doubtless reveal like criminal weakness. The foreign element of our population shows a higher criminal average than the native whites, as they occupy a decidedly lower social status.

While the Negro's criminal record exceeds that of the white, it does not appear that his presence in any community increases its criminal quality. In 1890 the Western division of States had 1,300 prisoners out of every million inhabitants; the North Atlantic States, 833.1, and the South Atlantic States, with their heavy Negro element, had only 831.7; Mississippi had 1,177, against 5,227 for Massachusetts. If the Negroes of the South were replaced by a white population there is no statistical indication that the moral character of that section would be improved by the interchange. There is nowhere any traceable casual connection between crime and race, the relation being between crime and condition. It should not occasion surprise that the free Negro shows a higher criminal record than did his slave progenitor. Under the surveillance of slavery there was little opportunity to commit crime, and punishment for offences was personally inflicted by the master without any public record. Slavery suppressed wrongdoing, but did not implant the corrective principle, so that when the physical restraint was removed there was no moral restraint to take its place. The increase in the criminal rate for the United States from 1880 to 1890 was 12.49 per cent. The parallel growth of education and crime is a noticeable phenomenon of the American people as a whole, and cannot be justly urged to the discredit of the Negro alone.

But, says the objector, in the North, where legal processes are acknowledged to be fair, and where the Negro has the fullest educational opportunity, he shows a criminal rate three to four times as great as his ignorant and oppressed brother in the South. And the conclusion is hastily reached that education makes the Negro a criminal. Referring to the above-cited statistics, it will be seen that while the Negro in Massachusetts seems to be five times as criminal as the Negro in Mississippi, it appears at the same time that the white man in Massachusetts is ten times as criminal as the white man in Mississippi. Shall we discount the superior education of the white man in the Bay State because he seems to be only one-tenth as saintly as his less enlightened white brother on the banks of the Mississippi? Or shall we foster the bliss of ignorance only when it is found under a black skin? Ordinarily one would explain the high criminal rate of the Northern States on the ground of congested population and more stringent enforcement of law; but logical processes seem to be of no avail against sweeping assertions to the detriment of the discredited Negro.

It is a common saying that the colored race has made greater progress since emancipation than any other people known to the history in a like space of time. In order to measure this progress, we need a knowledge of the starting-point as well as a fixed standard of calculation. We may say that the Negro began at the zero point, with nothing to his credit but the crude physical discipline of slavery. His progress should be measured in terms of his humble beginning and of the crude instruments with which he has had to work out his own salvation. He cannot be expected as yet to have reached the fulness of the stature of the Anglo-Saxon, who enjoys the advantage of centuries of inheritance and social opportunity.

Moral progress can hardly be gauged in terms of material units. The home lies at the basis of our social morality. The last census shows 60.1 per cent. of the white population of the United States to be single, 36.4 per cent. married, 3.0 per cent. widowed, 0.2 per cent. divorced, and 0.3 per cent. of unknown conjugal status. Among the Negroes 63.5 per cent. are single, 32.4 per cent. married, 3.5 per cent. widowed, 0.3 per cent. divorced, and 0.3 per cent. unknown. There is no glaring discrepancy between the two races as to the relative number of homes, size of family, or the permanence of domestic ties. In 1890 there were 100 Negro church communicants out of every 279 of the population against 100 out of 304 for the whites. The Negro is largely enrolled in patriotic, benevolent, fraternal, and social organizations, the aim of all of which is towards personal, moral, and social improvement. The facts also disclose that the Negro is engaged in settled and orderly industry to a degree that must be promotive of sobriety and good behavior. In 1890 only 36.4 per cent. of the white population were engaged in gainful occupations against 41.1 per cent. of Negroes who were thus engaged. People who but a brief generation ago were in a state of moral and social confusion and who have since formed definite family relations and enlisted themselves under the banner of the Christian church, and settled in regular industrial habits, might well be regarded as having made marvelous social and moral progress. While there remains much grossness and imperfection, yet no candid observer can fail to note the upward trend towards better and nobler modes of life.

In the domain of education the race has made most notable advancement. The rate of illiteracy has steadily declined, until now it is only 44.6 per cent. of persons over ten years of age. There is a school enrolment of 1,096,734, which indicates the eagerness to throw off the shackles of ignorance. When a people pass from an illiterate to a literate stage life takes on a new incentive and meaning. An impulse is imparted which yields ever-increasing momentum. Its influence can never be lost, but is carried forward to remotest generations. The ability to read and write is the minimum requirement of our economic and social scheme. It is the pass-key to social progress, and unlocks the secret and method of civilization. We should not, however, expect the Negro's imperfect grasp upon the literary symbols of knowledge suddenly to transform and uplift him to the level of Aryan attainment. The first effect of symbolic knowledge is necessarily potential rather than practical. It requires time for the new acquisition to become assimilated and to infiltrate into the life and react upon the conduct. The process of education

has just begun to do its beneficial work. The urgent
task now is to so strengthen and confirm the principles of knowledge that the Negro shall gain an intelligent conception of the object and aim, not merely
of labor, but of life.

It has become the fashion to say that the education
of the Negro is a demonstrated failure, and that the
effort expended upon his mental development has been
in vain. The mode of education undertaken by Northern philanthropy has been the chief object of attack.
But those who indulge in wholesale assertions are
craftily careful to avoid a bill of particulars. They
do not tell us that Howard University or Fisk or Atlanta has been a failure; but their chief reliance is
placed upon the frequent repetition of the charge,
and their only authority is arrogant assumption of
infallibility. When we consider that it was through
the inspiration of such institutions that the Negro
race received its upward impulse; that they trained,
for the most part, the teachers who are conducting
the public schools of the South; that their graduates
and sometime pupils are scattered throughout the
race as centers for good and are doing all within their
power to enlighten, guide, and restrain the ignorant
masses; that they are almost without exception advocates of peace and good-will between the races, it
is difficult to see upon what possible fact or argument
the assumption is based.

Let us take as an illustration of this type of education Howard University, situated at the National
Capital. This institution, during the thirty-seven
years of its history, has expended somewhere between
two and three million dollars in plant, equipment, and
current cost. As returns on this investment, it has
sent into the world 700 physicians, pharmacists, and
dentists, 300 lawyers, 200 ministers of the gospel, 400

teachers, 600 persons with general scholastic education, together with thousands of sometime pupils who have enjoyed the partial benefits of its course. These graduates and sometime pupils are found in every State and city where the colored population abounds, and are filling stations of usefulness and influence along all lines of high endeavor. They are preaching, practising, pleading, and teaching, and are guiding, directing, and inspiring the masses to a higher and better life. When the facts are carefully and dispassionately analyzed, it will probably appear that nowhere in the history of human experience has the expenditure of a like sum of money resulted in a higher degree of social good than the fifty millions contributed by Northern philanthropy for the enlightenment of this belated race.

But the colored race has received $100,000,000 from the public school funds of the Southern States, and we are told, with all the assurance of infallibility, that this sum has been misapplied because ignorance has not put on enlightenment, poverty has not given way to competence, and purity has not banished corruption. One hundred million dollars is a princely sum when viewed in the aggregate; but it is only when we remember that this amount has been distributed over a period of thirty-five years, scattered over an area of a million square miles, and applied to a population ranging from five to nine million souls, that we can appreciate its woful inadequacy to the task imposed. It would not average two dollars a year for each Negro child of school age. During 1901 South Carolina expended $726,825 for the education of 183,660 white children, and only $211,288 for that of 287,540 colored children. The educational cost of each white child was $3.95 against $0.74 for the Negro child. If, then, the educational facili-

ties for the white children of the South are wofully
inadequate and inefficient, as they are universally conceded to be, what can be said of those for colored
children? If it requires twenty-five dollars a year in
Massachusetts to educate a white boy who has the
stimulus of civilized inheritance and enlightened environment, how can we expect seventy-five cents to do
the same for a black boy in South Carolina who misses
these incentives? The condemnation of Negro education at this stage of the process is merely a preju-
diced pronouncement of judgment in advance of
adequate trial.

That the Southern whites impose a tax upon themselves to educate the Negroes has been so frequently
and so emphatically asserted that it has almost come
to be an accepted maxim. We are told that the whites
pay ninety-five per cent. of the taxes, and that Negro
education is almost a pure gratuity on their part.
This assumption rests upon a false notion of political
economy. According to the fundamental principles
of that science, labor pays every tax in the world.
And the fact that the laborer may not enjoy the
privilege of handing the tribute to the tax-taker is
no reason why he should be deprived of any public
privilege which his labor makes possible. The distribution of public benefits in proportion to tax-pay-
ing ability is widely at variance with the spirit of
American institutions. The public schools were in-
stituted in order to develop and maintain a higher
and more efficient citizenship. To this end the child-
less millionaire is laid under tribute for the educating
of the children of the prolific pauper. The Negro
may not contribute by direct taxation in proportion
to his scholastic requirements; yet, indirectly, public
burdens bear most heavily upon his shoulders. The
Negro is the laborer of the South and contributes his

full share to the public weal. He has a right to demand of the State the education of his children on equal terms with others, not merely as a civic charity, but as a public right. To limit, curtail, or abridge his educational opportunity would be an arbitrary misuse of power without justification on economic or moral grounds.

Ex-Superintendent Glenn, of Georgia, and Superintendent Shields, of Florida, have shown in their published reports that the colored people in these States, at least, pay the full cost of their own education. It would be easy enough to select a comparatively small number of individuals in New York or Massachusetts who pay the bulk of taxation in those commonwealths; but we never hear that they are being taxed for the less fortunate element of the community. The argument runs counterwise. The owners of wealth are rather regarded as the beneficiaries of the burden which is borne by the laboring classes.

Despite the hard industrial disadvantages under which he has labored, the Negro has made steady advancement in the accumulation of property. There is no reliable information as to the value of his holdings except in two or three States. A knowledge of the aggregate of value of this property, however, is of less importance than of its distribution throughout the whole race. In 1890 there were in the Southern States, including Delaware and the District of Columbia, 231,758 Negroes who owned their farms and homes, only 18,000 of which carried a mortgage incumbrance. Estimating five persons to the farm or household, this would give more than a million persons who lived on their own premises. The last census shows 156,372 Negro owners of farms. There were 746,717 Negro farmers, who, either as owner or tenant, operated farms aggregating 37,000,000

acres of land, and yielding in 1899 a productive value
of $250,000,000. The Negro operated 13 per cent.
of all the farms in the United States. In the South
Atlantic States 29.9 per cent. of the farms were operated by Negro farmers, 27.2 per cent. in the South
Central States, and 58.3 per cent. in Mississippi. In
the State of Governor Vardaman nearly three-fifths
of the farms are directed by black proprietors. These
700,000 farms contain a colored population of about
four million Negroes who have gained industrial self-
direction. There are more Negro farmers than farm
hands. These facts give us some indication of the
industrial power of the Negro in the Southern States.

A most significant indication of progress is the
emergence of a superior class. The talented tenth
constitutes the controlling factor in the life of any
people. The institution of slavery made no allowance
for superior attainment. Yet all slaves could not be
kept on the same low level, but there was marked
differentiation as to character, intelligence and ambition. The wider opportunities of freedom brought
a sudden awakening of power. Negro youths who
were deemed incapable of knowledge now dispute
academic honors with the choicest collegians of Harvard and Yale. The Negro aims at the same standard of attainment for which the Aryan strives.

There is a growing disposition to ignore the Negro
of superior attainment as an insignificant exception
or freak of nature, not to be calculated as a factor
in the ordinary equation. The white race is characterized by its best powers and capacities, the Negro
by his worst. The Southern white man is construed
to mean the traditional gentleman, instinct with dignity, comity, and grace, although we are perfectly
aware that numerically he represents only a small
percentage of the people whom he typifies. But when

reference is made to the Negro we are prone to think of a composite savage, and banish from the mind the superior man who has emerged from this dark and forbidden background. And yet it would be easy enough to isolate hundreds of thousands, if not millions, of Southern whites who, in intelligence, thrift and general respectability, would not rank above a corresponding number of Negroes that might be chosen.

Upon the enlightened Negro has been imposed unusual responsibility and opportunity for service. He becomes the inevitable leader and exemplar of his people. They look to him as their guide, philosopher and friend. Any people derive inspiration most readily from men of their own breed who have risen out of their own environment. When one colored man is elevated the whole race feels the uplifting effect of his promotion. As the individual rises he draws the whole race up toward his own level. Current philosophy seems to suppose that a lever can be put under the mass of the race and pry it up from the bottom, whereas the history of human development shows that races and nations and peoples are uplifted by the elevation of their choice individuals who draw them up toward the top. It is the part of sound statesmanship and wise philanthropy to encourage the better aspirations of this people. There is nothing to fear from a people who aspire. It is rather a vegetative race, without a soul that animates and spirit that strives, that forms a blight upon civilization.

The ignorant must be enlightened, the vicious must be restrained, the sick and afflicted must be soothed and healed, the lethargic must be inspired, and the hungry soul must be satisfied with spiritual solace. Under the intolerant social policy of the Anglo-Saxon these ministrations must be directed by members of

the benefited race. A million Negro children are
taught by Negro teachers. Three million church
communicants are led in paths of truth and righteousness by their own ministers; the sick are attended by
sympathetic physicians; the newspapers, magazines,
and other organs of public opinion by which the people are inspired to high endeavor are conducted by
men of their own blood. The members of this controlling class are scattered throughout the entire
race, as diffusive centers of light; and this little
leaven must ultimately leaven the whole lump. These
leaders should be carefully trained and qualified for
this function, which is second to none in its bearing
upon the general welfare of the American people.

It is charged that the enlightened Negro does not
restrain the evil tendency of the most vicious and degraded of his own race. It must always be remem-
bered that the Negro leader is not entrusted with
governmental function. He exerts only moral authority, and has no way of reaching the hardened
criminal, either in church or school or by personal or
social intercourse; for the criminally disposed of
every race shun ennobling contact, and are amenable
only to the rigid hand of the law. The white man
controls the machinery of government, and should
suppress and restrain the vicious and worthless, not
in a spirit of race vindictiveness, but for the common
good of all. The better class of colored people is being
rapidly recruited. In intelligence, thrift, purity of
life and decorum of manners its upward movement is
marked and unmistakable. In spite of obloquy, denunciation, ridicule, doubt and denial, it is steadily
climbing and lifting as it climbs.

The race question in America is a tough and
tangled one. Its issues are as intricate in their relations and as far-reaching in their consequences as any

problem which has ever pressed upon human wisdom for solution. Despite our pride of theory and cock-sure solutions that are so confidently projected and so vociferously proclaimed, it continues to baffle our wisdom and buffet our hopes. While we may not be able to see the distant scene, we should nevertheless proceed step by step in the direction of duty. Justice, intelligence, thrift and character are virtues of undisputed value, and apply to all men under all conceivable conditions. If the white man, North or South, in dealing with his weaker brother, will apply the principle of justice, and encourage him in the development of intelligence, thrift and character, he may safely free his mind from the dread of destiny which now occasions such anxious solicitude.

SOCIAL EQUALITY

A STRANGER to American institutions would be curiously impressed by the separate and distinct social areas which the two races occupy. Here are two peoples, domiciled in the same territory, vested with equal civil and political rights, speaking the same language, loyal to the same institutions, worshiping God after the same ritual, and linked together in a common destiny; and yet in all purely personal and pleasurable intercourse they are as far apart as if separated by interstellar space. " Social equality " is the shibboleth which divides the races asunder. This slogan, like a savage warwhoop, arouses the deepest venom of race, which slumbers only skin deep beneath a thin veneer of civilization. This expression cannot be defined according to the ordinary import and weight of words. Whoever coined it possessed a genius for summoning the evil spirit. The term has no exact lexical status, but it is surcharged with idiomatic meaning. We can no more determine its potency and power from the component words than we can judge the emblematic significance of " Old Glory " by the fabric and dyestuff that enter into its composition. As the sight of the flag evokes the patriotic zeal of the loyal beholder, or as the soldier makes frantic response to the alarm " to arms," so the tocsin " social equality " arouses the pride of class and wrath of race. " Social " and " equality " are two excellent, elegant words; but " social equality " must not be pronounced in good society, like two harmless chemical elements uniting to make a dangerous compound. This phrase has unbounded potency over the passion of the white man of the South. He religiously obeys its behest, at whatever sacrifice or cost of conscience. He bows down and worships before a verbal idol with fear and trembling, as a heathen before his graven God. The sanction of its decree is more binding than that of legal code, religious creed, or the claims of humanity. Pope has given a poetic setting to the moral conviction of mankind that conscience is the rightful arbiter of conduct:

> "What conscience dictates to be done,
>   Or warns me not to do;
> This teach me more than hell to shun,
>   That more than heaven pursue."

If in this elegant quatrain we substitute " social equality " for conscience, although we mar the meter, we adapt the meaning to the social creed of the South. The interpretation which that section places upon " social equality " constitutes the crux of the race problem, and conditions all modes of rights, privileges and opportunity, whether they be political, civil, educational or industrial. By reason of its exactions the Negro is not desired by the white man to vote for the same candidate, work at the same handicraft, enjoy the same public and civic privileges, to worship at the same shrine, or to be buried in the same graveyard. It is indeed the ruling passion strong in death. Race prejudice which this phrase evokes is not amenable to the formulas of logic; it is impatient of fact, and intolerant of argument and demonstration. It does not reason, it asserts and asseverates. Its traditional method is a word and a blow.

At one time it was the avowed policy of the domi-

nant South to furnish the Negro equal public opportunity with the whites, while insisting on the separation of the races in all purely social features. This
was the gospel according to the late Henry W.
Grady, who, before his untimely death, bid fair to
become not only the mouthpiece but the oracle of the
New South. Senator D. M. McEnery, of Louisiana,
in a notable speech in the United States Senate several years ago, said: "There never has been any
disposition on the part of the people of Louisiana
to deprive the Negro of his political and civil rights.
There has been and will continue to be determination,
fixed and unalterable, to deny him social privilege on
equality with the whites, and to prohibit him from
aspiring to any equality in social life, which nature
forbids." Passing by the gracious proffer to assist
nature in carrying out her inexorable decree, this deliverance shows plainly that the social policy of the
South is regarded as the primary factor, and political and civil regulations are but corollaries of the
leading proposition. In society, as in science, the
greater includes the less.

But of late we have heard a new voice from the
South. It is louder and less considerate of the
claims of humanity than the milder tones of the more
dignified and decorous leadership which it seeks to
supplant. This is the voice of Tillman and Vardaman and Baringer and Thomas Dixon. These new
oracles tell us that the Negro must be denied political,
civil, educational, and even industrial opportunity,
lest "social equality" should be the consummation of
it all. The Ten Commandments, the Golden Rule, the
Sermon on the Mount, the Declaration of Independence, the Constitution of the United States, and the
genius and tradition of American institutions are held
in open defiance by a narrow and provincial spirit.

The ethical and political foundations of social order are ruthlessly overborne by the fiat of a silly phrase. The question is of vital concern to every loyal American citizen. For if this spirit is allowed to prevail, and the Negro is, of set policy, suppressed below the level of American manhood, in deference to an absurd social theory, then his status will inevitably settle into a servile caste as rigid and inexorable as that which blights Oriental civilization. The enlightened patriotism that rose up in righteous wrath against human slavery cannot view with composure the establishment on American soil of an iniquitous caste which is even more repugnant to the genius of free institutions. The silent South, the survivors and descendants of the better type of the slave-holding class, the men and women in whose breasts not even the blighting influence of slavery could sour the milk of human kindness, are now held, as in a vise, by this narrow and intolerant spirit. They have no frantic dread of the social affiliation of the races. Indeed, according to their traditional social code, intimate personal association with the uncouth and uncultivated whites is almost as distasteful a contemplation. And yet the cry of social equality has been so persistently and boisterously dinned in their ears that an imaginary evil has assumed the semblance of a real danger. Their voice has been hushed; they have become tongue-tied, and are as completely divested of freedom, either of action or utterance, as the poor Negro who bears the brunt of it all. If liberal-minded Southern white men, like George W. Cable, or John Spencer Bassett, or Andrew Sledd, though still yielding allegiance to the prevailing social dogma, dare lift their voice, even in faintest whisper, in protest against the evil perpetrated in its name, they are forthwith lashed into silence by popular fury

and scorn. Race hatred is the most malignant poison
that can afflict the mind. It chills the higher faculties of the soul. The restiveness of the high-souled
sons of the South under restriction imposed by the
less enlightened of their own race is the only hopeful
rift that we can see in the dark and lowering cloud.

Every system of oppression seeks to justify itself.
The institutions of slavery ransacked science, history,
literature, and religion in quest of fact and argument to uphold the iniquitous system. There is almost an exact parallel between the methods employed
in support of human slavery and those that are now
being resorted to in justification of the decrees of
"social equality."

We are told that the separation of the races is
ordained of God, just as slavery used to be called a
" divine institution." It is strange indeed that those
who breathe out hatred and slaughter against their
fellow-men are ever prone to claim divine prerogative
in carrying out their iniquitous scheme. The alliance
of Providence with the type of men who are now
leading the propaganda of race hatred would reverse
all of our received notions of the divine attributes.

Physical dissimilarity is seized upon as a badge of
distinction, and a hasty judgment easily confuses
the index with the indicated potency. But, as is well
known, difference of race and color has never pre-
vented the closest intimacy of personal association.
The gentleman who drives to the station " cheek by
jowl " with his black coachman, but who becomes
furious on being made joint occupant with a black
seat-fellow in a railway coach, is actuated by an impulse other than purely physical repugnance. If race
friction rested solely upon physical basis we should
expect its rigor to be uniform wherever such distinctions prevail. But, as a matter of fact, we find

that it is subject to the widest latitude of variability, and is almost indefinitely modifiable by circumstances and conditions. It presents little of the fixity and inflexible character of natural law. The Teuton manifests it in a different degree from the Latin races, with whom ethnic peculiarities count for little or nothing against moral and spiritual homogeneity. Rio de Janeiro and Richmond, Virginia, are typical illustrations of the two spirits as respects the *entente* of dissimilar races. Prejudice is more pronounced, or at least assumes a different aspect, in the Southern than in the Northern State, being stimulated by the relative number or erstwhile status of the two elements. It becomes mild or virulent, according to incentive or occasion. In individual instances it almost or wholly disappears, and can be aroused only by playing upon class interests, prejudice, and pride. Grant Allen tells us somewhere that the same Englishman who seems to ignore race differences at home becomes the most intolerant of men when he takes residence in the colonies. If the separation of the races is a decree of Providence working through nature, what need of human help in carrying out that decree? The re-enactment of the laws of the Almighty leads naturally to the suspicion that those who so eagerly proffer this assistance are actuated by a wish rather than a conviction. The Negro is not credited with natural repugnance against associating with white men. The charge that they must be restricted in their eagerness for such association is the highest possible unwitting proof that the aversion between the races cannot be wholly accounted for by natural antipathy. The lion and the lamb do not enjoy a common bed, because such social intimacy is doubtless as distasteful to the lamb as to the lion. Natural antipathy is a reciprocal feeling.

There is little room to doubt that the feeling
against the Negro is of the nature of inspirited animosity rather than natural antipathy, and can be
accounted for, in large part, by the traditional place
which he has occupied in the social scheme. A people
who have yet made no considerable contribution to
the general culture of the human spirit, and whose
traditional relation with European civilization has
been of a servile sort, are not deemed eligible to the
ennobling circle of Aryan fellowship. The violent
severance of servile bonds, and the humiliation of
the Southern man's tough Teutonic spirit by outside
compulsion, engendered deep and long-abiding ani-
mosities.

But the chief cause of race estrangement is of a
political nature, if we be allowed to use that term,
not merely in the technical sense of statecraft, but
as comprehending the calculated policy of the ruling class towards the despised element. The cultivation of class consciousness is one of the most familiar
phenomena of history. The line of demarcation is
drawn at any easily discernible difference, whether it
be geographical, racial, natural, political, religious,
or minor distinctions of a physical or psychical nature. History is largely concerned with the conflict
of antithetic classes. The struggle between Greek
and Barbarian, Jew and Gentile, Christian and Mo-
hammedan, Catholic and Protestant, Norman and
Saxon, is but prototype of the conflict which now
wages about the color line. Evil disposition combined with shrewdly calculated design can always stir
up class friction. Two friendly baseball teams can
easily be wrought up to a pitch of murderous fury
against each other. The yellow press of this country can, within a few months, involve the United
States in war with a nation with whom we are now

on the closest terms of international friendship. A heterogeneous population, where the elements are, on any account, easily distinguishable, furnishes an easy prey for the promoter of strife. The fuse is already prepared for the spark. The peace and tranquillity of such a community depend upon the highest enlightenment and moral restraint in the leadership of the separable elements.

That the dominant South is determined to foster artificial barriers between the races is clearly seen in the utterances and action of its leaders. It was Henry W. Grady who laid down the platform: " We believe that there is an instinct, ineradicable and positive, which keeps the races apart. We add in perfect frankness, however, that if the South had any reasonable doubt of its existence it would, by every means in its power, so strengthen the race prejudice that it would do the work and hold the stubbornness and strength of instinct." The more recent leadership of the South, without the clear discernment and conscientious restraint of the brilliant Georgian, has seized upon his suggestion for sinister and selfish ends. They have harped upon the chord of race prejudice as a musician upon his favorite instrument. Seemingly dubious of the sufficiency of natural antipathy, they have sought to give it the requisite strength and stubbornness. The fire of race hatred has been fanned until it has become an uncontrollable flame. Sociologists tell us that the collective soul is less sensitive than the conscience of the individual. It responds to the shibboleths and slogans whose refrain is malice and strife. The soul of the mob is stirred by the suggestion of hatred and slaughter, as a famished beast at the smell of blood. Hatred is a great social dynamic, the ever-handy instrument of the unscrupulous demagogue. The rabble re-

sponds so much more easily to an appeal to passion
than to reason. To wantonly stir up the fires of race
antipathy is as execrable a deed as flaunting a red
rag in the face of a bull at a summer's picnic, or
of raising a false cry of " fire " in a crowded house.
And yet this is just what the politician is doing in
order to carry his crafty ends. He has raised the
cry of " Negro domination " when all the world
knows that the Negro is no more able to dominate
the South than the babies in the cradle. But it serves
its purpose by raising race animosity, which easily
overrides all arguments based on tax, tariff, or the
relative value of silver and gold.

The charge that the educated Negro is in quest
of social affiliation with the whites is absurdly un-
true. His sense of self-respect effectively forbids
forcing himself upon any unwelcome association.
Household intercourse and domestic familiarity are
essentially questions of personal privilege. The
choice of one's friends and intimate associates is the
most delicate phase of the pursuit of happiness.
Such matters are regulated wholly by personal preference and affinity of taste. The social integrity of
the white race is within its own keeping. The social
citadel is not subject to assault and battery. The
aphorism of Emerson is as true of races as of individuals : " No man can come near me except through
my own act."

The Negro is building up his own society based
upon character, culture, and the nice amenities of
life, and can find ample social satisfaction within the
limits of his own race. President Eliot, of Harvard
University, has told us in a recent utterance that the
white man of the North is not less averse than his
Southern brother to the social mingling of the races.
The Negro, too, has social sensibilities. He will

never complain against any white man, North or
South, because he is not invited to dine at his table,
sit in his pew, or dance with his daughter. But the
Negro ought not to be expected to accept that interpretation of " social equality " which would rob him
of political and civil rights, as well as of educational
and industrial opportunity.

For the Negro supinely to surrender his status of
political and civic equality would be as unmanly as a
silly insistence upon unwelcome social relations
would be unmannerly. The Negro and the white
man in this country must live together for all time
which we can foresee. They must mingle in business
and in public life. All their relations should be characterized by mutual respect, courtesy, and good will.
In all purely personal and social matters let each, if
he will, go unto his own company.

THE CITY NEGRO

THERE are two distinct branches of the Negro problem, viz., the rustic and the urban. The problem of the country Negro may be deferred, that of his urban brother is immediate and imperative. While the former may be preserved indefinitely, embalmed as it were in a state of nature, the latter demands immediate rescue from destruction.

The influx of rural population into large centers constitutes one of the most serious sociological movements of the last half century. The evils which flow in the train of this movement have been universally noted and commented upon. Such evils fall most heavily upon the poor Negroes, who are allured to the destruction of city life as moths by the glare of the candle. These unfortunate people rush from the country where they have a useful status and function to the city where there is no industrial *raison d'être* for them, and inevitably they sink to the bottom of the social scale, where they form the dregs, the scum, and menace of municipal life. A counterstream of tendency which will return this element to the place where it may become a helpful contributing factor is a sociological desideratum devoutly to be wished.

The urban Negro constitutes a larger per cent. of the race than is generally supposed. It is the prevalent belief that 90 per cent. of this race live in direct contact with the soil. There are nearly eight hundred cities and towns in the South, of more than

2500 inhabitants, containing about one and a quarter million Negroes. In Mississippi, Alabama, Arkansas, North and South Carolina the urban element constitutes from 6 to 12 per cent. of the total Negro population; in Georgia, Virginia, Louisiana, Texas, Florida, and West Virginia, from 16 to 20 per cent.; in Tennessee, Delaware, Maryland, Kentucky, and Missouri, from 27 to 55 per cent. It is quite noticeable that the city element is much larger proportionally in the border States than in the far South. It may occasion some surprise to note that more than half the Negro population of Missouri, two-fifths of that of Maryland, and more than a third of that of Kentucky, are found in the towns and cities. In the North and West the cities contain a still larger proportion of the race. When a Negro leaves the South he almost never proceeds to rural surroundings, but makes a bee-line for the large and attractive centers.

According to the census of 1900 there were seventy-two cities containing over five thousand Negro inhabitants; of these, five contained over 60,000; fifteen, over 20,000; thirty-two, over 10,000. Washington heads the list with 86,000; Baltimore, 79,000; New Orleans, 77,000; Philadelphia, 63,000; New York, 60,000, and Memphis, 49,000. The rate of increase for the city Negro during the last census decade was 30 per cent., against 18 per cent. for the country at large. Charleston, Richmond, and Nashville remained almost stationary, while Memphis, Louisville, and Atlanta made surprising gains. On the whole the Northern cities show the largest percentage of growth. Philadelphia increased by 56 per cent.; New York, 66 per cent., and Chicago, 111 per cent. The Negro element of the Windy City, now numbering 30,000, more than doubled itself in a single decade. Already the alarmist has informed

us that the great cities of the North are threatened
with a black deluge. At the present rate of growth
Philadelphia, New York, and Chicago would each
contain three-quarters of a million Negroes by the
middle of this century. But, as a matter of fact, it
is impossible to predict, except in the vaguest and
most general terms, the permanent growth of the
Negro element in large cities. This growth depends
wholly upon immigration. So far as the facts have
been ascertained, it appears that the Negro in the
North is not a self-sustaining quantity except
through fresh reinforcement from the South. The
mobile Negro element shifts from place to place according to temporary attraction. A given city will
hold just so many of this class in solution before
reaching the point of saturation, resulting in a black
precipitation. The Negro element in Washington
increased by 56 per cent. between 1880 and 1890, but
dropped to 13 per cent. during the last decade; the
growth in Nashville dropped from 79 per cent. from
'80 to '90, to a paltry 2 per cent. for the subsequent
decade. It seems quite evident that such cities as
Charleston, Nashville, and Richmond have about
touched high-water mark so far as the Negro population is concerned, and even the Capital of the nation does not seem subject to much further expansion in that direction. It is misleading to predict the
permanent tendency of the Negro population by its
spasmodic movement during a decade of unusual
commotion and unrest.

The census defines a city as a place of 8000 or
more inhabitants. There were in 1900 forty-one
places with over 8000 Negroes, making a total of
more than a million black souls. This exceeds the
city population of the United States in 1830. A
clearer idea of the significance of these numbers can

be had by the following comparisons: If all the
white residents should withdraw from Washington,
Baltimore, New Orleans, Philadelphia, New York,
and Memphis, the black residue would form municipalities of the respective sizes of Grand Rapids, Se-
attle, Wilmington, Del., Des Moines, Evansville, and
Portland, Me.   The Negro element constitutes the
majority of the population in Charleston, Savannah,
Montgomery, Jacksonville, Shreveport, Vicksburg,
Natchez, Baton Rouge, Athens, Ga., and Winston,
N. C.

A noticeable feature of the city Negro is the tendency to segregate into certain sections and localities. This is more strikingly apparent in the North
than in the South.   Every large city has its white
wards and its black wards, which the politician understands as well as the seaman knows the depths and
shallows of the sea.   In 1890, and the tendency has
been accentuated since that time, one ward in Philadelphia contained 9000 Negroes, three wards in Chicago contained 9000, and three wards of New York
contained 13,000.

The predominance of the female element is perhaps
the most striking phenomenon presented by the urban
Negro population.   The females are in the vast majority in all of the large cities, except Chicago.

About one-half the colored race in cities are engaged in gainful occupations, but are confined mainly
to three or four lines of unskilled or menial pursuits.
Colored women are engaged almost as extensively as
the men, their sphere of gainful activity being confined chiefly to domestic service and " taking in wash-
ing."   We have not the prescient power to foresee
the time when this condition will be materially different.   These people should be made efficient along
the lines of work that inevitably devolves upon them.

The number of Negroes following mechanical pursuits is quite considerable in the South, but fades away to the vanishing point as we proceed toward the North.   Even in the South, the Negro mechanic is fast giving way to conquering European workmen. If we may read the shadow which coming events cast before them, it seems clear that within half a century Negro workmen along lines of higher mechanical skill will be as rare in Atlanta and Richmond as they are in Boston and Philadelphia.

The Negro has hardly as yet entered upon such pursuits as merchant, dealer, and pedler, which perhaps are the chief business of the city.   Indications, however, are not wanting that the future will show greater activity in this direction.

Teachers, preachers, doctors, and lawyers enjoy a larger income than any other class of colored wage-earners.   Although they constitute an insignificant fraction of the population, nevertheless, it is a signally potential one.   There is almost total absence of the merchant, the manufacturer, and the non-professional man of practical affairs, who constitute the ruling power among the whites.   This gives the professional class a unique position and influence in Negro society.

The Negro death rate is unmistakably higher than that of the whites; quite enough so to give rise to most serious and searching inquiry as to causes and remedies.   New Orleans, Charleston, Savannah, and Richmond show the highest death rates for both races, which is due, we might infer, to the unsanitary situation of these cities.   In such Northern cities as New York, Philadelphia, Chicago, and Boston the Negro death rate is not perceptibly higher than in the large centers of the South.   It is known, however, that the colored population of these cities is made up largely of young adults who are not subject to high death rate.

Before we become too much alarmed as to this high mortality for the Negro, let us consider several explanatory factors. It is known that the environment of the city Negro is most miserable. He lives in large numbers in byways and alleys that are not fit for human occupation. In spite of all that can be said of the one-room cabin in the South, it possesses one virtue which the city tenement sadly misses, and that is ample ventilation. There is not a cabin in the State of Virginia that is so unfit for human habitation as are scores of blocks of alley houses in Washington City. Dr. John S. Billings tells us that " . . . if we could separate the vital statistics of the poor and ignorant whites, the tenement-house population of our Northern cities, from those of the mass of the white population, we should undoubtedly find a high rate of mortality in this class." The physical and social environment of the city Negro constitutes one of the causes of his high mortality.

The death rate, on the whole, shows a tendency to decrease. But because of the limited data and the fluctuating conditions, little reliance can be placed upon this indication. It is known that the population of these cities has received an enormous reinforcement of Negro adults whose presence would of course lower the general mortality rate. The excess of the colored death rate over that of the whites is due mainly to the great preponderance of infant mortality.

This is the outcome of carelessness, ignorance, and neglect on the part of Negro mothers. As an indication of what proper sanitary treatment will do to lower the rate of infant mortality, the record of the Board of Children's Guardians of Washington, D. C., may be cited. The infants that come to them are mainly abandoned waifs, and therefore the most unpromising of any possible class of children. These infants are placed in homes and subjected to a sanitary and dietary regime under direction of the board, and the result is that the death rate among them is perhaps not half as great as among the corresponding class of the population at large.

The Negro is especially prone to diseases of a pulmonary character. This conclusion does not admit of the least doubt.

While the general death rate for Negroes is much higher than for the whites, the mortality due to pulmonary affections shows the widest discrepancy. This dread enemy of the human race seizes upon the Negro as its favorite victim. It seems to be as prevalent in the most Southern cities as in higher latitudes. Charleston and Savannah are no better off in this regard than Chicago and Boston. Where is to be found deliverance from the effects of this scourge?

The difference between Negro and white mortality in the country at large is a matter of great pertinence to this inquiry. While this matter has not been studied for the entire country, yet the indication is unmistakable that the country negro is more vigorous and healthy than his city brother.

A careful study of census data gives rise to certain clear conclusions: (1) The Negro death rate is nearly double that of the whites in all of our large cities; (2) this rate is due mainly to excess of infant mortality; (3) consumption and allied pulmonary complaints carry off proportionately about three Negroes to one white person; (4) Negro death rate seems to be slightly decreasing, and (5) the mortality of the city Negro is almost double that of his country brother, which is not much in excess of the rate for the white race in rural districts.

The movement toward the cities should be checked; a higher sense of parental duty should be inculcated; simple sanitary and health instruction should be given to the people, and municipalities should be prevailed upon to maintain better sanitary regulations in the alleys and shade places where the Negroes are forced to live.

" The education of the Negro " has become a cant phrase whose sing-song sound is constantly dinged in our ears. By the frequency of its repetition we are led to believe that it stands for a fixed and definite quantity in the educational equation. The Negro race is ever referred to as a unit, and its circumstances and conditions as requiring a unitary mode of treatment. Our educational philosophers seem to think that the whole race stands in need of a single programme of instruction. They make no allowance for discreet differentiation.

The educational needs and circumstances of the city Negro must be carefully differentiated from those of the rustic masses. The general economic conditions are so different from those of the rural districts and the educational provisions are so glaringly disproportional that we must separate the two in any scheme of profitable discussion. In the cities the funds are quite sufficient to maintain the schools for the average length of term, and to provide the requisite appliances and facilities of instruction. The duplication of schools for the two races works to much less economic disadvantage in the cities, where the numbers of both races are sufficient to supply adequate school constituencies, than in the country, where the population is sparse and far between. The education of the city Negro makes no claim on outside philanthropy. The cities are able to educate their own children and do not stand in need of philanthropic aid. There is no more reason for Baltimore, Richmond, New Orleans, and Atlanta to seek outside aid to educate their children than that they should appeal for like support for their police departments.

The teachers in city schools for colored children are generally of the colored race, Baltimore and Charleston forming notable exceptions. In Charleston all such teachers, and in Baltimore the majority of them, are of the white race. The Negro teachers compare quite favorably with their white co-laborers, and Southern superintendents are not sparing in according them the measure of commendation and encouragement which is their just due.

The status of the city Negro seems to furnish a contradiction of the prevalent belief that education will solve the race problems. Experience seems to show that the problems grow in difficulty as general intelligence increases. This is no discredit to education or a derogation of its function. It simply shows that the case was wrongly diagnosed in the first instance. In the city of Washington, and in a corresponding degree the same may be said of other cities, the educational facilities for colored children are practically as good as any offered the most favored class of children anywhere on the face of the earth. These schools have been crowded for a quarter of a century and have now more than fifteen thousand in attendance, a higher average than prevails in white schools. And yet the race problem at the national Capital is not solved. It is a mild criticism of Negro education to say that it has not had satisfactory reaction upon the mass life of the race.

It is on this account that there has recently sprung up such a widespread movement to modify the plan and policy of Negro education so as to bring it into closer relation with the actual life of the people for whom it is designed. In rural districts the pressing problem is better schools and more of them, but in the cities the question is one of readjustment and wise adaptation.

The perfection of the city schools is of the highest importance to the race at large, for it is in the urban centers that the torch must be lighted and passed on to the remotest rural ramifications.

If our great cities were not constantly supplied with fresh life and vigor from the country they would soon wither up for lack of self-sustaining vitality. The tree is cut from the mountain side and shaped and fashioned into instruments of use and ornamentation, but the supply can be sustained only by fresh growth on the original heath. The city constantly draws in fresh supplies of physical, intellectual, and moral energy only to develop, exploit, and exhaust it. The great drawback to the Negro element is that it is exhausted, without being either developed or utilized.

Mr. George W. Cable in a recent contribution has emphasized the importance of what he calls the " citification " of the Negro. The value of this sagacious suggestion must be accepted with a word of caution. The cities are indeed the centers of light, the storehouses of advantage and opportunity. Without the opportunity of urban contact it is hardly possible for one either to develop or exploit his better faculties. The great men of America were, as a rule, born in the country, but nurtured in the city. With the Negro, however, the situation is not so simple. He shares the disadvantages without the benefits. He does not enter into the larger opportunities of urban life. There is a certain advantage of education and contact, but his culture is apt to assume a pale and sickly cast for lack of the sunlight of opportunity. The city Negro grows up in the shade. He is completely overshadowed by his overtowering environment. As one walks along the streets of our great cities and views the massive buildings and sky-seeking structures, he finds no status for the Negro above the cellar floor. There is perhaps no place on earth where so much culture runs to seed, and so much intelligence goes to waste, as among the Negro element of our large cities. The younger element of the race at least is practically as well educated as the whites. And yet they count for almost nothing in the higher business and industrial life of the community. It is scarcely necessary to inquire into the cause of this condition of things or to apportion responsibility. The fact cannot be disputed. So far only the more fortunate class of city Negroes has been considered. But there are those who are completely crushed by the weight of superimposed conditions and sink to the bottom of the social scale. These constitute the slum element, and furnish the hospital and the jail constituency. Let us, however, be careful to avoid extremes. Large numbers of city Negroes are sober, industrious, church-going, law-abiding citizens. There are also exceptional individuals who are able to breast the blows of hard circumstances and have their merit recognized and rewarded. But the picture in its characteristic features is not too gloomily drawn. The " citification " of the country Negro as a means of solving the race problem should be accepted, if not with the traditional grain of salt, at least with prudent hesitation.

On the other hand, the country Negro has very

little opportunity for getting hold of the machinery of civilization. The discipline of the plantation system has been destroyed. Every well-ordered plantation was a school in which were taught the crude elements of civilization. Industry, order, and obedience are the cardinal virtues of the industrial world. The slave regime was based upon false notions of political economy and therefore encouraged only the mechanical or marketable virtues in the slave, and suppressed all higher outcroppings of intelligence and personal dignity. A black man was looked upon as a machine and not as a being in whom the image of God could be made manifest. And so the school of slavery appealed merely to the physical side, and left the higher faculties untouched, or, worse still, smothered and suppressed. As the whites are withdrawing to the cities the Negroes are gaining in density in the purely rural sections of the South, and the opportunities for improvement in manners and methods of life are meager enough. The public schools hold for only a few months, and with the most poorly equipped teachers and facilities. The knowledge thus gained is mostly of the mechanical sort and has very little potential value. The number of Negroes who *can* read and write runs up into the millions. But the number who *do* read and write and who use these accomplishments as a means of conducting the ordinary processes of life and of acquiring a larger hold on civilization would probably not amount to ten per cent. of the number who are reckoned as literate. We must make an immense distinction between the technical and the practical illiteracy of the Negro race. The country schools in the South cannot qualify their own teachers. The rural Negro if left to himself would be in a most pitiable plight. He needs the sympathy and help of his more

fortunate city brother. As the city has need of the
country for new life and fresh physical, moral stamina, just so the country must draw upon the city for
intelligence, system, and civilized method.

The country Negro, however, has certain advantages; he is on terms of equality with his environment. He is not confronted by suggestions of inequality at every turn. Nature is a mother who is
equally kind and beneficent to all of her children.
An acre of ground will yield as much for the black
as for the white tiller. The markets are color-blind.
No one inquires into the color of the producer of
the best produce in the market except as a matter
of idle curiosity. No labor organization has yet
placed a boycott upon Negro farm labor. The farm
offers for the Negro the only really unhampered
field which is open to him on an unlimited scale. The
city Negro of education and culture, on the contrary,
is forced into menial employment, because higher
forms of occupation are pre-empted by the more
favored class. There are plenty of Negro domestics
who have sufficient educational advantages to conduct
independent undertakings. But they find the avenues so crowded, and the competition so fierce, that
the balance of success is on the side of the white
competitor. The best brain and energy of the Anglo-
Saxon race are engaged in the city industries. There
are a dozen competitors for every dollar in sight.
In the great majority of cases the Negro is handicapped by his color. In those branches of business
involving the social feature, as most branches do, he
is placed at a serious disadvantage. His own race
has not yet been educated up to the necessity of
patronizing him, as a sort of race protective tariff.
The white merchant affords the black customer every
facility for spending a dollar. His courtesy is as

expansive as the Negro's pocketbook. But this courtesy turns into coldness and scorn when the Negro asks the merchant to give his son or daughter a place in his store so that he may accumulate business knowledge and experience. In communities where the Negro constitutes a half, a third, or a fourth of the population, and where his educational facilities are practically as good as those of the whites, we find that he does not conduct one per cent. of the business. This accumulated intelligence should seek an outlet. This can be found in the country. It requires as great intelligence, thrift, and patience to make a farm productive as to succeed in a city enterprise.

It is to be feared that the city environment too often develops in the colored boy or girl a love for leisure and ease and a positive disinclination for downright hard work. They prefer to affect the fine manners and fine attire of the ultra-fashionable of the white race, and are strenuously opposed to "hanging up the fiddle and the bow and taking up the shovel and the hoe." Indeed, this is one of the dangers of superimposing the superficialities of civilization upon a backward race. It indisposes them to hard work. The Puritans gained the discipline of work by trying to persuade the rocky hillsides of New England to yield up a living. This has become a fixed trait of character and is handed down by heredity. It is this predisposition to work which makes the Yankee so great a force in the world. The work which devolves upon the city Negro is of an intermittent character, and lacks the discipline of steadiness and consecutive endeavor.

RELIGION AS A SOLVENT OF THE RACE PROBLEM

RELIGION may be treated as a sociological phenomenon whose manifestation is as evident and whose effect is as easily measured as any other data with which the student of social subjects has to deal. The influence of the church upon the Negro is just as evident as that of the school. In current discussion of the race problem this potent and pervasive factor is all but wholly ignored. The proclaimed purpose of Christianity is to establish peace and good will among all the children of men. Before discussing the bearing of Christianity upon the Negro let us see to what extent he is susceptible to its influence.

The Negro as we know him in America is of a deeply religious nature. He is widely noted for his emotional and spiritual susceptibilities. His weird, plaintive, melodious longings are fraught with spiritual substances and meaning, not unlike the lamentations of the Jews in captivity; only the Negro does not yearn for an earthly restoration, but for the Promised Land beyond the skies. These plantation melodies, this blind, half-conscious poetry, breaking through the aperture of sound before the intellect had formulated a definite form of statement, reveal the Negro's passive Christian virtues of meekness, humility, and lowliness of spirit, and express the spiritual strivings of his race.

The conversion of the Negro to the Christian faith is as marvelous, and perhaps as momentous, as any event in the history of the church. There were no

147

religious orders devoted to his evangelization, no zealous missionary propagandism, no concerted movement on the part of his captors to convert the black heathen whom the lust for lucre had brought within their gates.   Here and there a kindly mistress or pious planter might have been moved by pangs of pity to free the soul of the black bondman from the shackles of sin, if only the body might remain in subjection to the galling gyves of an iniquitous system.   "Servants, obey your masters," was the only Scripture text which it was deemed prudent to explain in the depth and plenitude of its meaning. While sitting in the back pews and upper galleries the Negro caught the suggestion of the Christian cult, which was so peculiarly adapted to his ethnic characteristics that it met with an enthusiastic and ready response.   To a race thus spiritually predisposed, the lines of the hymnist convey a special meaning:

> "This is the way I long have sought
> And mourned because I found it not."

It is doubtful whether any race, however great its superiority, can impose its intellectual, æsthetic, or religious cult upon another, either by persuasion or force, unless the recipient race is ready to adopt the suggestion and interpret it in terms of its own ethic aptitude.   Culture is a centrifugal as well as a centripetal process.   The inner spring of motive and action must vibrate in sympathetic resonance with the waves of influence which proceed from without, before they can be awakened into life and power.   Mankind had been observing the phenomenon of falling apples pattering upon the ground ever since the serpent beguiled the first pair; but it was reserved for

Sir Isaac Newton, whose mind was alert on the suggestive, to utilize this familiar occurrence as a key to unlock the hidden mysteries of the universe. This new cult of grace was seized upon by the Negro with Pentecostal enthusiasm and fervor, because it relieved his overburdened soul and satisfied his longings as nothing else could do.

The evangelization of the transplanted African is the only assured fresh conquest of Christianity in modern times, if, indeed, it is not the only undisputed triumph of this faith outside of the range of the Caucasian. For four centuries a continuous stream of missionary influence has been steadily playing upon the American Indian; and yet, to-day, the red aborigine can scarcely be said to be any nearer evangelization than when Columbus first planted his Catholic cross in the virgin soil of a New World. The rise of the missionary spirit is the most unselfish and creditable movement of modern times; but the conversion of the world to the standard of the Cross is discernible only to the eye of faith, which realizes the substance of things hoped for, the evidence of things not seen. On the other hand, the conversion of the Negro is an established fact. The sanction of his religion is as prevalent and as potent as in the case of his white neighbor from whom it was derived. In the United States the Negro has a higher average of church membership than the whites, and constitutes one-fifth of the numerical strength of all the Protestant denominations. This race has a sufficient grasp upon the spirit, meaning, and method of Christianity to propagate and transmit it, although perhaps not yet able to formulate a theological statement of its doctrine. The highest evidence of ignition is furnished by the fact that the lighted torch has become a new center of diffusion, giving light unto all who come within the range of its radiant influence. Several independent Negro denominations in America are supporting foreign missions in the darker continent of Africa, conducted by their own men and means. Where else has Christianity made such manifestation of its power since the rise of the Protestant sect?

But we are accustomed to the reproach that the Negro's religious profession has little beneficial influence upon his practical life. It is unfortunately true that there is a wide discrepancy between creed and conduct. This discrepancy is, of course, intensified by ignorance and grossness of life. At best, the heavenly treasure is placed in earthen vessels. He is indeed a poor judge of human nature who expects to find, in any people, an exact adjustment between practical conduct and religious standard. When we consider the broad function of the Negro church, and the original grossness and degradation with which it has had to deal, it will be seen that, although religion has not yet done its perfect work, the wholesomeness of its influence has been not only manifest, but marvelous. Imagine the moral status of this people if the religious influence had been withdrawn! Who is he that condemneth? The practical conduct of the white Christian furnishes the roughest approximation to the standards of his faith. The keynote and kelson of Christianity is love for God and man. When the white Christian violates the vital precepts of his faith, in his treatment of the Negro, he furnishes an example and an excuse for his weaker brother to transgress, though it may be in a more flagrant manner.

The most notable feature of Negro church life is its tendency toward ecclesiastical independence. After receiving the original suggestion from the white race, the Negro evinced a decided inclination to worship God under his own vine and fig tree.   The Baptist and Methodist denominations, representing the independent spirit, contain 98 per cent. of all colored Protestant communicants.   The Presbyterian, Episcopalian, and Congregational churches, which have enjoyed the largest measure of white assistance, contact, and control, have flourished, at the expense of much watering, only as a root out of dry ground. Although these churches appeal generally to the more cultivated classes, yet their numerical feebleness is in no wise offset by any superior vigor of spiritual aggressiveness or force.   Even in these denominations there is an ambition, expressed or suppressed, for a larger measure of ecclesiastical self-control.   Presbyterian and Congregational missionary societies have spent many millions of dollars among the freedmen of the South, but the result is seen rather in the intellectual and moral uplift than in religious proselytism.   The real religious advantage consists largely in reflex influence upon the Methodist and Baptist denominations.   These churches have flourished because of their ecclesiastical independence, and not on account of any theological tenets or administrative polity.

It is almost as rare to find a white pastor of a colored congregation as to come across the reverse relationship.   We see the same tendency in the Northern States.   Wherever two or three dozen colored people are gathered together, there will be found a Negro church, of an independent type, springing up in the midst of them.   No people take a greater pride in their churches or give so large a share of their means to support them.   The church is not merely a religious institution, but embraces all the complex functions of Negro life.   It furnishes the broadest field for the exercise of talent, and is the only sphere in which the Negro has shown initiative and executive ability. Frederick Douglass began his public life as a local preacher in the A. M. E. Church, and if a wider career had not providentially opened up to him he doubtless would have risen to a position of ecclesiastical dignity and power.

In politics, education, and business the white man manages and controls the Negro's interests; it is only in the church that the field is undisputed. Upon the failure of the reconstruction governments the Negro politicians sought careers in the church as the most inviting field for the exploitation of their powers. The Negro preacher is a potential politician, whose natural qualities of organization and leadership being denied scope and exercise in the domain of secular activity, seek them in the religious realm. When the Negro preacher makes occasional excursions into the political field we are apt to condemn his conduct as irrelevant to his calling, but he is merely giving vent to pent-up powers on the slightest show of opportunity or pretext of duty.

The Negro ministry is often upbraided for its delinquencies and shortcomings. But when we consider all of the circumstances of the case, there is no more remarkable body of men in America than these black preachers who guide the people in the ways of truth and righteousness. There is a professional body of men, some twenty-five thousand strong, who, like Melchizedek of old, sprang into existence without announcement or preparation. They show unmistakable ability for leadership and guidance. The priesthood has always been upbraided for its carnal imperfections, notwithstanding the high and sacred character of its function. The Negro ministry does not escape blame and censure; but no one can say that the moral and spiritual trend of its leading has not been upward. Under the influence of education and orderly training this ministry is rapidly attaining to a higher and higher degree of orderliness and spiritual decorum. There are increasing thousands of Negro churches where no breath of suspicion attaches to the clerical reputation, and where the services are conducted with intelligence, simplicity, and in the beauty of holiness.

The Negro church has stood, and still in large measure stands, for the home, the school, and the State. It has been and is the greatest enlightening, uplifting, purifying, and inspiring influence which actuates the life of the benighted masses.

It was the consolation of religion that solaced and sustained the Negro slave under burdens as heavy as any that the human race has ever been called upon to bear. It was the manifestation of the religious spirit that gained for him the confidence and sympathy even of his oppressors, and played no small part in effecting his emancipation. If the Negro had remained a heathen, and had adhered to the repugnant religious rites of his ancestors, can any one believe that the Christian sentiment of this nation would have exerted itself so strongly in his behalf? Would a race of heathens have ever been incorporated into the body politic of this nation?

It is probably true that the educated Negro is not so deeply interested in religion as were his ignorant forebears. This is due in large part to the revolt of culture against the grotesque excesses of ignorance, partly to the cold, critical, intellectual indifferentism of the times, and in large measure to the haughty attitude of the white Christian whose spiritual arrogance causes his black brother to offend. But there still abides that deep subconscious religious feeling which a larger enlightenment and the sobering influence of adversity will again waken into life and power.

Stern moral qualities are necessary to save a backward race, in contact with civilization, from physical destruction. Such races usually fade before the breath of civilization, as a flower is withered by the chilling blast of autumn. The Indian is gone, the Australian has followed him, the scattered fragments of the isles of the sea are rapidly passing away. These people have not perished so much by force and violence as through the disintegrating influence inherent in the vices of civilization. The backward races cannot stand the vices of the Aryan; what makes the one drunk, but makes the other bold. Vice is destruction; virtue is preservative. The thief, the robber, the murderer, the drunkard, the adulterer, and, not less, those who indulge in the more refined and recondite modes of sin, are destructive of the stability of social order. The criminal and moral status of the Negro race is threatening its physical continuance. After we have made all possible allowance for historic causes and plead all possible exculpatory excuses, the plain, unpleasant, unvarnished fact remains: The American Negro must conquer his vices or be destroyed by them.

It is true that perhaps ninety-five per cent. of the colored people are orderly and well-behaved; but this is not sufficient, any more than it would be satisfactory for a fruiterer to assure us that ninety-five per cent. of the apples in a barrel are sound. It is also true that the Negro has no monopoly of sin. There is no caste in crime which is a failing of weak human nature; and yet the criminal is a special bane and burden to the people to whom his base blood binds him. One might argue the failure of the sort

of Christianity to which the Negro has been subjected, because it has not banished sin and ushered
in the era of righteousness. This religion has been
in the world for two thousand years, and yet history fails to tell us of a single people from whom
it has removed the earth-stains of wickedness and sin.
In portions of Asia and Africa where this gospel once
held sway the surviving influence is so faint as to be
scarcely perceptible. Parts of Europe after many
centuries of Christian endeavor are sunken in the
depths of vileness and iniquity. Many of the cities
of our own country that are covered with a forest of
church towers are, if we believe reports and rumors
of corruption, as rotten as Nineveh and Tyre. Do
we say in such cases that religion is a failure, and
that the people are incapable of understanding and
applying the principles of Christianity? The Negro
needs, what all mankind needs, a higher, purer, and
more effective application of his professed religion
to the daily affairs of life.

Religion constitutes the only effective sanction the
world has yet devised over the conduct of the ignorant and unawakened masses. No enlightened ruler
of backward races, from Marcus Aurelius to Edward
VII, has ever failed to utilize religious adherence as
an aid to wise and salutary control. This conduct
does not always spring from high spiritual motive,
but is resorted to as a matter of administrative prudence. The sneer of the poet Goethe contains a
valuable half-truth:

" Whoso has art and science found, religion too has he;
Who has nor art nor science found, religion his should be."

The value of knowledge, culture, æsthetic taste, and
social pride as aids to conduct is a matter of casuistic

dispute: but all will agree that where such auxiliaries are wanting the absence can be made good only by the mystic power of faith. The combined experience of mankind shows that it is impossible to bring a backward race under a wholesome, moral order without the quickening power of spiritual motive. Intellectual doctrine and moral maxims are not sufficient. China to-day stands as a living, or rather as a dying, embodiment of what a scheme of morality will do for a race without the mystic religious element. Morality, without religion, especially to an unawakened people, is as impotent and void of effect as a cannon ball without the propulsive power of gunpowder.

A new people stand especially in the need of religious guidance. An old-stablished race, as history has often demonstrated, may exist for ages on the forms of faith after the vital spirit has departed. They are carried forward by the spiritual inertia acquired in a more virile and pious period. The foundation of the Roman greatness was laid in the good old days of stern and robust Roman faith and virtue. The anchor-sheet of our own Republic was forged in the furnace of faith. It is absolutely essential for a people to begin right. The opening words of Genesis form the granite foundation of all true race building—" In the beginning, God."

This brings us to the importance of religious instruction in colored schools, whether under public or private control. For the sake of avoiding argument we may hold in abeyance the larger aspect of this question, and limit our discussion to its application to this unfortunate class. The missionaries who came South directly after the war were not educators in the modern significance of that term, many of them were not even educated; and yet they worked wonders in transforming the life of a new people.

They were filled with the love of God and his dark and benighted creatures, and imparted a measure of their moral and spiritual zeal to the people among whom they came to labor.   There was not an unbeliever among them.   Suppose they had left their Bibles at home; does any one believe that they could have imparted such a lasting and wholesome impulse? In this instance surely the letter killeth and the spirit maketh alive.   You do not arouse the lethargic energies of a people seeking a newness of life by imparting information to the mind or skill to the fingers, but by quickening the spirit.   The public schools, with their more competent secular agencies, have supplanted the missionary in the educational world; but, alas! the subtle spirit is wanting.   It is one of the greatest misfortunes of the race that this moral and spiritual influence was too early withdrawn.

The home, the church, and the school are the only places where religious instruction can formally be imparted.   The average Negro home is no more capable of imparting religious than intellectual knowledge.   The Sunday school has the child only one hour a week, whereas the ordinary church service is too stiff and formal to be of much advantage to the average child.   Thus it can readily be seen that the great bulk of Negro children are growing up in moral and spiritual illiteracy, without a saving knowledge of the truth.

There does not exist the same ground for controversy over introducing the Bible in Negro schools as in the case of the white race.   With the Negro there are practically only two religious denominations, with no great diversity of theological tenets.   He has no inherited doctrinal bias. Schismatic differences have not been burned into his soul by the hot iron of per-

secution and martyrdom. The Irishman is a Catholic, the Scotchman a Presbyterian, the Yankee a
Congregationalist for reasons whose roots strike deep
in the soil of conflict and suffering. The Negro has
no serious controversy over Scriptural interpretation.
He is never tried for heresy. He does not wrangle
over questions of the higher criticism. After all
these things does the white Christian seek. The
time-honored dispute as to the proper mode of baptism is about the only Scriptural text that the Negro
approaches with controversial heat. The fundamental agreement among the Negro race as to the
interpretation and value of Bible teaching renders
such instruction comparatively easy of accomplishment.

Again, religion furnishes the only sanction that
can enable the overridden races to contemplate
the trend of modern civilization with composure of
spirit. They form an insignificant part in the world's
rivalry for material and political supremacy. The
exceeding weight of humiliation under which the Negro labors can be relieved only by a firm grasp upon
the spiritual and eternal verities. When a contestant
feels that a prize is beyond his grasp he is apt to console himself by depreciating its value. The humble
slave on bended knee, with marvelous sagacity, gave
utterance to a far-reaching philosophy: " You may
have all the world; give me Jesus." Although this
utterance has been made the butt of much ridicule in
recent years, it may yet prove that the intuition of
the soul is a safer criterion than the deductions of
the intellect. Can the heavily handicapped Negro,
with his present enfeebled energies and hereditary
ineptitude for affairs, compete with the Anglo-Saxon,
the modern war-lord of creation, for the power and
glory of this world? Is he not much more likely to

solve his problems by adhering to high moral and spiritual precepts than by joining the great white throng which bows down and worships before the shrine of " the almighty dollar "?

The historic development of races verifies the truth of Scripture: "Seek ye first the Kingdom of God and His righteousness, and all these things shall be added."

There are more than twenty million persons of African blood in the Western Hemisphere. These people have been brought here and are permitted to remain and to insinuate themselves into the civilization and culture of this continent because of their passing Christian graces of meekness and lowliness.

The presence and promise of the Negro in the Western world is a striking fulfilment of that Scripture saying which is at once a beatitude and a prophecy: " Blessed are the meek for they shall inherit the earth." The Negro is not only preserved by his passive virtues, but he holds them as a lash over the conscience of the Anglo-Saxon, to scourge him to the observance of the requirements of the faith to which he avows allegiance. The history of religion abounds in anomalies. The European derived his creed from Jew, but as soon as the transference was finished the new convert turned in persecution upon the race through which the cult had been transmitted. The American Negro secured his first notion of the Christian religion from the Anglo-Saxon, but now, with acknowledged justice, denounces him bitterly for his failure to keep the precepts of the faith which he transmitted to others.

Moral and spiritual qualities are of the essence of eternal good, and carry their own reward. The Negro holds a warmer place in the sympathies of his fellow-men, because it can be said, " Behold, he prayeth."

And what if men should fail to recognize moral and spiritual excellence? They do not depend upon human recognition for their value. For if God is our Father, it matters little whether Abraham affects ignorance of us or Israel acknowledges us or not.

In estimating the benefits of Christianity to the natives of the Sandwich Islands a pious missionary recounted the inestimable blessing in that it had prepared thousands of the dwindling race for their heavenly home. To the Hawaiian this must be bitter irony. The salvation of the soul is an individual and not a collective phenomenon. It is poor consolation to the Indian race to be assured that an encroaching Christian civilization has merely hastened its departure to the happy hunting-ground in the sky. But the mission of Christianity is to bring about social salvation, as well as the salvation of souls. However the complex problems of race may eventuate, whether the Negro is to be absorbed in the great body of the American people, or to be perpetuated in racial integrity, whether he is to be banished to some distant continent, or perish from the face of the earth, religion is absolutely essential either as a solvent or as a salve.

So far we have dealt with the effect of religion upon the Negro alone, but its effect upon the white race is an equally important factor.

The real question is, What power is there in Christianity to wean men from race prejudice? If we listen to some of the good ministers of the Gospel, who with incredible suddenness turn philosophers and propose off-hand solution for all sociological problems, religion has little or nothing to do with this question.

We are led to believe that the white man is all-wise, all-good, and altogether without sin, while the Negro is passively or actively responsible for all of the evils of the situation; that the white man is bearing his burden with fortitude and grace, while the Negro should be thankful for whatever treatment he receives or escapes.

They tell us that the Negro must be patient, that his hand must be trained to work, that the ballot must be taken from him, that his civil privileges must be limited, that he must be constantly impressed with a sense of inferiority; but few indeed have courage to demand of the white race to apply the simple principles and precepts of the religion of Jesus in dealing with their black brethren of the same household of faith.

Mr. James Bryce, in his notable lecture on the world-wide race problem, asserts that religious sanction is less strong than the bond of blood. This is contradictory to the plain letter and spirit of the Gospel. We have fallen upon such evil days that quotation of Scripture, however direct or unequivocal, is not regarded as serious argument. When Jesus was chided with seeming indifference toward His kindred after the flesh, He responded: " Who is my mother and who are my brothers? For whosoever shall do the will of my Father which is in heaven, the same is my brother and sister and mother."

A strong religious sanction can command amity among diverse races or enmity among kindred ones, and it will be so. The Apostle Paul found the new cult of grace sufficient to solve the ethnological problems of his day. For, through the eye of faith, he could discern neither " Jew nor Greek, Barbarian, Scythian, bond or free, but Christ is all and in all."

The unifying power of religion alone can allay the frictional strife among the sons of men.

Mr. James Bryce, in commenting upon this superior pacifying power of Mohammedanism, says: " Can one of the causes be that Christianity achieves less because it aims at more? " Then in answer to his own question he rejoins: " Christians, of course with many noble exceptions, have failed to rise to the level of the higher teaching, while Moslems have risen to the level of the lower." And yet the teachings of the two religions are identical as respects those who are of the same household of faith. There is the crux of the whole question—Christianity has not solved the race problem because Christians, in adequate numbers, have not risen up to the level of their creed. Emerson tells us that " every Stoic was a Stoic, but in Christendom where is the Christian? "

It is worthy of note that the Catholic states are superior to the Protestant countries in controlling the virulence of race prejudice. Macaulay tells us that it was the policy of this church that caused the disappearance of animosity between Saxon and Norman in England. In Brazil the African element is as large or larger in proportion than it is in the Southern States, and yet race friction is unknown. Recently the United States has driven a Catholic power from the Western Hemisphere in the interest of free institutions; but if the victor shall derive from the vanquished the secret and method by which to subdue race prejudice, so that the race relations shall be as kindly and as congenial in Washington as they are in Havana, he will derive from the vanquished Spaniard as valuable a lesson as he can hope to bestow upon his long suffering victim.

In fostering the spirit and power of initiative, in awakening the dominant forces which conquer and control, the Protestant religion clearly leads the van of progress. It solves all physical and natural problems, but seems to fail to produce a harmonious adjustment among the different breeds of men.

But Christianity has not yet been able to wean the Anglo-Saxon of his race prejudice. With him ethnic ties are cherished more fondly than bond of faith or moral and spiritual kinship. Blood is not only declared to be thicker than water, but its consistency and spissitude surpass the cohesive power of civilization, morality, and religion. With him philanthropic interest and personal repugnance are not incompatible terms. While he professedly loves the soul, he avowedly dislikes the bodies of those whose blood differs from his own. He will build schools and colleges, establish asylums and hospitals, give of his substance and his service to carry the light to the darksome places of the earth, but his tough Teutonic spirit balks at the concrete brotherhood of man.

A learned bishop of the Episcopal Church is reported to have said: " I care not if a Negro be as learned as Socrates or as pious as St. John, yet he could not sit down at my table." Such race intolerance would doubtless be astounding both to Socrates and St. John. Household intimacy and the details of personal intercourse may indeed fall outside the sphere of one's Christian duty; but to hold such things to be of higher sacredness and sanction than one's religious creed merely shows the arrogant spirit which actuates those who worship at the shrine of race idolatry.

It required two revelations to convince the Apostle Peter that what God had cleansed was no longer common or unclean. Will it require still another to teach the Teuton so?

We read in Isaiah of the type of soul that characterizes the Kingdom of God, as being without form or comeliness, and when we shall see him there is no beauty that we should desire him. We did deem him stricken, smitten of God and afflicted, and hid, as it were, our faces from him; and we console ourselves that this has exclusive reference to the attitude of the stiff-necked Jew toward the Messianic prophecy. But does it not equally describe the supercilious attitude of the white Christian to-day toward an humble black people whom he holds in despite? But if the Christian religion has not overcome, it has markedly modified this rancorous spirit.

The great work which Northern philanthropy has accomplished was inspired mainly by religious motive. Without the love of God the love for man becomes a dead formulary. For love of knowledge men will hazard their lives in quest of some new or unknown fact or process of knowledge; the soldier, in a burst of patriotic fervor, gives up his life to his country; the student of science is carried away with zeal and enthusiasm for screeching things that fly in the air or creeping things that crawl on the earth or for slimy things that swim in the sea. But it is only the man or woman whose soul is full of the love of God that devotes his life and powers to the salvation of the souls and bodies of dying men.

It is in matters of religion that the two races will find the surest basis of mutual helpfulness and co-operation. Through contact and assistance from the white race the Negro will be enabled to maintain a higher standard of concrete morality, thus insuring more rational modes of worship and orderly habits of life. On the other hand, the white race will be a great debtor. Culture and refinement are not essential conditions of spiritual enlightenment, but the inevitable outcome. It does not always appear in a pleasing outward garb. The spiritually minded have usually been despised and rejected of men. The haughty Caucasian can learn from the despised Negro valuable lessons in meekness, humility, and forgiveness of spirit, the brightest stars that shine in the galaxy of the Christian graces. The Negro Christian must purify himself of grossness and carnal corruption, and the white Christian must descend from his pharisaical attitude, whose pious hauteur finds vent in the prayer, "I thank the Lord that I am not as other men," until they, too, shall meet upon a common plane of truth and righteousness and brotherly kindness.

Christianity will solve the race problem if, as we profess to believe, it is destined to gain full sway over the innate wickedness of the human heart. Right and wrong may co-exist for ages, but finally the evil will be swallowed up in good. Universal slavery existed for well-nigh two thousand years after the advent of the Christian dispensation, but in the fullness of time the influence of this religion destroyed the iniquitous system wherever its power prevailed. Christianity is incompatible with caste. Spiritual kinship transcends all personal and social relations.

The solution of the race question depends upon the simple recognition of the Fatherhood of God and the Brotherhood of Man, and the application of the Golden Rule to the affairs of life. Let the Negro lay stress of emphasis upon the Ten Commandments and the white man upon the Golden Rule, and all will be well.

PLEA OF THE OPPRESSED

" Lord, Teach us How to Pray "

O Thou who heard the plaintful plea
Of our forebears on bended knee,
And broke their bonds and set them free,
    To Thee we pray,
    To Thee we pray.

In broken word and wailing tone,
In deep, unutterable groan,
They made their tribulations known;
    Hear us, we pray,
    Hear us, we pray.

In this dark day of sore distress,
In deepest gloom of wilderness,
When threatening ills so hardly press;
    Help us this day,
    Help us this day.

If slighting scorn of race would seek
Its vial of wrath to venge and wreak
Upon this lowly folk and meek,
    Spare us, we pray,
    Spare us, we pray.

They need not fear, our Strength and Stay,
Who keep thy Law, walk in the way,
When all the world might look and say:
    " Behold, they pray ! "
    " Behold, they pray ! "

But when we stray from Thy command,
And feel Thy sore afflicting hand,
We humbly bow; we understand:
      May we obey,
      May we obey.

If some Thy saving help deny,
With wild, inane, distracted cry,
Like Job's wild wife, would curse and die,
      Forgive, we pray,
      Forgive, we pray.

If time-taught wisdom nostrums find
In cunning hand or knowing mind,
Show the blind leaders of the blind
      'Tis vanity,
      'Tis vanity.

Thy righteous Law is all our trust,
Who builds on else but builds on dust;
The Mighty should, the Lowly must
      Rely alway,
      Rely alway.

Lord, since of stones Thou raiseth seed
As choice as any boasted breed,
Vouchsafe to us the larger meed,
      We humbly pray,
      We humbly pray,
        Amen.

THE LAND OF GOSHEN

THERE is much speculation as to the ultimate destiny of the Negro population in the United States. History furnishes no exact or approximate parallel. When widely dissimilar races are thrown into intimate contact it is inevitable that either extermination, expulsion or separate racial types will be the outcome. So far as the present problem is concerned, extermination and expulsion have few serious advocates, while amalgamation has no courageous ones. The concensus of opinion seems to be that the two races will preserve their separate identity as co-inhabitants of the same territory. The main contention is as to the mode of adjustment, whether it shall be the coordination or subordination of the African.

All profitable speculation upon sociological problems must be based upon definitely ascertained social tendencies. It is impossible to forecast coming events unless we stand within the pale of their shadow. The Weather Bureau at Washington, discerning the signs of air and cloud and sky, makes probable predictions of sunshine or storm. Such predictions are not for the purpose of enabling us to affect or modify approaching events, but to put ourselves and our affairs in harmony with them. Sociological events have the inevitableness of natural law, against which speculations and prophecies are as unavailing as against the coming of wind and tide. Prescient wisdom is serviceable only in so far as it enables us to put ourselves in harmony with foreknown conditions. Plans and policies for the solution of the race problem should be based upon as full a knowledge of the facts and factors of the situation as it is possible to gain, and should be in line with the trend of forces which it is impossible to subvert. Social tendencies, like natural laws, are not affected by quackery and patent nostrums. Certain of our sociological states-men are assuming intimate knowledge of the eternal decrees, and are graciously volunteering their as-sistance to Providence. They are telling us, with the assurance of inspiration, of the destiny which lies in store for the black man. It is noticeable, however, that those who affect such familiarity with the plans and purposes of Providence are not usually men of deep knowledge or devout spirit. The prophets of evil seem to derive their inspiration from hate rather than love. In olden times, when God communicated with man from burning bush and on mountain top, He selected men of lowly, loving, loyal souls as the chosen channel of revelation. To believe that those who breathe out slaughter and hatred against their fellow-men are now his chosen mouthpiece is to as-sume that Providence, in these latter days, has grown less particular than aforetime in the choice of spokes-men.

The most gifted of men possess very feeble clair-voyant power. We do not know the changes that even a generation may bring forth. To say that the Negro will never attain to this or that destiny requires no superior knowledge or foresight except audacity of spirit and recklessness of utterance. History has so often changed the " never " of the orator into accomplished results, that the too-frequent use of that term is of itself an indication of heedlessness and incaution. It is safe to follow the lead of Dr. Lyman Abbott, and limit the duration of the oratorical " never " to the present generation. When, there-

fore, we say that the Negro will never be expelled or
amalgamated or that he will forever maintain his
peculiar type of race, the prediction, however emphatically put forth, does not outrun the time which
we have the present means of foreseeing.   The fortune of the Negro rises and falls in the scale of public
regard with the fluctuation of mercury in the bulb
of a thermometer, ranging alternately from blood
heat to freezing point.   In 1860 he would have been
considered a rash prophet who should have predicted
that within the next fifteen years colored men would
constitute a potent factor in State legislatures and
in the national Congress.   On the other hand, who,
in 1875, would have hazarded his prophetic reputation
by predicting that during the following quarter of a
century the last Negro representative would be
driven from places of local and national authority,
and that the opening of a new century would find the
last two amendments to the Constitution effectually
annulled?   No more can we predict what change
in public feeling and policy the remote or near future
may have in store.   But of one thing we may rest
assured, the coming generations will be better able
than we are to cope with their own problems.   They
will have more light and knowledge, and, let us hope,
a larger measure of patience and tolerance.   Our
little plans of solution that we are putting forth with
so much assurance and satisfaction will doubtless
afford ample amusement in years to come.

> "We call our fathers fools,
>   So wise we grow;
> Our wiser sons, no doubt, will
>   Call us so."

The late Professor Freeman, in his " Impressions
of the United States," suggests a unique solution of

the race problem; viz., let each Irishman kill a Negro and get hanged for it. In this way America would be speedily rid of its race problems, both Ethiopic and Celtic. We read this suggestion and smile, as no doubt the author intended we should. And so we smile at the panaceas and nostrums that are being put forth with so much ardor of feeling. Many such theories might be laughed out of existence if one only possessed the power of comic portrayal. While we muse the fire is burning. But alas, we lack the discernment to read aright the signs of the times.

Physical population contains all the potential elements of society, and the careful student relies upon its movement and expansion as the controlling factor in social evolution. It is for this reason that the Federal census is so eagerly awaited by those who seek careful knowledge upon the race problem in America. There are certain definitely ascertainable tendencies in the Negro population that seem clearly to indicate the immediate, if not the ultimate destiny of that race. Amid all the conflicting and contradictory showings of the several censuses since emancipation, there is one tendency that stands out clear and pronounced; viz., the mass center of the Negro population is moving steadily towards the Gulf of Mexico. Notwithstanding the proffer of more liberal political and civil inducements of the old abolition States of the North and West, the mass movement is in the Southerly direction. The industrial exclusion and social indifference of the old free States are not inviting to the African immigrant, nor is the severe climate congenial to his tropical nature. The Negro population in the higher latitudes is not a self-sustaining quantity. It would languish and gradually disappear unless constantly reinforced by fresh blood from the South. Although there has been a steady

stream of immigration to the North for the past
forty years, yet 92 per cent. of the race are found in
the States which fostered the institution of slavery
at the time of the Civil War.   The thirty-one free
States of the North and West do not contain as
many Negroes as Alabama.   There is no likelihood
that the Negro population will scatter itself equally
throughout the different sections of the country. We
should not be misled by the considerable Northern
movement of the last census decade. This period was
marked by unusual unrest in the South, and many
of the more vigorous or more adventurous Negroes
sought refuge in the cities of the North.   But evidently this tendency is subject to sharp self-limitation.

In the lower tier of the Southern States, comprising
Georgia, Florida, Alabama, Mississippi, Louisiana,
Texas and Arkansas, there has been a steady relative
gain in the Negro population, rising from 39 per
cent. of the entire race in 1850 to 53 per cent. in
1900.   On the other hand, the upper tier, including
Delaware, Maryland, Virginia, West Virginia, North
Carolina, South Carolina, Tennessee, Kentucky and
Missouri, showed a decline from 54 to 37 per cent.
during the same interval.   The census shows an unmistakable movement from the upper South to the
coastal and Gulf States.   The Negro constitutes the
majority of the population in South Carolina and
Mississippi, and also in Louisiana, outside of the city
of New Orleans.   The colored race forms the more
numerous element in the group of States comprising
South Carolina, Georgia, Florida, Alabama, Mississippi and Louisiana, a contiguous territory of 290,-
000 square miles.   Within this region the two races
seem to be growing at about the same pace.   During
the last decade the Negro rate of increase exceeded
the white in Florida, Alabama and Mississippi, but

fell below in South Carolina, Georgia and Louisiana.

But the State as the unit of area gives us a very imperfect idea of the relative and general spread and tendency of the Negro element. The movement of this population is controlled almost wholly by economic and social motives, and is very faintly affected by State boundaries or political action. The Negro is segregating in the fertile regions and along the river courses where the race was most thickly planted by the institution of slavery. This shaded area extends from the head of the Chesapeake Bay through eastern Virginia and North Carolina, thence through South Carolina, middle Georgia and Alabama and Mississippi to the Mississippi River. Leading off from the main track, there are darkened strips of various width, along the Atlantic Ocean through eastern Georgia and northern Florida and along the banks of the Chattahoochee, Alabama, Mississippi, Sabine and Brazos rivers leading to the Gulf of Mexico. The South is dotted with white belts as well as with black ones. Western Virginia and North Carolina, the southern and northern extremes of Georgia and Alabama, and the peninsula part of Florida are predominantly white sections. There are scores of counties in which the Negro does not constitute ten per cent. of the population. The Negro element not only does not tend to scatter equally throughout the country at large, but even in the South it is gathering more and more thickly into separate spaces. The black belts and white belts in the South are so interwoven as to frustrate any plan of solution looking to political and territorial solidarity. The measures intended to disfranchise the Negro in eastern Virginia operate against the ignorant whites in the western end of the State. The coming political contest in the South will not be between

whites and blacks, but it will be over the undue power
of a white vote based upon the black majority. The
black counties are the more populous, and therefore
have greater political weight. The few white voters
in such counties are thus enabled to counterbalance
many times their own number in the white districts.
This gives rise to the same dissatisfaction that comes
from the North because the Southerner's vote is
given added weight by reason of the black man whose
representative power he usurps. A closer study of
the black belts reveals the fact that they include the
more fertile portions of the South. The master settled his slaves upon the rich, productive lands, and
banished the poor whites to the thin and barren
regions. These belts are best adapted to the culture
of cotton, tobacco, rice, and sugar cane, the staple
productions in which the South has advantage over
other sections of the country. The Negro, by virtue
of his geographical distribution, holds the key to the
agricultural development of the South.

A clearer idea of the distribution of the Negro
population can be had by taking the county as
the unit of area. The number of counties in which
the Negroes outnumber the whites has risen from 237
in 1860 to 279 in 1900. This would make a section
as large as the North Atlantic division of States.
Within these counties there are, on the average, 130
Negroes to every 100 whites. In 1860 there were 71
counties in which the Negroes were more than twice
as numerous as the whites, which number had swollen
to 108 in 1900. The region of total eclipse shows a
tendency to spread more rapidly than the penumbra
surrounding it. The average ratio of Negroes in
these densely black counties is about three to one.
In some counties there are from ten to fifteen Negroes
to every white person. The future of such counties,

so far as the population is concerned, is too plainly foreshadowed to leave the slightest room for doubt.

There seems to be some concert of action on the part of the afflicted States. The revised constitutions have followed with almost mathematical exactness the relative density of the colored element. The historic order has been Mississippi, South Carolina, Louisiana, North Carolina, Alabama and Virginia. Georgia and Florida have not followed suit, for the simple reason that they do not have to. But political action does not affect the spread of population. The Negro finds the South a congenial habitat. Like flora and fauna, that race variety will ultimately survive in any region that is best adapted to its environment. We can no more stop the momentum of this population than we can stop the oncoming of wind and wave. To the most casual observer it is clearly apparent that the white race cannot compete with the Negro industrially in a hot climate and along the miasmatic lowlands. Where the white man has to work in the burning sun, the cadaverous, emaciated body, drooping spirit and thin, nasal voice bespeak the rapid decline of this breed. On the other hand, the Negro multiplies and makes merry. His body is vigorous and his spirit buoyant. There can be no doubt that in many sections the Negro element is gradually driving out the whites. In the struggle for existence the fittest will survive. Fitness in this case consists in adaptability to climate and industrial environment. In the West Indian archipelago the Negro race has practically expelled the proud Caucasian, not, to be sure, *vi et armis*, but by the much more invincible force of race momentum. This seems to be the inevitable destiny of the black belts in the South. For example, in the State of Georgia the number of counties in which the

Negro population more than doubles the whites was 13 in 1860, 14 in 1870, 18 in 1880, 23 in 1890, and 27 in 1900. In the same interval the counties in which the Negro constitutes the majority had risen from 43 to 67. This does not imply that the white population in the Southern States is not holding its own; but the growth of the two races seems to be toward fixed bounds of habitation.

Numerous causes are coöperating toward this end. The white man avoids open competition with the black workman and will hardly condescend to compete with him on equal terms. Wherever white men and women have to work for their living, they arrogantly avoid those sections where they are placed on a par with Negro competitors, and if indigenous to such localities they often migrate to regions where the black rival is less numerous. For this reason European immigration avoids the black belts as an infected region. The spectacle of black and white artisans working side by side at the same trade, of which we used to hear so much, is rapidly becoming a thing of the past. The line of industrial cleavage is almost as sharp as social separation. The white man does not desire to bring up his family amidst a Negro environment. The lynchings and outrages and the rumors of crime and cruelty have the effect of intimidating the white residents in the midst of black surroundings, who move away as rapidly as they can find it expedient to do so. Only a few Jewish merchants and large planters are left. The large plantations are becoming less and less profitable, and are being broken up and let out to colored tenants, to enable the landlord to move to the city, where he finds more congenial social environment for himself and children.

The rise and development of manufacturing industries in the South also adds emphasis to the same tendency. The poor whites are being drawn off in considerable numbers from the rural districts as operatives and workmen along lines of higher mechanical skill. In the black belts the Negro is protected by the masses around him. One may ride for hours in many portions of the South without meeting a white face. The great influx of Negroes into the large cities comes from regions where the Negro is thinly scattered among the whites, rather than from the regions of greatest density. These factors, operating separately and coöperating conjointly, will perpetuate these black belts of the South. The bulk of the Negroes seems destined to be gathered into these dark and dense areas.

If, therefore, we are accorded so large a measure of prevision, it is the part of wisdom to arrange our plans in harmony with the social movement which we have not the power to subvert. The first essential of a well-ordered society is good government, which affords satisfaction to the people living under it. The Negroes in the South are not satisfied with the present mode of government, not only because it was not formulated in harmony with their sensibilities, but because it lamentably fails to protect life and property. Perhaps there is no other government of European type which so ruthlessly disregards the rights and feelings of the governed since the effacement of the Boer republics in South Africa. The first need of the South is a brand of statesmanship with capacity to formulate a scheme of government which will command the hearty good will and cheerful coöperation of all the citizens, and at the same time leave the controlling power in the hands of those best qualified to wield it. This is the desideratum devoutly to be wished. The amiable African can be ruled much more effectively by the wand of kindness than by a rod of iron. Strange to say, Southern statesmanship has never seriously tested this policy. European powers in control of tropical races have found that reconciliation is essential to effective control. The weaker element must feel that they are a constituent part of the governmental order and are responsible for the maintenance, authority and discipline. But Southern statesmanship has been characterized by broken pledges and bad faith and open avowal to humiliate a third of the population. The Democratic party claimed to have won the election in 1876 upon a platform which, in clearly avowed terms, accepted the amendments to the Constitution of the United States. But the Democratic States forthwith proceeded to revise their constitutions with the undisguised purpose of defeating the plain intendment of these amendments. This on the plea that if the Negro were eliminated from politics, the government should be equitable and just, guaranteeing to all equality before the law. But as soon as these plans are adopted the very statesmen who were most instrumental in bringing them to pass are urging more drastic and dreadful measures. They are demanding the repeal of the Fourteenth and Fifteenth Amendments, which, by indirect tactics, they have already annulled. Has the Negro any reason to feel that the demanded appeal would stop this reactionary movement? There can never be peace and security and permanent prosperity for whites or blacks until the South develops a brand of statesmanship that rises above the pitchfork variety.

The next great need of these black belts is moral and industrial regeneration. This can be effected only through the quickening touch of education. Outside help is absolutely necessary. These people

unaided can no more lift themselves from a lower to
a higher level than one can sustain the weight of his
body by pulling against his own bootstraps.   The
problem belongs to the nation.   Ignorance and degradation are moral blights upon the national life and
character. They are wasteful of the national resource.
The cotton area is limited, and cotton-stuff will become more and more an important factor in our national, industrial and economic scheme.   And yet
thousands of acres of these valuable cotton lands are
being washed away and wasted annually by ignorant
and unskilled tillage.   The nation is contemplating
the expenditure of millions of dollars to irrigate the
arid regions of the West.   But would it not be a wiser
economic measure to save the cotton area of the
South through the enlightenment of the peasant
farmers?   The educational facilities in the black
counties outside of the cities are almost useless.   The
reactionary current against the education of the
Negro in the South is deep and strong.   Unless the
nation, either through statesmanship or philanthropy,
lends a helping hand, these shade places will form a
continuing blot upon the national escutcheon. There
should be better school facilities and social opportunities, not only as a means of their own betterment, but
in order that contentment with the rural environment
to which they are well suited may prevent them from
flocking into the cities, North and South, thus forming a national municipal menace.

The Negro's industrial opportunities lie in the
black belts.   He occupies the best cotton, tobacco,
rice and sugar lands of the South.   The climate
shields him from the crushing weight of white
competition.   Agriculture lies at the base of the life
of any undeveloped race.   The manufacturing stage
is a later development.   The exclusion of the Negro

from the factories is perhaps a blessing in disguise. The agricultural industries of the South are bound to become of greater and greater national importance and the Negro is to become a larger and larger industrial factor. The cotton area is limited, but the demand for cotton stuffs increases not only with the growth of our own national population, but with the expansion of our trade in both hemispheres. A shrewd observer has suggested that the time seems sure to come when a pound of cotton will be worth a bushel of wheat. When cotton regains its ancient place and again becomes king, the Negro will be the power behind the throne.

It is interesting to notice from the last census the extent to which Negroes are owning and managing their own farms. The large estates are being broken up into small farms and let out to Negro tenants at a higher rate of annual rental. This is but the first step toward Negro proprietorship. There is a double field for philanthropy. First, to furnish school facilities so that the small farmer may become intelligent and skilled in the conduct of his affairs; and second, to make it possible for him to buy small tracts of land. The holders of the old estates do not care to atomize their plantations, but would gladly dispose of their entire holdings. There is a vast field for philanthropy with the additional inducement of five per cent. Already such attempts have been made. Some Northern capitalists have undertaken such a movement in the neighborhood of Tuskegee Institute, which promises to have far-reaching effect upon the betterment of black belt conditions. There are also indications of Negro villages and industrial settlements to afford better social and business opportunities. Colored men of ambition and education will be glad to seek such communities as a field to exploit their powers. The secret and method of New England may thus be transplanted in these darksome places by the sons of Ethiopia. Thus those that now grope in darkness may yet receive the light.

Mr. John Temple Graves has, in a recent notable utterance, advocated the separation of the races, and has elaborated his doctrine with great rhetorical pains. But mass movement of the Negro race seems clearly to indicate immediate, if not the ultimate, outcome to be separateness rather than separation.

No one can tell what the ultimate future of the Negro is to be; whether it is to be worked out in this land or on some distant continent. We may, however, be permitted to foretell the logical outcome of forces now at work, without assuming the prophet's prerogative.

SURPLUS NEGRO WOMEN

A NOTABLE article entitled " The Duty of Surplus women," * by Mrs. Charlotte Perkins Gilman, excites a deep and abiding interest. The original and unique suggestion that judicious migration from regions of less to regions of greater masculine density might form a panacea for matrimonial helplessness, will doubtless delight the heart of spinsterdom. The practical wisdom of the suggestion has the sanction of historical precedent and high social prestige. Did not the forlorn maidens of old England brave the dangers of the deep in response to the matrimonial demand of a thriving colony? The thrifty farmer, restive under enforced bachelorhood, eagerly resorted to the market place, and gladly exchanged his precious pounds of tobacco for the priceless boon of a bride.

But Mrs. Gilman's article seems to contemplate only that fraction of the female world implied in the somewhat doleful soliloquy: " Here I am, free, white and twenty-one (or over?) " What of the lot of those surplus women who are not white, and not so very free? Is the ennobling sisterhood of woman to be limited to the color line? The struggle of the colored woman towards purity and refinement involves as deep and as dark a tragedy as any that marks the history of human strivings. If any would gain a true knowledge of the inner soul of black folks, let him contemplate the position of their women, whose pathetic situation must fill the soul with infinite pity.

The enormous preponderance of colored females

* *New York Independent*, January, 1905.

over males, especially in our large cities, is a persistent and aggravating factor which has almost wholly escaped the attention of our sociological philosophers. The census of 1900 gives 4,447,568 Negro females against 4,393,221 Negro males, leaving an excess of 54,347 of the gentler sex in the United States. This gives a residue of thirteen left-over women to each thousand of the male population. But this is utterly insignificant when compared with the excesses revealed by the statistics of the large cities. The predominance of the female element is perhaps the most striking phenomenon of the urban Negro population.

The subjoined figures will show this excess in fifteen cities of more than 20,000 Negroes.

EXCESS OF COLORED FEMALES, 1900

CITY	Females	Males	Excess of females	No. females to each 100 males
Washington..........	48,354	38,348	10,006	126
Baltimore..........	44,195	35,063	9,132	126
New Orleans.........	42,585	35,129	7,456	121
Philadelphia.........	33,673	28,940	4,733	116
New York...........	33,534	27,132	6,402	124
Memphis............	25,359	24,551	808	103
Louisville...........	20,297	18,842	1,455	108
Atlanta.............	20,921	14,806	6,115	143
St. Louis...........	18,020	17,496	524	103
Richmond...........	17,878	14,354	3,524	123
Charleston..........	17,552	13,970	3,582	125
Nashville...........	16,775	13,269	3,506	125
Chicago.............	14,077	16,073	*1,996	88
Savannah...........	15,344	12,746	2,598	120
Norfolk.............	10,738	9,492	1,246	113
Total,	379,312	320,221	59,091	118

* Surplus Males.

These cities with an aggregate Negro population of 699,533 show a female excess of 59,091. Chicago is the only city where the females are not in the majority, which is doubtless due to the fact that a new city is always first settled by the men, who pave the way for a subsequent female influx. If every Negro male in these cities should be assigned a helpmeet there would still remain eighteen left-over females for every one hundred couples. In Atlanta this unfortunate residue reaches the startling proportion of 43 out of a hundred. Washington and Baltimore have respectively 10,006 and 9,132 hopeless females, for whom there are neither present nor prospective husbands. No such astounding disproportion prevails anywhere among the white race. The surplus women who give Mrs. Gilman such anxious solicitude scarcely exceed one in a hundred even in such man-forsaken cities as New York and Boston. If then the evil be a threatening one among the white race with such an insignificant surplus, what must be said of its multiplied enormity when we turn to the situation of the black race, where the excess is more than one-sixth of the male sex? Preponderance of one sex over the other forbodes nothing but evil to society. The maladjustment of economic and social conditions upsets the scale where nature intended a balance. The argument of Mrs. Gilman is as correct as it is courageous. " Where women preponderate in large numbers," she says, " there is a proportionate increase in immorality, because women are cheap; where men preponderate in large numbers there is also immorality because women are dear."

This argument is perfectly general in its scope, and has special application to the Negro only because aggravated conditions add a graver emphasis. These left-over, or to-be-left-over, Negro women, falling as they do in large part in the lower stratum of society, miss the inhibitive restraint of culture and social pride, and, especially if they be comely of appearance, become the easy prey of the evil designs of both races. The question is a painfully delicate one. It is a disordered nature that delights in stirring up filth for the sake of its stench. The only justification for holding up such a dark and forbidden picture to the gaze of the world is that a clear knowledge of the enormity of the evil may lead to the consideration of constructive measures of relief.

The problem is for the most part an economic one, and the treatment must partake of the nature of the disease. It is easier to account for this unfortunate condition than it is to propose a remedy. Negro women rush to the city in disproportionate numbers, because in the country there is little demand for such services as they can render. They cannot remain at the hard, bone-breaking labor of the farm. The compensation of rural workers is so meagre that the man alone cannot earn a reasonable livelihood for the whole family. The girls, when they are of age and become conscious of their great deprivations, are enticed away by the glare and glitter of city life. They would escape the ills they have by fleeing to those they know not of. The situation is anomalous. The Negro man has no fixed industrial status in the cities. He loiters around the ragged edge of industry, and is confined to the more onerous and less attractive modes of toil. He who gives up the freedom and independence of rural life to drive an ash cart or dig in a city sewer surely is not wise. On the other hand, the Negro woman finds an unlimited field of employment in the domestic and household industries. These surplus women can hardly be expected to migrate back to the country in quest of marriage. They have just fled from the material poverty and social dearth of rural environment, and it is not likely that they will give up the flesh pots of the city for the dreary drudgery from which they have just escaped.

In order to forestall mischievous misinterpretation, it seems necessary to say that which should need no saying; namely, that the upward ambition and aspiration of colored women is the most encouraging indication of Negro life. The women of any race are the conservators of its moral stamina, which in turn lies back of all social progress. Any one who gains intimate knowledge of the better side of Negro life must be deeply impressed with the evident superiority of the progressive colored women over the average man of like opportunity. This superiority is manifested not only in cultivation and character, but in their fearless and aggressive attitude towards race rights and privileges. In many instances they are forced to a life of perpetual spinsterhood because of a dearth of men of the requisite ambition and progressive spirit. But we should not allow our appreciation of the advancement of the upper ten to render us oblivious of the needs and necessities of the lower ninety.

The great bulk of colored women in our cities, being shut out from higher avenues of work, must seek employment in domestic service. A study of the occupation of colored women in the city of Washington, where the attainments of the upper ten have been widely exploited, will throw much light on this subject.

OCCUPATION OF COLORED FEMALES IN THE DISTRICT
OF COLUMBIA, 1900.

```
All occupations ..............................23,448
Domestic and personal service.................21,018
Dressmaking and needlework...................  1,617
Professional service ..........................   519
All other occupations..........................   294
```

It is interesting to note that nearly one-half of the
females are engaged in gainful occupations, a circumstance which tells its own story.   There are ten
thousand surplus women of color at the National
Capital; this fact, together with the low economic
status of the men, renders it imperative that a large
proportion of the women should enter the great
bread-winning contest.   Seven-eighths of them are
engaged in domestic and personal service.   The 519
assigned to professional service are mainly engaged
in teaching.   These figures show us plainly the field
in which these women must labor for all time that we
have the data to foresee.   If we take the country at
large it will be found that the Negro woman is confined almost exclusively to agricultural and domestic
pursuits as means of gaining a livelihood.

COLORED FEMALES EMPLOYED IN THE UNITED
STATES, 1900.

```
All occupations ..............................1 316,872
Domestic and personal service..............   681,947
Agriculture .................................   582,001
Professional service ........................    15,601
All other occupations........................    37,323
```

Thus it will be seen that for the entire country
domestic service absorbs fifty-two per cent. of this
class of wage earners.   In the cities it constitutes
almost the exclusive avenue of remunerative work.

If we take the Negro race as a whole, male and

female, it will be found that out of 3,998,963 engaged in all occupations, 2,143,176 are agricultural workers and 1,324,160 are found in domestic and personal service; these two fields of effort furnished a livelihood for 86 per cent. of the entire race. It is a hard, but nevertheless a painful, concrete fact, that an intolerant spirit effectually shuts out the Negro from manufacturing industries and from trade and transportation. The two great industrial problems before the Negro are (1) to gain greater efficiency in the two available lines of industry, and (2) to press upon the borders of the higher mechanical and industrial pursuits in quest of larger opportunity.

But when we restrict attention to the status of the colored women in the large cities we find that they are shut in to a single line of remunerative activity. Here is a field of labor which is large, wide open, and undisputed. There is little danger that the Negro domestic will be banished from the household by white competition, unless on the score of superior efficiency. The ultra-fashionable may indulge in the fad of English servants, but in the long run the Negro will be found to return to favor. The colored woman possesses sacrificial virtues and altruistic devotion in the highest degree. In her ignorant and degraded condition she was able to take the children of her refined mistress, and by the wealth of her natural affection, foster for herself a fondness and an endearment sometimes beyond that they bore their own mothers. She still possesses that sacrificial quality which gives her the preference, even though she falls short in point of competency, in close personal and subordinate relations. The immediate pressing problem growing out of the situation is how to make these women more competent and efficient in this broad field of labor.

There should be in every city with a large Negro population a school of domestic service whose scheme of training should be of such simple and easy character as to be available to every girl of moderate intelligence and ambition. This would indeed be industrial education that counts. It is preparing laborers for a field that is already white unto harvest. There can be no dispute as to the advantage and even the necessity of such training. There is no adequate agency at present devoted to this task. Hampton and Tuskegee do not aim to accomplish it any more than do Fisk and Howard. In the very nature of the case the problem is a local one and must be worked out by local agencies. Here is a wide field for practical philanthropy based upon sound economy. A project looking forward to the higher efficiency of domestic service in our large cities must command the good will and hearty cooperation of all elements, white and black, whatever their school of belief or social opinion. There should be more strenuous and vigilant activity to guard these girls against the dangers of sordid city association, and to surround them with wholesome moral and religious environment. There is no problem of our city life to-day that appeals more imperatively to the religious and charitable agencies that are devoted to civic righteousness and social purity. But after all has been said and done the treatment can only be temporary and palliative. Society cannot contemplate with satisfaction the permanence of any considerable body of unmarried women, whose existence is indeed without " excuse or explanation," in either social or divine economy. It is to be hoped that either city conditions will so improve that men will be attracted in sufficient numbers to claim the surplus city spinsters, or that country conditions will so improve that they will gladly avail themselves of rural matrimonial opportunities.

The large and remunerative field of domestic service has not received adequate attention on the part of the leaders of the colored race. The contemptuous attitude of the more favored of this race towards this department of labor has had much to do with the low estimate in which such service and servants are held. This feeling is but a survival or reaction of the influence of slavery, which taught the Negro to despise all those with whom work was a necessity. He saw all dignity and honor and glory attach to those who neither toiled nor spun. Even to-day it is hard for the average Negro to have much respect for a white man who works with his hands, or to think of him as other than " po' white trash." Slavery inculcated the drudgery, but not the gospel of work. This servile estimate of labor is still potent and persistent. That all labor is honorable is a formal phrase rather than a serious feeling with the average Southerner, white or black. The few Negroes whom circumstances enabled to rise swiftly above the level of menial labor, not unnaturally, brought forward the traditional attitude of contempt for those left below. Menial service served and serves as a reminder of the old relationship of master and slave. A sharp line of cleavage suddenly developed between the favored few and the less fortunate many. There was an absence of that sympathetic relationship and mutuality of good-will that prevails in a well-established order where different ranks and social grades are recognized and understood.

Some negroes still hesitate to advocate preparation for domestic service for fear of being accused of proposing menial service for the whole race. The whites who persist in limiting the Negro's function in society to the servile sphere impel them to this hesitant attitude. But the plain demands of the situation require the application of sanity and common sense. Class differentiation is becoming a recognized phenomenon of Negro development. No one formula of treatment can be applied to these nine million people with such varied aptitudes and opportunities. The mutual dependence of the more fortunate and the less favored—of the upper ten and the lower ninety—is gaining a wide and deeper appreciation. More than half of the Negro women who are forced to earn a living are employed in the domestic industries. The bulk of the following of the great Catholic Church in America falls among those who are engaged in the humbler spheres of service, but many of them are rapidly gaining wealth, and power, and fame. The wise and far-seeing leadership of this great organization discourages estrangement between the high and low, learned and ignorant, rich and poor, who are of the same household of faith. Nor are the humble workmen led to despise their lowly calling, but rather to dignify their office by diligence and fidelity to duty. A more enlightened leadership among the Negroes will assume a similar attitude towards the toiling masses who look for wise guidance and direction. Those who have been benefited must become enlarged so as to appreciate the obligation that opportunity confers; while those who are left in the humbler places must be encouraged to become workmen "that maketh not ashamed."

Advocacy of adequate preparation for immediate and available service on the part of those who can secure no other is in no sense inconsistent with the higher needs and aspirations of the race. Every American boy and girl who is made of the true metal

will make for the highest place within the reach of
his faculties or the range of his opportunities. President Roosevelt and Booker T. Washington, alike,
will endeavor to procure for their children the highest form of service they are capable of performing.
The humblest citizen will, and ought, to do the same.
What right can be more sacred than the right to
better one's condition? The old-fashioned, homely
Negro mother who washed and ironed till her fingers
bled and burned, in order that her children might
improve their status, exhibited a spirit that should
elicit the highest admiration. The Negro woman is
handicapped by such an unfavorable environment
that it seems almost inhuman to make her the butt
of witticism and ridicule as is sometimes done, because
from the depth of her lowliness she dares aspire to
the highest and best things in life. It is a cheap
philosophy and a false leadership that would belittle
or ridicule the higher aspirations of the least of
these. The Negro women of our large cities, especially the surplus fifth, need all the stimulus of high
ideals to sustain them under the heavy burdens which
unfortunate social conditions compel them to bear.

These surplus women present a pressing social
problem which calls for immediate and special treatment. The remedy suggested is not proposed as a
solution of the vexed race problem, but merely as the
means of simplifying one of its most serious and
aggravating factors.

RISE OF THE PROFESSIONAL CLASS

In a homogeneous society where there is no racial cleavage only the select members of the favored class occupy professional stations. In India it is said that the populace is divided horizontally by caste and vertically by religion; but in America the race spirit serves both as a horizontal and vertical separation. The isolation of the Negro in all social and semi-social relations necessitates independent ministrative agencies from the lowest to the highest rungs of the ladder of service. It is for this reason that the colored race demands that its preachers, teachers, physicians and lawyers shall be for the most part men of their own blood and sympathies. Strangely enough this feeling first asserted itself in the church —that organization founded upon the universal fatherhood of God and brotherhood of man. In the estimation of its founder there is neither Jew nor Greek, Barbarian, Scythian, bond or free. According to a strict construction of its requirements there is no difference in kind among those who are spiritually akin. And yet the organic separation of the races first asserted itself in the matter of religion. Whenever the colored adherents became sufficiently large to excite attention they were set apart, either in separate communion or in separate assignment of place in the house of worship. When the Negro worshiper gained conscious self-respect he grew tired of the back pews and upper galleries of the white churches, and sought places of worship more compatible with his sense of freedom and dignity. Hence arose the Negro church and the Negro clergy. This

was the first professional class to arise, and still relatively the most numerous. The religious interests
of the race are almost wholly in the hands of the
colored clergy. Outside of the Catholic Church it is
almost as difficult to find a white clergyman over a
colored congregation as it is to meet with the reverse
phenomenon. The two denominations, Methodists
and Baptists, that are wholly under Negro ecclesiastical control, include well-nigh the entire colored
race.

The proportional number of church communicants
for the colored race exceeds that for the white race.
In 1890 the colored race had one communicant to
every 2.79 of the Negro population, while the whites
had one out of every 3.04.

This vast host of church members is almost wholly
under colored ecclesiastical control. There is need
for at least 25,000 trained men to administer to the
spiritual needs of this multitude. Herein lies one of
the most powerful arguments for the higher education of select members of the Negro race. The tendency of the times is to require of candidates for the
professions sound academic training as a preparatory
basis for their professional equipment. It is idle to
say that because the Negro race is ignorant and undeveloped therefore its clergy need not measure up
to the average of professional requirements. It
surely requires as much discretion, resourcefulness
and sense to meet the needs of the lowly as to administer to those who are already exalted. It is true
that the Negroes have been gathered in the church in
great multitudes under the guidance of men who had
little academic equipment for their work; but we
know full well that this is but the first step in their
spiritual development, and that their future welfare
requires not only men of consecration, but men of

definite training for their work. Let us not forget
also that the Negro church has a larger function
than the white church. Therefore, the Negro preacher
must be not only the spiritual leader of his flock,
but also the general guide, philosopher, and friend.

The rise of the colored teacher is due almost wholly
to the outcome of the Civil War. The South soon
hit upon the plan of the scholastic separation of the
races, and assigned colored teachers to colored schools
as the best means of carrying out this policy. Hence
a large professional class was at once injected into
the arena. As the Negro preacher is responsible for
the spiritual life of the race, so the Negro teacher
is charged with its intellectual enlightenment. The
2,000,000 Negro children of school age constitute
the charge committed to the keeping of the 30,000
Negro teachers. There were at the inception a great
many white laborers who generously entered upon
this work, of whom there still remains a goodly sprinkling. But their function was and is mainly to prepare colored men and women for the responsible
tasks. It was inevitable that many of the teachers,
for whom there was such a sudden demand, should
have been illy prepared for the task imposed. It was
and still is in many cases a travesty upon terms to
speak of such work as most of these teachers were
able to do as professional service. We find here as
strong an argument for the secondary and higher
education of the Negro as was furnished by ecclesiastical necessities. The duty imposed upon Negro
teachers is as onerous and requires as high a degree
of knowledge and professional equipment as that
imposed upon any other class engaged in educational
work. The special needs of their constituency call
for a higher rather than a lower order of training,
preparation and fitness.

The colored doctor and lawyer have only recently entered the field in anything like sufficient numbers to attract attention. The same spirit that demanded the Negro preacher has also operated in favor of the Negro doctor. The relation between patient and physician is close and confidential. The social barrier between the races often operates against the acceptability of a physician of the opposite race. The success of the colored physician has often been little less than marvelous.

The colored lawyer has not been so fortunate as his medical confreres. The relation between client and attorney is not necessarily close and personal, but partakes of a business nature. The client's interest is also dependent upon the court and jury, with whom the white attorney is generally supposed to have greater weight and influence. For such reasons the Negro lawyer has not made the headway that has been accomplished in the other professions.

It must be said for the professions of law and medicine that the applicants are subjected to a uniform test, and therefore colored and white candidates are on the same footing. Colored practitioners, therefore, must have a fair degree of preliminary training and professional preparation.

Macon B. Allen was the first colored attorney regularly admitted to practice in the United States. He was admitted in Maine in 1844. It is claimed by some that the husband of Phyllis Wheatley was a lawyer. Robert Morris was admitted to the Boston bar in 1850, on motion of Charles Sumner, where he practiced with splendid success until his death, in 1882. Prof. John M. Langston was admitted to the Ohio bar in 1854. James Durham was born a slave in Philadelphia in 1762. His master was a surgeon. He purchased his freedom and became one of the most noted physicians in New Orleans. His practice is said to have been worth $3,000 a year. The following account attests the success of a black physician:

" Dr. David Ruggles, poor, blind, and an invalid, founded a well-known water-cure establishment in the town where I write (Northampton, Mass.), erected expensive buildings, won fashionable distinction as a most skilful and successful practitioner, secured the warm regard and esteem of this community, and left a name established in the hearts of many who feel that they owe their life to his skill and careful practice."

Dr. John V. Degrass was admitted in due form as a member of the Massachusetts Medical Society in 1854.

The above are only samples of negroes in the learned professions before the Civil War. Of course, there was a large number of ministers and teachers. Out of such meager beginnings has grown the great number of professional colored men and women of to-day.

The colored preachers are quite as numerous in proportion to the population as the white, and in some cases more so. In West Virginia there are 425 whites and 802 blacks to each minister of the respective races. One might expect a preponderance of colored ministers for two reasons: (1) There is a larger relative church membership; and (2) the colored population has not more than half the density of that of the white in the area under consideration. In the State of Missouri, for example, 735 colored preachers cover the same territory as 3,439 white ministers; and while each of the former has on an average 375 persons to the parish to the latter's 735, yet his geographical area is five times as extensive. If we turn to the States where the Negroes predominate we may expect to find a reversal of conditions. In Mississippi and South Carolina the colored parish is smaller in area but more populous than that of the whites. The clerical demand of the Negro population is fully supplied in a numerical sense, albeit there is much need for a higher standard of professional equipment for its most arduous and delicate duties.

In no case has the colored race as many teachers in proportion to the population as the white. In some cases, like South Carolina and Alabama, the disproportion is glaring, the number of persons to each teacher being 217 to 775 in the former, and 262 to 718 in the latter, in favor of the more fortunate race. It must be said, however, that the number of persons to each teacher does not necessarily represent the actual distribution of work between the races; for it is known that in every Southern State there are white teachers working among colored people. These are mainly in private and philanthropic schools, however, and do not materially affect the general equation, or rather the inequality, of educational conditions. If we take geographical conditions into account, and the fact that the two sets of teachers operate over the same area, it will be seen that the disparity is greatly enhanced. Taking all in all, it appears that the Negro teaching force is in no sense adequate to the task imposed upon it.

The colored lawyers and doctors form so small a proportion of the general population as scarcely to merit mention as a professional class. In Texas there is one Negro doctor in 9,000 and one Negro lawyer in 40,000 of the population, while in South Carolina there are 22,000 and 29,000 Negroes to a colored practitioner in the respective professions. In

Alabama there is one black doctor to look over 24,000 patients, and each colored lawyer has 52,000 clients. The work in these professions is conducted mainly by the whites, although the twelfth census will undoubtedly show a large increase in the colored practitioners. Where numbers are small, proportions are sensitive. The number of persons to each practitioner will be materially reduced. The argument which we sometimes hear that Negroes are leaving the farm and shop to rush into the learned professions is not borne out by the collected facts in the case. In Alabama, for instance, only one Negro in 50,000 has entered upon the practice of law and one in 25,000 upon the profession of medicine. While it is true that there is no large demand for colored men in these professional pursuits, especially outside of the large centers, nevertheless the steady progress of the people in property, intelligence, and diversified material and commercial interests calls for a conservative increase in the number of professional colored men both in medicine and in law.

It cannot be claimed that the colored race has developed superlative names in the several professions. There are not a few ministers of piety and eloquence. The teacher in the public service must maintain the average proficiency of the system to the satisfaction of the white superintendents. The Negro lawyers are in open competition with their white colaborers, and must render satisfactory service, else they would have no clients. Colored physicians generally have a good record for professional skill and integrity. There is no movement affecting the lot and life of the colored race so suggestive of its educational needs as the relative size of the professional class.

EMINENT NEGROES

THE individual is the proof of the race, the first unfoldment of its potency and promise. The glory of any people is perpetuated and carried forward by the illustrious names which spring from among them. As we contemplate the great nations and peoples, whether of the ancient or of the modern world, their commanding characters rise up before us, typifying their contribution to the general welfare of the human race. On the contrary, no people can hope to gain esteem and favor which fails to produce distinguished individuals illustrative and exemplary of its possibilities.

For four centuries the African race has been brought in contact with the European in all parts of the globe. This contact has not been of an ennobling character, but of the servile sort, affording little opportunity for the development of those qualities which the favored races hold in esteem. And yet there have arisen from this dark and forbidding background not a few striking individual emanations. This race, through a strain of its blood, has given to Russia her national poet and to France her most distinguished romancer. Toussaint L'Ouverture, the Negro patriot, is the most commanding historical figure of the entire West Indian Archipelago. In South America persons of Negro blood have gained the highest political and civil renown.

The Anglo-Saxon deals with backward peoples on

a different basis from the Latin races. While he has a keener sense of justice and is imbued with a spirit of philanthropic kindness, yet he builds up a barrier between himself and them which it is almost impossible to overcome. To him personal solicitude and good will and racial intolerance are not incompatible qualities. On the other hand, the Latin races, while possessing a much lower order of general efficiency, accept on equal terms all who conform to the prevailing standards. Under the Latin dispensation color offers not the slightest bar to the individual who exhibits high qualities of mind or soul. We need not be surprised, therefore, to find that the colored men who have reached the highest degree of fame should have sprung from the Latin civilization. The persons of African blood who are most nearly comparable with names of the first order of renown among Europeans are Toussaint L'Ouverture, of Haiti; Alexander Pushkin, of Russia; Alexander Dumas, of France. In France, Italy or Spain color is only a curious incident. The Afro-American, therefore, belongs in a category by himself. His circumstances and conditions are so different from those of his European brother that although of the same color they are not of the same class.

Several lists of distinguished colored men have been prepared, the most important of which, perhaps, was published by Abbé Grégoire, and was prepared to answer the argument of Thomas Jefferson and others, who undertook to prove the Negro's intellectual inferiority. This work contains accounts of Negroes in all countries who have reached eminence and distinction in all lines of endeavor. An account of the part played by colored men in the Revolutionary War contains the deeds and achievements of noted Negroes. Rev. William J. Simmons brings the former work nearer to date and includes many colored men now living. A list of distinguished colored women has also been compiled.

Numerous magazine articles have appeared on this subject from time to time. The two which are perhaps of the greatest importance, and which include the substance of the rest, appeared in the *International Quarterly Review* and in the *North American Review*.

An interesting syllabus has recently been prepared by Mr. A. O. Stafford on " Negro Ideals," which gives a good outline of the efforts of the Negro toward better things.

It is with some hesitancy that a few names of the more distinguished Afro-Americans are here presented. In such a restricted list it is inevitable that many should be omitted who are equally worthy as some who are mentioned. The names here presented have not been selected because of general distinction, but rather for technical, artistic, and intellectual achievements in the scholastic sense.

Only those have been included of whose achievements the world takes account. There is no name in the list which may not be found in Appleton's Cyclopedia of American Biography. Nothing is great or small except by comparison. The names here presented are at least respectable when measured by European standards. It is true that no one of them reaches the first, or even the second degree of luster in the galaxy of the world's greatness. The competing number has been so insignificant and the social atmosphere has been so repressive to their budding aspirations that it would be little short of a miracle of genius if any member of this race had reached the highest degree of glory. It is true that if not one of these had ever been born the bulk and quantity of science, literature, and art would not be appreciably affected.

While these contributors must be measured in terms of European standards in order that there may be a sane and rational basis of comparison, yet there is another measure which takes account of the struggles and strivings out of which they grew. In the light of European comparison it appears that they represent more than the marvelous vision of a one-eyed man among the blind, but rather the surprising visual power of a one-eyed man among two-eyed men. The significance of these superior manifestations, however, must not be measured solely by their intrinsic value. They serve both as an argument and an inspiration. They show the American people that the Negro, at his best, is imbued with their own ideas and strives after their highest ideals. To the Negro they serve as models of excellence to stimulate and encourage his hesitant and disheartened aspirations.

One will be struck by the versatility and range of names in the list. They cover well-nigh every field of human excellence. It will be noticed that the imitative and esthetic arts predominate over the more solid and severe intellectual acquisitions. Is this not the repetition of the history of culture? The poet and the artist precede the scientist and the engineer. This meager fruitage does not furnish cause for self-complacent glorification on the part of the Negro, but is only an index of the promise of the tree of which they are the initial bearings. With its extended range and scope, the rising generation can look upon them in the light of promise rather than fulfilment.

" That which they have done but earnest of the things that we shall do."

Phyllis Wheatley was born in Africa and was brought to America in 1761. She was bought from the slave market by John Wheatley, of Boston, and soon developed remarkable acquisitive faculties. In sixteen months from her arrival she could read English fluently. She soon learned to write, and also studied Latin. She visited England in 1774 and was cordially received. After returning to Boston she corresponded with Countess Huntington, the Earl of Dartmouth, Rev. George Whitefield, and others, and wrote many poems to her friends. She addressed some lines to General George Washington, which were afterwards published in the *Pennsylvania Magazine* for April, 1776. General Washington wrote a courteous response and invited her to visit the Revolutionary headquarters, which she did, and was received with marked attention by Washington and his officers. Her principle publications are " An Elegiac Poem on the Death of George Whitefield "; " Poems on Various Subjects, Religious and Moral," published in London in 1773, and republished as ".The Negro Equalled by Few Europeans," two volumes, Philadelphia, 1801. The letters of Phyllis Wheatley were printed in Boston in 1864, collected from the proceedings of the Massachusetts Historical Society.

Benjamin Banneker was born November 9, 1731, near Ellicotts Mill, Md. Both his father and grandfather were native Africans. He attended a private school which admitted several colored children along with the whites. Although his early educational facilities were scanty, young Banneker soon gained a local reputation as a miracle of wisdom. In 1770 he constructed a clock to strike the hours, the first to be made in America. This he did with crude tools and a watch for his model, as he had never seen a

clock.   Through the kindness of Mr. Ellicott, who
was a gentleman of cultivation and taste, he gained
access to his valuable collection of books, and was
thus inducted into the study of astronomy.   In this
study he gained great proficiency, and constructed
an almanac adapted to the local requirements of
Pennsylvania, Virginia and Maryland.   This was the
first almanac constructed in America, and was published by Goddard & Angell, Baltimore.   Banneker's
Almanac was published annually from 1792 to 1806,
the year of his death.   It contained the motions of
the sun and moon; the motions, places, and aspects
of the planets; the rising and setting of the sun, and
the rising, setting, southing, place, and age of moon,
etc., and is said to have been the main dependence of
the farmers in the region covered.   He lived mainly
from the royalties received from this publication.
Banneker sent a copy of this almanac to Thomas
Jefferson, which elicited a flattering acknowledg-
ment on the part of the philosopher and statesman.
Banneker assisted the commissioners in laying out
the lines of the District of Columbia.   A life of Banneker was published by Hon. J. H. B. Latrobe, Baltimore, 1845, and another by J. S. Norris, 1854.
That Thomas Jefferson believed in the intellectual
capacity of the Negro and appreciated the force of
the argument that the treatment of this race found
justification in its assumed low state of mental possibility is revealed by his letter to Benjamin Banneker,
the black astronomer:

Sir:
   I thank you sincerely for your letter of the 19th instant and
for the almanac it contained.   Nobody wishes more than I do
to see such proofs as you exhibit that nature has given to our
black brethren talents equal to those of the other colors of
men, and that the appearance of a want of them is owing

merely to the degraded condition of their existence, both in Africa and America. I can add with truth that nobody wishes more ardently to see a good system commenced for raising the condition both of their body and mind to what it ought to be as fast as the imbecility of their present existence and other circumstances which cannot be neglected will admit. I have taken the liberty of sending your almanac to M. de Condorcet, secretary of the Academy of Sciences at Paris and member of the Philanthropic Society, because I considered it as a document to which your color had a right for their justification against the doubts which have been entertained of them.

I am, with great esteem, sir,
Your most obedient humble servant,
THOMAS JEFFERSON.

MR. BENJAMIN BANNEKER,
Near Ellicotts Lower Mills, Baltimore County.

Lemuel Haynes was born in Hartford, Conn., July 18, 1753. His father was an African, his mother a white woman. He received his honorary degree of A. M. from Middlebury College in 1804. After completing a theological course he preached at various places and settled in West Rutland, Vt., in 1788, where he remained for thirty years and became one of the most popular preachers in the State. He was characterized by a subtle intellect, keen wit, and eager thirst for knowledge. His noted sermons from Genesis 3 and 4 were published and passed through nine or ten editions. His controversy with Hosea Ballou became of worldwide interest. The life of Lemuel Haynes was written by James E. Cooley, New York, 1848.

Ira Aldridge was born at Belair, Md., about 1810. There is some dispute as to the exact composition of his blood; some claim that he was of pure African descent, while others contend that he was of mixed extraction. He was early brought in contact with Mr. Kean, the great tragedian, and in 1826 accompanied him to Europe. Mr. Kean encouraged his dramatic aspiration, and on one occasion, at least, permitted him to appear as Othello, while he himself took the part of Iago. As an interpreter of Shakespeare he was very generally regarded as one of the best and most faithful. He appeared at Covent Garden as Othello in 1833, and in Surrey Theater in 1848. On the Continent he ranked as one of the greatest tragedians of his time. Honors were showered upon him wherever he appeared. He was presented by the King of Prussia with the first-class medal of arts and sciences, accompanied by an autograph letter from the Emperor of Austria; the Grand Cross of Leopold; a similar decoration from the Emperor of Russia, and a magnificent Maltese cross, with the medal of merit, from the city of Berne. Similar honors were conferred by other crowned heads of Europe. He was made a member of the Prussian Academy of Arts and Sciences and holder of the large gold medal; member of the Imperial and Arch Ducal Institution of Our Lady of the Manger in Austria; of the Russian Hof-Versamlung of Riga; honorary member of the Imperial Academy of Arts and Sciences in St. Petersburg, and many others. Aldridge appeared with flattering success in Amsterdam, Brussels, Berlin, Breslau, Vienna, Pesth, The Hague, Dantzic, Konigsberg, Dresden, Berne, Frankfort-on-the-Main, Cracow, Gotha, and numerous other cities in the leading parts of the standard plays of the times. He was an associate of the most prominent men of Paris, among whom was Alexander Dumas. When these two met they always kissed each other, and Dumas always greeted Aldridge with the words " *mon confrere.*" Aldridge died at Lodz, in Poland, in 1867.

Col. George W. Williams was born in Pennsylvania in 1849. He was educated in public and private schools and completed his theological training at West Newton Theological Seminary. His " History of the Negro Race in America " is the sole existing authority on the subject of which it treats, and forms, without doubt, as valuable a literary monument as any yet left by a colored man.

Paul Laurence Dunbar died while a young man, being under thirty years of age. He made an impression on American literature that can never be effaced. He published " Oaks and Ivy," " Majors and Minors," " Lyrics of Lowly Life," and "Lyrics of the Hearthstone," together with half a dozen volumes of fiction and short stories. Several of his works have been reprinted in England. Speaking of his early poems, William Dean Howells says: " Some of these (poems in literary English) I thought very good. What I mean is, several people might have written them, but I do not know any one else at present who could quite have written his dialect pieces. There are divinations and reports of what passes in the hearts and minds of a lowly people whose poetry had hitherto been inarticulately expressed, but now finds, for the first time in our tongue, literary interpretation of a very artistic completeness."

Henry O. Tanner, son of Bishop B. T. Tanner, of the African Methodist Church, was born in Pittsburg, Pa., in 1859. His early educational opportunities were good, having studied at the Pennsylvania Academy of Fine Arts, and subsequently at Paris. His pictures have been hung on the line in many a salon exhibition, and now the government of France has crowned the long list of medals and prizes which Mr. Tanner has received by buying one of his most important works, " The Raising of Lazarus," for the Luxembourg Gallery. The picture has already been hung in the Luxembourg Gallery, and in the course of time will naturally be transferred to the Louvre. Other notable pictures by the same artist are " Nicodemus," owned by the Academy of Fine Arts, Philadelphia; " The Annunciation," which now hangs in the Memorial Hall, Philadelphia; " The Betrayal," in the Carnegie Gallery, at Pittsburg.

Dr. Daniel H. Williams, of Chicago, is widely known throughout the medical profession. He has performed several noted operations that taxed the skill of surgical science. In 1897 Dr. Williams performed an operation on account of a stab wound of the heart and pericardium, a report of which published in the *Medical Record*, March 27, 1897, attracted the attention of the entire medical and surgical fraternity, and was reprinted in the medical journals of nearly every country and language. It has also been referred to in most recent works on surgery, especially in " International Text Book on Surgery " and Da Costa's " Modern Surgery."

An article on " Ovarian Cysts in Colored Women," by Dr. Williams, published in the *Philadelphia Medical Journal*, December 29, 1900, had for its purpose the refutation of the idea that had been almost universal among surgeons, that colored women did not have ovarian tumors. The record of the cases collected by Dr. Williams furnishes sufficient data to sustain his contention. It is also shown in this article that the same may be said of fibrous tumors. This article has been considered of such value to the profession that it has been copied extensively in medical literature, and notably in some of the best German and French medical journals.

Dr. Williams has performed various important operations that have been published in medical journals and widely commented upon in the medical world.

He was surgeon-in-chief of the Freedmen's Hospital at Washington, D. C., from 1893 to 1897.

Charles W. Chestnut was born in Cleveland, Ohio. By his own effort he rose to the rank of court stenographer. Mr. Chestnut has written several works of fiction which, according to competent critics, place him among the foremost story-tellers of the time. " The Wife of My Youth," " The House Behind the Cedars," and " The Marrow of Tradition " are published by Houghton, Mifflin & Co., Boston, Mass.

Prof. W. S. Scarborough was born in Georgia in 1852, was graduated from Oberlin College in 1875, and is President of Wilberforce University. He is a member of the American Philological Society and of the Modern Language Association. He has published " First Lessons in Greek " (New York, 1881), and the " Theory and Functions of the Thematic Vowel in the Greek Verb."

Prof. W. E. B. DuBois was born in Massachusetts about forty years ago. He was graduated from Fisk University and subsequently from Harvard, after which he studied two years in Germany and earned his Ph.D. degree from Harvard. He has been a teacher in Wilberforce University, associate in sociology at the University of Pennsylvania, and professor of history and political economy at Atlanta University. His chief works are " The Suppression of the African Slave Trade," published in the Harvard Historical Series; " The Philadelphia Negro," published under the auspices of the University of Pennsylvania; " The Souls of Black Folks "; and numerous special studies and investigations that have appeared in the proceedings of the Atlanta conferences and the bulletins of the Bureau of Labor, as well as sundry magazine articles. Mr. DuBois has done more to give scientific accuracy and method to the study of the race question than any other American who has essayed to deal with it.

It is generally believed that while the Negro possesses the imitative he lacks the initiative faculty; that while he can acquire what has already been accumulated, he cannot inquire into the unrevealed mystery of things. As an illustration of how easy it is for the achievements of the Negro to escape his fellow co-laborers, the following incident may be regarded as typical. The Patent Office sent out circulars inquiring as to the number and extent of colored patentees. One of the leading patent attorneys responded that he had never heard of the Negro inventing anything except lies; yet the Patent Office record reveals 250 colored patentees and more than 400 patents. Many of these show the highest ingenuity and are widely used in the mechanical arts.

Granville T. Woods was born in Ohio, and is fifty years old. He has more than twenty patents to his credit. Mr. Woods is the inventor of the electric telephone transmitter, which he assigned to the American Bell Telephone Company for a valuable consideration. The transmitter is used in connection with all the Bell telephones.

Elijah T. McCoy, of Detroit, Mich., has taken out thirty patents, mainly devoted to the improvement of lubricating devices for stationary and locomotive machinery. His inventions are in general use on locomotive engines of leading railways in the Northwest, on the Lake steamers, and on railways in Canada.

There are numerous colored people who have achieved distinction in fields calling for practical energy, moral courage, sound intelligence, and intellectual resource. Mr. Frederick Douglass and Prof. Booker T. Washington are, in general average of distinction, the most renowned of their race, although their fields of exertion are not mainly intellectual, in the academic sense of the term—and yet Mr. Douglass was one of the most eminent American orators, and his autobiography forms an integral part of the literature of the anti-slavery struggle; and Mr. Washington's "Up from Slavery" is one of the most popular books printed in the first year of the twentieth century. As Mr. Douglass's life is woven in the warp and woof of the great epoch ending in the Civil War, so Mr. Washington's life and work have become a vital part of current educational literature, and his place in the history of education is assured.

WHAT WALT WHITMAN MEANS TO THE NEGRO

WALT WHITMAN is the poet of humanity. He sings the song universal for all who suffer, love, and hope. No class or clique or clan can lay claim to him and say, " He is mine." To his " feast of reason and flow of soul " he invites all mankind.

"Of every hue and caste am I, of every rank and religion."

The processes of nature are uniform in their operations and apply with equal favor to all classes and conditions of men. The rain falls, the grass grows and the sun shines kindly alike for all who place themselves in harmonious relations to their beneficent design. And so comes Walt Whitman, adorning himself to bestow himself upon whoever will accept him, scattering his good will freely over all.

As we ascend higher and higher in the scale of moral and spiritual excellence, the ephemeral distinctions among men, based for the most part upon arrogance and pride, grow fainter and fainter, and finally vanish away. The great moral and spiritual teachings of mankind have always reprobated the spirit of caste. Buddha teaches: " There is no caste in blood, which runneth of one hue; nor caste in tears, which trickle salt withal."

It was revealed to the Apostle Peter in a vision that he should not call any man common or unclean. St. Paul, viewing mankind from his spiritual altitude, saw " neither Greek nor Jew, Barbarian nor Scythian, bond nor free." It is but natural to expect exalted sentiments from Walt Whitman, for he, too, dwells upon " the radiant summit." From this lofty elevation he looks with equal eye on all below. He announces himself " meeter of savages and gentlemen on equal terms." True, it does not require the gift of inspiration to establish the identity of all men when reduced to their lowest terms. Even so unspiritually minded a poet as Shakespeare recognizes the sameness of the fool and the philosopher in their final physical analysis. But Whitman's conception of equality is all-comprehensive in its scope; it is not limited to the lower plane of animal existence, but extends to the higher region of spiritual kinship. Specifying the circumstances of his spiritual illumination with the definiteness of a Methodist convert, he tells us:

" Swiftly arose and spread around me the peace and knowledge that pass all the argument of the earth,
And I know that the hand of God is the promise of my own,
And I know that the spirit of God is the brother of my own,
And that all the men ever born are also my brothers, and the women my sisters and lovers,
And that a kelson of the creation is love."

His cosmic breadth of view is no shallow sentimentality or vain intellectual pretense, but is based upon the unifying power of the love of God.

Let no favored fraction of the human family fancy that they find in him their pet poet or special pleader. He himself rebukes such unwarranted presumption:

" No friend of mine takes his ease in my chair;
I have no chair, no church, no philosophy."

There is no variety of the human race that cannot find in him that which is adapted to its peculiar needs.

Compelled by circumstances to view all objects under a racial angle of vision, the Negro, not unnaturally, seeks in Whitman some peculiar significance and specialty of meaning. The automorphic tendency is so strongly rooted in human nature that a people are apt to form their ideals in their own image and stamp upon them the impress of their own physical and social peculiarities. This circumstance renders any type unsuited to artistic or literary uses among a people of different " clime, color and degree." " Shakespeare," says a learned critic, " ought not to have made Othello black, for the hero of a tragedy ought to be white." But Walt Whitman tells us that in his literary treatment he does not " separate the learn'd from the unlearn'd, the Northerner from the Southerner, the white from the black."

As the Negro is portrayed in modern literature, he usually plays a servile, contemptible or ridiculous rôle. He is sometimes used to point a moral, but seldom to adorn a tale. We find the Negro appearing in several forms of literature.

1. In the unadorned, didactic discussions of the race problem which have filled our newspapers, magazines, and book-stalls, both in anti-slavery times and since the war. Such works are mainly preceptive in their aim, and, strictly speaking, cannot be called literature at all.

2. In the dialect story he is portrayed as being ignorant, superstitious, degraded and clownish, cutting jim-crow capers and apish antics for the amusement and delight of white lookers-on. By a strange literary inconsistency, however, he is made to express the wisest philosophy in the crudest forms of speech. If there be any virtue, or if there be any praise, ascribed to him, it is of the unaspiring, sycophant, servile sort, leaving the world to believe of the race

that " their morals, like their pleasures, are but low."

3. In anti-slavery poetry the Negro is pictured in his pitiable helplessness, and is sometimes endowed with manly qualities and courage, to serve as a more effective object-lesson of the wrongs and cruelties of slavery.   Whittier, Lowell, and Longfellow tuned their lyres to human liberty and did noble service for freedom by means of their songs.   But on close scrutiny we find that for the most part these have the patronizing or apologetic tone.   They are not intended to please, but to teach.   They do not appeal to the taste, but to the moral judgment.   The sermonic purpose is apparent in every line.   This class of poetry reaches the high-tide mark in the kindly conceived lines of the poet Cowper, who, with conscious satisfaction of feeling, pays the Negro the negative compliment of not being outside of the pale of humanity:

> " Fleecy locks and black complexion
>   Cannot forfeit nature's claim."

It is no depreciation of the kindly intent and useful purpose of this class of poetry to say that it is " sicklied o'er with the pale cast of thought."   Contrasted with it, how refreshing are the lines of Whitman:

> " You whoever you are!
> You daughter or son of England!
> You of the mighty Slavic tribes and empires! you Russ in
>   Russia!
> You dim-descended, black, divine-soul'd African, large, fine-
>   headed, nobly-form'd, superbly destin'd, on equal terms
>   with me!"

4. In recent years it has been quite customary to discuss the race question through the agency of the

novel. Authors of no less distinction than Grant Allen, W. D. Howells, and Paul Bourget have handled the subject in this fashion. The Negro is made the tragic representative of his own fate. These stories usually breathe the spirit of despair and death. They hold up no model, no ideal, no ambition, no aspiration for the youth of this race.

The growth and expansion of modern literature is co-extensive with the rise and development of African slavery. This literature is tinged throughout with the contemptuous disdain for the Negro which he is made to feel in all the walks and relations of life. In it he finds himself set forth in every phase of ridicule, and derided in every mood and tense of contempt. It appears in our text books, in works of travel, in history, fiction, poetry, and art.

The same spirit does not obtain in the Oriental and classical literatures. These never refer to the Negro except in terms of endearment and respect. The gods of Homer are not too fastidious to spend a holiday season of social intercourse and festive enjoyment among the blameless Ethiopians.

It is true that many of the choicest works of the human mind have been produced during this modern period. This literature possesses all of the qualities which Macaulay ascribes to the works of Athenian genius. It is " wealth in poverty, liberty in bondage, health in sickness, society in solitude." " It consoles sorrow and assuages pain and brings gladness to eyes which fall with wakefulness and tears." But for the Negro to derive therefrom such wholesome, beneficial effects, he must be " self-balanc'd for contingencies," so as to steel his feelings against rebuff, insult, and ridicule. He must exercise the selective instinct, which " from poisonous herbs extracts the healing dew."

The poet Virgil paints a pathetic picture. After the wandering Æneas had suffered many vicissitudes by land and sea, he came at length to Tyre, the land of the ill-fated Dido; and while waiting in the sacred grove an audience with her Sidonian majesty, he feasted his mind on the works of art which embellished the temple of Juno. But when he saw, represented in art, the woes and miseries of his race; when he saw the Trojan forces fleeing before the Greeks, and beheld the body of the god-like Hector dragged around the walls of Troy, and saw the aged Priam extending his feeble hands in helpless pity, his heart failed him and his eyes melted with tears. Out of this pathetic fullness of soul he exclaimed to his faithful companion in woe: " O Achates, what spot is there, what region is there, throughout the whole earth, which is not full of our misfortunes? "

Like father Æneas, the Negro sees that his woes and misfortunes are universal, confronting him everywhere—in art and literature, in statue and on canvas, in bust and picture, in verse and fiction, in song and story. But in the literary realm of Whitman all are welcome; none are denied, shunned, avoided, ridiculed, or made to feel ashamed. Indeed, Whitman's whole theory is a protest against such exclusion. He has in his inimitable way described the degrading effects of European literature upon America. This degradation holds with added force when we apply it to modern literature and the Negro. Whitman says:

No fine romance, no inimitable delineation of character, no grace of delicate illustration, no picture of shore or mountain or sky, no deep thought of the intellect, is so important to a man as his opinion of himself is; everything receives its tinge from that. In the verse of all those undoubtedly great writers —Shakspere just as much as the rest—there is the air which to America is the air of death. The mass of the people, the laborers and all who serve, are slag, refuse. The countenances of kings and great lords are beautiful; the countenances of mechanics ridiculous and deformed. What play of Shakspere as represented in America is not an insult to America, to its marrow and to its bones?

As a matter of course the Negro can get no standing in that school of literature which runs wild over the " neck, hair, and complexion of a particular female."

Walt Whitman's poetic principle does not depend upon superficial distinctions, but upon the eternal verities. He does not believe the " jay is more precious than the lark because his feathers are more beautiful, or the adder better than the eel because his painted skin contents the eye." He is " pleased with the homely woman as well as the handsome." This concession would bankrupt almost any other poet by depriving him of half of his stock in trade. Truly his poems " balance ranks, colors, races, creeds, and sexes." He does not relegate the Negro to the backyard of literature, but lets him in on the ground floor.

But let none imagine that because Whitman includes the weak as well as the mighty, the lowly and humble as well as the high and haughty, the poor as well as the rich, the black as well as the white, that he depreciates culture, refinement, and civilization. Although he widens the scope, he does not lower the tone. True, he is " no dainty *dolce affettuoso*." He hates pruriency, fastidiousness and sham. " He is stuff'd with the stuff that is coarse and stuff'd with the stuff that is fine."

I know that his bold, bald manner of expression sometimes grates harshly upon the refined sensibilities of the age. But he speaks with the unblushing frankness of nature. To the pure all things are pure. "Leaves of Grass" must not be judged by isolated lines, but we must consider the general drift of its purpose and meaning. Whitman does not despise the perfumeries, graces, and adornments of life, but he will not be intoxicated by their exhalations. He maintains his soberness and sanity amid these enticing allurements.

> "He says indifferently and alike, How are you, friend? to the
> President at his levee,
> And he says, Good day, my brother, to Cudge who hoes in
> the sugar-field,
> And both understand him and know his speech is right."

And yet he urges us to preserve all the solid acquisitions of civilization.

> "Earn for the body and for the mind whatever inheres and
> goes forward."

> "Produce great persons, the rest follows."

> "Charity and personal force are the only investments worth
> anything."

All truly great souls spend themselves in selfless service. Whitman would drag none down, but would lift all up. He would ring in for the world " the nobler modes of life, with purer manners, sweeter laws." He would bring mankind everywhere " flush " with himself.

America has broken the shackles which bound four millions of human beings to a degraded life. But the bondage of the body is nothing compared with the slavery of the soul. Whitman sounds the keynote of the higher emancipation. A great poet is necessarily a great prophet. He sees farthest because he has the most faith. The time must come when color will not be interchanged for qualities. When all other considerations will not wait on the query, "Of what complexion is he?"—when men and women cease to make graven images of their physical idiosyncrasies, and cease to bow down to them and serve them—then the accidental will yield to the essential, the temporary and fleeting to those things which abide.

The providence of God is mysterious and inscrutable, but His ways are just and righteous altogether. Suffering and sorrow have their place in divine economy. If the woe and affliction through which this race have passed but lead to the unfoldment of their latent æsthetic and spiritual capabilities, then the glory of tribulation is theirs. But can it be that they are to be forever the victims of contempt, caricatured in literature, and despised in all the ennobling relations of life? Can it be for the purpose of making a race despicable in the eyes of mankind that this people have endured so much and suffered so long? Was it for this that their ancestors were ruthlessly snatched from their native land, where they basked in the sunshine of savage bliss and were happy? Was it for this that they endured the hellish horrors of the middle passage; that the ocean bed was calcimined with the whiteness of human bones, and ocean currents ran red with human blood? Was it for this that they groaned for three centuries under the taskmaster's cruel lash? that their human instincts and upward aspirations were brutalized and crushed? Was it for this that babes were inhumanly torn from mothers' breasts; that the holy sentiment of mother-love—that finest, that divinest feeling which God has embedded in the human bosom —was stifled and smothered? Was it for this that our Southland was filled with sable Rachels " weeping for their children and would not be comforted for they were not "? Was it all for this? In the name of God I ask, was it for this?

Whitman points to a higher destiny. He looks through the most degraded externals and forecasts the glorious possibilities of this people. He leads the Negro from the slave block and crowns him with everlasting honor and glory.

" A man's body at auction,
  (For before the war I often go to the slave-mart and watch
    the sale),
  I help the auctioneer, the sloven does not half know his
    business.
Gentlemen, look on this wonder,
Whatever the bids of the bidders they cannot be high enough
    for it,
For it the globe lay preparing quintillions of years without
    one animal or plant,
For it revolving cycles truly and steadily roll'd.
In this head the all-baffling brain,
In it and below it the makings of heroes,
Examine these limbs, red, black, or white, they are cunning
    in tendon and nerve,
They shall be stript that you may see them.
Exquisite senses, life-lit eyes, pluck, volition,
Flakes of breast muscle, pliant backbone and neck, flesh and
    flabby, good-sized arms and legs,
And wonders within there yet.
Within there runs blood,
The same old blood! the same red-running blood!
There swells and jets a heart, there all passions, desires,
    reachings, aspirations,
This is not only one man, this the father of those who shall
    be fathers in their turns,
In him the start of populous states and rich republics,
Of him countless immortal lives with countless embodiments
    and enjoyments."

No Negro, however humble his present station, can read these lines without feeling his humanity stirring within him, breeding wings wherewith to soar. Whitman has a special meaning to the Negro, not only because of his literary portrayal; he has positive lessons also. He inculcates the lesson of ennobling self-esteem. He teaches the Negro that " there is no sweeter fat than sticks to his own bones." He urges him to accept nothing that " insults his own soul."

"Long enough have you dream'd contemptible dreams,
  Now I wash the gum from your eyes."

"Commence to-day to inure yourself to pluck, reality, self-
  esteem, definiteness, elevatedness."

Surely he would lead this race "upon a knoll."

He has also taught his fellow-men their duty concerning the Negro. Catching his inspiration from
the hounded slave, he has given the golden rule a
new form of statement which will last as long as
human sympathies endure:

"I do not ask the wounded person how he feels, I myself
  become the wounded person."

"Whoever degrades another degrades me."

He will accept nothing that all cannot have a
counterpart of on equal terms with himself. Listen
to his "Thought":

"Of quality—as if it harm'd me giving others the same chances
  and rights as myself—as if it were not indispensable to
  my own rights that others possess the same."

These are the lessons that Whitman would teach the
world.

But one asks, What did he do practically in his
lifetime for the Negro? Beyond the fact that he
imbibed the anti-slavery sentiment of his environments, and that this sentiment distills throughout
"Leaves of Grass," I do not know. Nor does it matter in the least. Too large for a class, he gave himself to humanity. These are his words:

"I do not give lectures or a little charity,
  When I give, I give myself."

"I give nothing as duties, what others give as duties I give
  as living impulses."

He knows no race, but scatters his charity alike

over all the families of the earth. He believes in
Euclid's axiom that the whole is greater than any of
its parts. He does not love a race, he loves mankind.

I am a Christian and believe in the saving merits
of Jesus Christ to redeem mankind, and to exalt them
that are of low degree. It is nevertheless true that

> " In faith and hope the world will disagree,
>   But all mankind's concern is charity."

Whitman has given the largest human expression of
this virtue.

On this first meeting of the Walt Whitman Fellowship all men can equally join in celebrating the merits
of their great comrade, who, in robust integrity of
soul, in intellectual comprehension and power, in
catholic range of sympathy, and in spiritual illumination, is to be ranked among the choicest of the sons
of men.

FREDERICK DOUGLASS

THE highest function of a great name is to serve as an example and as a perpetual source of inspiration to the young who are to come after him. By the subtle law known as "consciousness of kind" a commanding personality incites the sharpest stimulus and exerts the deepest intensity of influence among the group from which he springs. We gather inspiration most readily from those of our class who have been touched with the feeling of our infirmities and have been subject to like conditions as ourselves. Every class, every race, every country, and indeed every well-defined group of social interests has its own glorified names whose fame and following are limited to the prescribed sphere of influence. Indeed, human relations are so diverse and human interests and feelings so antagonistic that the names which command even a fanatical following among one class may be despised and rejected by another. He who serves his exclusive class may be great in the positive degree; the man who serves a whole race or country may be considered great in the comparative degree; but it is only the man who breaks the barrier of class and creed and country and serves the human race that is worthy to be accounted great in the superlative degree. We are so far the creatures of local and institutional environment, and so disposed to borrow our modes of thought and feeling from our social medium, that even an appeal to the universal heart must be adapted to the spirit and genius of the time and people to whom it is first made. Even the Saviour of the world offered the plan of salvation first to the Jews in the traditional guise of the Hebrew cult.

It is essential that any isolated, proscribed class should honor its illustrious names. They serve not only as a measure of their possibilities, but they possess greater inspirational power by virtue of their close sympathetic and kindly touch. Small wonder that such people are wont to glorify their distinguished men out of proportion to their true historical setting on the scale of human greatness.

Frederick Douglass is the one commanding historic character of the colored race in America. He is the model of emulation of those who are struggling up through the trials and difficulties which he himself suffered and subdued. He is illustrative and exemplary of what they might become—the first fruit of promise of a dormant race. To the aspiring colored youth of this land Mr. Douglass is, at once, the inspiration of their hopes and the justification of their claims.

I do not on this occasion intend to dwell upon the well-known facts and circumstances in the life and career of Mr. Douglass, but deem it more profitable to point out some of the lessons to be derived from that life.

In the first place, Mr. Douglass began life at the lowest possible level. It is only when we understand the personal circumstances of his early environment that we can appreciate the pathos and power with which he was wont to insist upon the true measure of the progress of the American Negro, not by the height already attained, but by the depth from which he came. It has been truly said that it required a greater upward move to bring Mr. Douglass to the status in which the ordinary white child is born than is necessary on the part of the latter to reach the presidency of the United States. The early life of this gifted child of nature was spent amid squalor, deprivation and cruel usage. Like Melchizedek of old, it can be said of him that he sprung into existence without father or mother, or beginning of days. His little body was unprotected from the bitter, biting cold, and his vitals griped with the gnawing pangs of hunger. We are told that he vied with the dogs for the crumbs that fell from his master's table. He tasted the sting of a cruel slavery, and drank the cup to its very dregs. And yet he arose from this lowly and degraded estate and gained for himself a place among the illustrious names of his country.

We hear much in this day and time about the relative force of environment and heredity as factors in the formation of character. But, as the career of Mr. Douglass illustrates, there is a subtle power of personality which, though the product of neither, is more potent than both. God has given to each of us an irrepressible inner something, which, for want of better designation, the old philosophy used to call the freedom of the will, which counts for most in the making of manhood.

In the second place, I would call attention to the tremendous significance of a seemingly trifling incident in his life. When he was about thirteen years of age he came into possession of a copy of the "Columbian Orator," abounding in dramatic outbursts and stirring episodes of liberty. It was the ripened fruit of the choicest spirits, upon which the choicest spirits feed. This book fired his whole soul and kindled an unquenchable love for liberty. It is held by some that at the age of puberty the mind is in a state of unstable equilibrium, and, like a pyramid on its apex, may be thrown in any direction by

the slightest impression of force. The instantaneity
of religious conversions, which the Methodists used
to acclaim with such triumphant outbursts of halle-
lujah, may rest upon some such psychological foundation. When the child nature stands at the parting
of the ways, between youth and adolescence, it yields
to some quickening touch, as the fuse to the spark,
or as the sensitized plate to the impressions of sunlight. There are "psychological moments" when
the revealed idea rises sublimely above the revealing
agent. According to the theory of harmonies, if two
instruments are tuned in resonant accord the vibra-
tions of the one will wake up the slumbering chords
of the other. Young Douglass' soul was in sympathetic resonance with the great truth of human brotherhood and equality, and needed only the psychological suggestion which the "Columbian Orator" supplied. In a moment, in the twinkling of an eye, it
burned deep into his soul and made an ineffaceable
impression upon his consciousness of the gospel of
brotherhood and equality of man. It was the same
truth which could only be impressed upon the Apostle
Peter in the rhapsodies of a heavenly vision. The
age of revelation is not past, and will not pass so
long as there remains one soul that yearns for spiritual illumination. There comes at times into our
lives some sudden echo of the heavenly harmony from
the unseen world, and happy is that soul which beats
in vibrant harmony with that supernal sound. When
the gospel of liberty first dawned upon the adolescent
Douglass, as he pursued the pages of the "Columbian Orator," there is no rendition of either the old
or the new school of psychology that can analyze
the riot of thought and sentiment that swept through
his turbulent soul. This was indeed his new birth,
his baptism with fire from on high. From that

moment he was a possessed man. The love of liberty bound him with its subtle cords and did not release him until the hour of his death on Anacostia's mist-clad height.

Our educational philosophers are ransacking their brains to prescribe wise curricula of study for colored youth. There is not so much need of that which gives information to the mind or cunning to the fingers as that which touches the soul and quickens the spirit. There must be first aroused dormant consciousness of manhood with its inalienable rights, privileges, and dignity. The letter killeth, the spirit maketh alive. The " Columbia Orator " contributed more towards arousing the manhood of Mr. Douglass than all the traditional knowledge of all the schools. Of what avail is the mastery of all branches of technical and refined knowledge unless it touches the hidden springs of manhood? The value of any curriculum of study for a suppressed class that is not pregnant with moral energy, and that does not make insistent and incessant appeal to the half-conscious manhood within is seriously questionable. The revelation to a young man of the dignity, I had almost said the divinity, of his own selfhood is worth more to him in the development of character and power than all the knowledge in all the de luxe volumes in the gilded Carnegie libraries.

In the third place, Negro youth should study Mr. Douglass as a model of manly courage. In order to acquire a clear conception of principles let us discriminate sharply in the use of terms. Courage is that quality which enables one to encounter danger and difficulties with firmness and resolution of spirit. It is the swell of soul which meets outward pressure with inner resistance. Fortitude, on the other hand, is the capacity to endure, the ability to suffer and

be strong. It is courage in the passive voice. True
courage sets up an ideal and posits a purpose; it cal-
culates the cost and is economic of means, though
never faltering in determination to reach that end.
Bravery is mere physical daring in the presence of
danger, and responds to temporary physical and
mental excitation. He who is eager to fight every
evil which God allows to exist in society does not
display rational courage. Even our Saviour selected
the evils against which He waged war. The caged
eagle which beats his wings into insensibility against
the iron bars of his prison-house is accounted a fool-
ish bird. On the other hand, " the linnet void of noble
raze " has gained the everlasting seal of poetic disapproval. It is not genuine courage to go through
the world like the knight in the tale with sword in
hand and challenge on lips to offer mortal combat to
every windmill of opposition.

Mr. Douglass was courageous in the broadest and
best significance of the term. He set before him as
the goal of his ambition his own personal freedom
and that of his race, and he permitted neither prin-
cipalities nor powers, nor height nor depth, nor
things present nor things to come, to swerve him
from the pursuit of that purpose.

When we speak of moral courage we indulge in
tautology of terms; for all courage is essentially
moral. It does not require courage to go with your
friends or against your enemies; it is a physical impulse to do so. But true moral courage is shown
when we say no to our friends.

Mr. Douglass reached the climax of moral courage when he parted with William Lloyd Garrison, his
friend and benefactor, because of honest difference
of judgment, and when for the same motive he refused to follow John Brown to the scaffold at Har-

per's Ferry. It required an iron resolution and sublime courage for Douglass to deny the tender, pathetic, paternal appeal of the man who was about to
offer up himself as a sacrifice for an alien race. John
Brown on the scaffold dying for an alien and de-
fenseless race is the most sublime spectacle that this
planet has seen since Christ hung on the cross. That
scaffold shall be more hallowed during the ages to
come than any throne upon which king ever sat. Who
but Douglass would decline a seat on his right
hand?

In the fourth place, Mr. Douglass stands out as
a model of self-respect. Although he was subject to
all of the degradation and humiliation of his race,
yet he preserved the integrity of his own soul. It
is natural for a class that is despised, rejected and
despitefully used to accept the estimate of their
contemners, and to conclude that they are good for
nothing but to be cast out and trodden under foot.
In a civilization whose every feature serves to impress a whole people with a sense of their inferiority,
small wonder if the more timid and resigned spirits
are crushed beneath the cruel weight. It requires
the philosophic calm and poise to stand upright and
unperturbed amid such irrational things.

It is imperative that the youth of the colored race
have impressed upon them the lesson that it is not
the treatment that a man receives that degrades him,
but that which he accepts. It does not degrade the
soul when the body is swallowed up by the earthquake or overwhelmed by the flood. We are not
humiliated by the rebuffs of nature. No more should
we feel humiliated and degraded by violence and
outrage perpetrated by a powerful and arrogant social scheme. As a man thinketh in his heart, so is he.
The inner freedom of soul is not subject to assault

and battery. Mr. Douglass understood this principle well. He was never in truth and indeed a slave; for his soul never accepted the gyves that shackled his body.

It is related that Mr. Douglass was once ordered out of a first-class coach into a "Jim Crow" car by a rude and ill-mannered conductor. His white companion followed him to the proscribed department, and asked him how he felt to be humiliated by such a coarse fellow. Mr. Douglass let himself out to the full length of his robust manhood and replied, "I feel as if I had been kicked by an ass." If one will preserve his inner integrity, the ill-usage and despiteful treatment others may heap upon him can never penetrate to the holy of holies, which remains sacred and inviolable to an external assault.

The fifth lesson which should be emphasized in connection with the life of Mr. Douglass is that he possessed a ruling passion outside the narrow circle of self-interest and personal well being. The love of liberty reigned supreme in his soul. All great natures are characterized by a passionate enthusiasm for some altruistic principle. Its highest manifestation is found in the zeal for the salvation of men on the spiritual side. All great religious teachers belong to this class. Patriots and philanthropists are ardently devoted to the present well-being of man. The poet, the painter, and the sculptor indulge in a fine frenzy over contemplative beauty or its formal expression. The philosopher and the scientist go into ecstasy over the abstract pursuit of truth. Minds of smaller caliber get pure delight from empty pleasure, sportsmanship or the collection of curios and bric-à-brac. Even the average man is at his highest level when his whole soul goes out in love for another. The man who lives without altruistic enthusiasm goes through the world wrapped in a shroud.

There have been few members of the human race that have been characterized by so intense and passionate a love for liberty as Frederick Douglass. His love for liberty was not limited by racial, political or geographical boundaries, but included the whole round world. He believed that liberty, like religion, applied to all men " without one plea." He championed liberty for black men, liberty for white men, liberty for Americans, liberty for Europeans, liberty for Asiatics, liberty for the wise, liberty for the simple; liberty for the weak, liberty for the strong; liberty for men, liberty for women; liberty for all the sons and daughters of men. I do not know whether he permitted his thoughts to wander in planetary space or speculated as to the inhabitability of other worlds than ours; but if he did, I am sure that his great soul took them all in his comprehensive scheme of liberty. In this day and time, when the spirit of commercialism and selfish greed command the best energies of the age, the influence of such a life to those who are downtrodden and overborne is doubly significant. Greed for gain has never righted any wrong in the history of the human race. The love of money is the root, and not the remedy of evil.

In the sixth and last place, I would call attention of the young to the danger of forgetting the work and worth of Frederick Douglass and the ministration of his life. We live in a practical age when the things that are seen overshadow the things that are invisible.

What did Douglass do? asks the crass materialists. He built no institutions and laid no material foundations. True, he left us no showy tabernacles of clay.

He did not aspire to be the master mechanic of the colored race. The greatest things of this world are not made with hands, but reside in truth and righteousness and love. Douglass was the moral leader and spiritual prophet of his race. Unless all signs of the times are misleading, the time approaches, and is even now at hand, which demands a moral renaissance. Then, O for a Douglass, to arouse the conscience of the white race, to awaken the almost incomprehensible lethargy of his own people, and to call down the righteous wrath of Heaven upon injustice and wrong.

JEFFERSON AND THE NEGRO

THE recurring anniversaries of the birth of Thomas Jefferson elicit expressions of gratitude and esteem second only to that for George Washington. For strength and intensity of discipleship and for attachment to the tenets that he taught, his name is honored beyond all names in American politics. The authorship of the Declaration of Independence has fixed his fame forever among those who love liberty and hate oppression. The vital clause in this world-renowned document transcends the narrow exigencies of the situation with which it specifically dealt, and makes it the greatest state paper of all times. The specific charges against the British monarch are caustic enough, and adroitly drawn, but they no longer burden our memory nor quicken our emotion. If we should strike from the document the appeal to the universal heart touching the inalienable right to liberty and equality of privilege, it would rarely be disturbed from its resting-place in the appendix of our school histories. Abraham Lincoln, who, after Jefferson, possessed perhaps the most illumined understanding of any American statesman, deemed it the crowning proof of the political genius of the author of the great Declaration that " in the concrete pressure of a struggle for national independence, he had the coolness, foresight, and capacity to introduce into a merely revolutionary document an abstract truth applicable to all men and all times, and so embalm it there that to-day and in all coming days it shall be a rebuke and a stumbling-block to the harbingers of appearing tyranny and oppression."

It is among the glaring anomalies of our national history that the political party which from the days of Jefferson to the present time has stood for the enslavement and suppression of the Negro race professes the greatest admiration for his teachings and assumes almost the exclusive right to cherish his memory.   And yet the welfare of this unfortunate race, not merely its release from physical bondage, but, to use his own felicitous expression, " the emancipation of human nature," was ever a burden upon the heart of this great apostle of liberty.   It is doubtful whether among all the tributes of praise and honor which these anniversaries of his birth evoke one word will be said about his devotion to that cause for which he labored as strenuously as for any other.   Indeed, the Negro race is the chief beneficiary of his doctrine.   The luminary which he lit in the sky of liberty can never be blotted out till all men shall be blessed by its kindly light.   Though for a time it may be obscured by the shifting mists of doubt, evasion, and denial, it will endure as long as sun and moon and stars.

It is said that the Northern States, after finding slavery unprofitable in their barren clime and ice-bound latitude, disposed of their slaves at a profit and turned abolitionists for easement of conscience. However this may be, it is well known that economic principles and moral notions are so closely interwoven that it is hard to say where the one begins and the other ends.   It is a sad comment upon human nature that no people, as such, have ever cried out against the oppression of the weak so long as it inured to their material profit.   " Go sell all thou

hast and give to the poor " is the hardest condition
the Saviour imposed upon His followers. Idolatry
will never be destroyed by the makers of images, nor
the rum traffic by saloon-keepers. There were, indeed, a number of choice spirits like Edward Coles,
of Virginia, a devoted disciple of Jefferson, who had
the courage to make the sacrifice which his conscience
demanded. There were thousands of individuals who
did the same thing; but never enough to make it a
general policy.

Those who make a close study of the economic condition of Virginia during the latter half of the eight-
eenth century are easily persuaded that the Old Do-
minion was ready to follow closely upon the heels of
New England in the matter of the emancipation of
the slaves. The agricultural resources of the colony, under a century and a half of reckless tillage,
had been well-nigh exhausted. The old baronial estates were rapidly falling to pieces, and were passing
through the hands of the sheriff. The production of
tobacco by slave labor had ceased to be a bonanza.
Under such conditions it was inevitable that enlightened public sentiment would animadvert to the moral
evil of slavery; the same moral leaven that had leav-
ened the conscience of New England was at work in
Virginia. The Negro element in Virginia has scarcely
more than doubled itself in one hundred years. Unless the estates of Washington and Jefferson were
cared for because of sentimental reasons, they would
now be the homes of the owl and the bat. If it had not
been for the rise of the lower Southern States and
the new valuation put upon slaves by the invention
of the cotton-gin, Virginia would have early arrayed
herself in the column of the anti-slavery States.
But just as New England carried on the slave trade
with Southern neighbors for many years after the

system had ceased to be profitable on her own soil, so Virginia became the slave market for the newer and richer States to the South of her. The close geographical touch and ties of blood kinship strengthened, no doubt, by the rise of a meddlesome spirit in the North, kept Virginia in sympathy with the slave regime. The rise of the anti-slavery spirit, however, was not the sole product of Puritan principles, but had an exact counterpart in the more southern colony. The moral sense of a community does not rest upon geographical latitude, but upon a long chain of cause and consequence, which the careful student can trace as clearly as the causal connection in the more exact domains of knowledge.

Jefferson was of Welch and Scotch extraction, with little of the Anglo-Saxon in his makeup. His passionate devotion to moral principle, which was redeemed from fanaticism only by his robust intellectual sanity, may be considered in part at least as an attribute of blood. As with George Washington, the circumstances of his blood and birth would hardly entitle him to rank with the exclusive aristocratic set. Like Washington also, by force of personal worth and dint of strenuous endeavor, he made his merits known and received the fullest recognition among circles of the highest social consideration; but, unlike Washington, he was never completely assimilated by the upper set among whom he moved. He never forgot the rights and privileges of the under man. It was the ambition of his life to found an aristocracy upon character and culture, instead of lineage and wealth. No one ever gave the aristocratic pretensions of his day such rude shocks as he. It was Jefferson who abolished the law of entail and primogeniture in Virginia, and disestablished the Church of England. He never failed to exert his influence for the curtail-

ment and even for the abolition of slavery.   The
aristocrats hated him with bitter and malignant
hatred.

The struggle against the oppression of the mother
country and the wrongs and cruelties of slavery were
in harmony with the impulse of his soul.   Perhaps no
man ever lived who has done so much to impress
the minds of the common people, whom others were
disposed to ignore and despise, with a sense of liberty and personal dignity, as the author of the
Declaration of Independence.   This he was able to
do without the gift of oratory, without the glamour
of military glory, without the potent spell of religious mystery, but by sheer force of intense conviction and intellectual acumen.

It is generally believed that Jefferson was himself a wealthy slaveholder, who inconsistently enough
gave occasional utterance against the system of
which he was a beneficiary; but that his serious and
sustained endeavor lay wholly in other directions.
As a matter of fact, the question of emancipation
and the subsequent welfare of the Negro race was
one in which he never lost a vital interest.   It is
known that this was one of the first questions to
which he gave attention at the beginning of his career, and at the age of eighty-two, just one year
before his death, we find him writing to an Aboli-
tionist: " My own health is very low, not having
been able to leave the house for three months.   At
the age of eighty-two, with one foot in the grave,
and the other uplifted to follow it, I do not permit
myself to take part in new enterprises, even for bet-
tering the condition of men, not even the great one
which is the subject of your letter, and which has
been through life one of my greatest anxieties."

In the early part of his public career he proposed

an amendment to the Constitution of Virginia for the emancipation of slaves born after a certain date, and that they should be educated at public expense "in tillage, arts, and sciences, according to their geniuses." His marvelous foresight comprehended the entire scheme of industrial preparation of the Negro, which is nowadays being exploited with as much gusto and freshness of enthusiasm as if it were a new discovery. As a member of the Legislature, in 1778, he brought in a bill forbidding the further importation of slaves in Virginia, which was adopted without opposition.

The last article of the Declaration of Independence as the author drafted it was an indictment against the King for his complicity in the slave trade. This article, which was rejected by his more conservative colleagues, contained the only underscored words in the whole document: " He has waged cruel war against human nature itself, violating its most sacred rights of life and liberty in the persons of distinct peoples, who never offended him; captivating and carrying them into slavery in another hemisphere to incur miserable death in their transportation thither. This piratical warfare, the opprobrium of infidel powers, is the warfare of the Christian King of Great Britain. Determined to keep open market where MEN should be bought and sold, he has prostituted his negative for suppressing every legislative attempt to prohibit or to restrain this execrable commerce."

There is much dispute as to whether the Declaration of Independence was intended to include the Negro race. The language of this clause leaves not the slightest room for doubt of its intendment, at least so far as the author was concerned. He intended nothing short of the " emancipation of human nature."

Speaking of a temporary check placed upon the slave traffic in Virginia, he said: " This will in some measure stop the increase of this great political and moral evil while the minds of our citizens are ripening for the complete emancipation of human nature." As still further proof that Jefferson included the Negro in his universal scheme of liberty and equality, we read from a letter written to Edward Coles in 1820: " I had hoped that the younger generation, receiving their early impressions after the flame of liberty had been kindled in every breast, would have sympathized with oppression wherever found, and proved their love of liberty beyond their own share of it." And again: " What a stupendous, what an incomprehensible machine is man! Who can endure toil, famine, stripes, imprisonment, and death itself, in vindication of his own liberty, and the next moment be deaf to all those motives whose power sustained him through his trial, and inflict on his fellow-men a bondage, one hour of which is fraught with more misery than ages of that he arose in rebellion to oppose."

If such unmistakable utterances by the author of the instrument do not make clear its intendment, then all the laws of critical interpretation are of no avail. In a recent political controversy we heard this great document reduced to an airy abstraction by the leaders of a party that was supposed to espouse its principles. But the spirit of Jefferson must surely rise up and condemn all those who would deprive any race or class of the blessings which flow from this great Declaration.

Jefferson presented a plan for the government of

the great Northwest Territory, according to which
slavery was to be abolished after the year 1800. This
provision was lost by a bare majority of one. The
author, commenting bitterly upon the miscarriage
of his propaganda of liberty, said: " Thus we see
the fate of millions unborn hanging upon the tongue
of one man, and heaven was silent at that awful moment! " With characteristic sagacity he clearly
foresaw the strategic value of gaining the great
Northwest country to the side of liberty. It was,
indeed, in this region that the issue became most
acute, and the struggle between the two economic
regimes became most intense.

Jefferson adopted two principles that the modern
statesman would do well to heed: (1) That the Constitution should be liberally interpreted where human
rights are involved, and (2) that a just cause, if
persisted in, will prevail in the long run. It is the
policy of this day to make the most lax constitutional interpretation, not in favor of, but against
the rights of man, and there is also danger of forgetting that old homely motto that truth is mighty
and in the end will prevail.

Thomas Jefferson loved humanity and did not
despise it because of the outward semblance that it
wore. On one occasion he had as his guest at Monticello a colored man of education and taste, by name
of Julius Melbourn. There were in the company
at dinner Chief Justice Marshall, Mr. Wirt, Mr.
Samuel Dexter, of Boston, and Dr. Samuel Mitchell,
of New York. On this occasion the race question
was the theme for discussion. About the same arguments as to the Negro's incapacity and the decrees
of Providence which are still resorted to were brought
forward and ably presented. Mr. Jefferson showed
clearly the faith that was in him by declaring that,

" As regards personal rights, it seems to me most palpably absurd that the individual rights of volition and locomotion should depend upon the degree of power possessed by the individual. I should hardly be willing to subscribe to the doctrine that because the Chief Justice has a stronger mind or a more capacious and better-formed brain than I that, therefore, he has the right to make me his slave." Jefferson informed his colored guest that it was his intention to make instruction at the University of Virginia free to all sects and colors. In a letter to Benjamin Banneker, the Negro astronomer, Mr. Jefferson expressed his interest in the moral and intellectual improvement of the colored race, and wished them every opportunity to demonstrate to the world their intellectual and moral worth.

Mr. Jefferson in his notes on Virginia expressed the conviction that there were irreconcilable differences between the races, and that they could not live together on terms of amity. In defining the shortcomings of the Negro, however, he makes full allowance for unfavorable circumstances and lack of opportunity, and hazards his statements with great hesitancy and caution. There is entire absence of that cock-sureness and assumption of omniscience of which we hear so much nowadays. Jefferson's plan for the colonization of the emancipated race was a much more simple, sensible and humane project in his day than at the present time. It should not be without significance, however, that Jefferson, De Tocqueville, and Abraham Lincoln, all three of whom were men of as great a degree of enlightenment as any who have ever discussed American policies, were of the same mind as to the final solution of the race problem.

But how could a man be a slaveholder and at the

same time entertain such doctrines of liberty and
equality? This charge has stood for more than a
century, not only against the author of the Declaration of Independence, but against all those who participated in the great events leading up to and growing out of the Revolutionary struggle. Jefferson
was a man of glaring inconsistencies, even above his
fellow. Indeed, every man who thinks great thoughts
and does great deeds is apt to encounter the charge
of inconsistency. The man of one idea who never
puts even that one into execution can easily be consistent, because he has no hosts of conflicting
thoughts and deeds among themselves. But the man
of thoughts and deeds always repels the charge of
inconsistency with the retort, " Do I contradict myself; well, then, I contradict myself; I am large, I
contain multitudes." When a great American President wants to place the fiscal scheme of the country
on a firm basis he simply does so, and would gladly
forget that he at one time advocated free silver.
When a great party wants to annex some distant
island of the sea, without their let or hindrance, it
proceeds to do so, even though it once professed to
subscribe to the Declaration of Independence. Jefferson was a man of superlative political genius, and
at the same time possessed a high order of talent for
well-nigh every other branch of human pursuit. You
cannot fetter genius by the delicate cords of consistency. It breaks them violently asunder, and follows
the freshly imparted impulse. When President Jefferson saw that the purchase of Louisiana would
inure to the lasting good of his country he struck
the bargain with the great Napoleon, although it ran
counter to all of his political teachings.

No man more keenly appreciated the inconsistency
of the American attitude on the question of slavery

than did Thomas Jefferson. The above recital shows this most plainly. And yet he retained the slaves which came to him as patrimony. Slavery on the Jefferson estate was of the mild, patriarchal sort, and the owner continued it partly from the force of inertia, and partly as a duty to those thrust upon his charge. To use his own words: " My opinion has ever been that until more can be done for them, we should endeavor with those whom fortune has thrown in our hands, to feed and clothe them well, protect them from ill uses, and require such reasonable labor only as is performed voluntarily by freemen." Mr. Bacon, who was for twenty years the manager at Monticello, has given us a splendid account of the kindly and patriarchal dispensation that prevailed on Mr. Jefferson's estate. When the British soldiers carried off some thirty or forty of his slaves he complained of their unnecessary harshness and severity, but did not forget to add that if they would give the men their freedom it would be right.

We do not hold men responsible for participating in the prevailing customs of their time, although it must ever be a source of regret that the author of the Declaration of Independence did not personally set the example which he never failed to urge upon the conscience of his fellow-men.

THE ARTISTIC GIFTS OF THE NEGRO

WHAT contribution has the Negro race ever made or ever can make to the general culture of the human spirit? asks the critic, with a scornful disdain that allows no answer. Ridicule and contempt have characterized the habitual attitude of the American mind toward the Negro's higher strivings. The faintest suggestion as to his higher possibilities is received either with a sneer or with a smile. The African was brought to America to be a hewer of wood and a drawer of water. Requisition was made upon his physical faculties alone to perform this manual and menial mission. His function was supposed to be as purely mechanical as that of the ox which pulls the plow. No more account was taken of his higher susceptibilities than of the mental and moral faculties of the lower animals. Indeed, the Negro has never been regarded in his own right and for his own sake, but merely as a coefficient which is not detachable from the quantity whose value it enhances. The servant exists for the sake of his master. The black man's status is fixed and his usefulness is recognized on the lower level of crude service. His mission is to administer to the wants of the higher, or as it is more fitting to say, the haughtier race. " The Negro is all right in his place " phrases a feeling that is deep seated and long abiding. This historical bias of mind is brought forward in current discussion. It is so natural to base a theory upon a long-established practice that one no longer wonders at the prevalence of this belief. The African has sustained servile relations to the Aryan for so long a time that it is easy, as it is agreeable to the Aryan pride, to conclude that servitude is his ordained place in society. The dogma of Carlyle that "the Negro is useful to God's creation only as a servant" still finds wide acceptance. Much of our current social philosophy on the race problem is but a restatement of the ancient prejudice in terms of modern phraseology. Why awaken the higher faculties of the race when only the lower ones are demanded in our scheme of economy? What boots it to develop higher taste and finer feelings in a people who must of necessity perform the rougher grade of the world's work? Is it not preposterous that black men should ponder over Shakespeare and Dante and black maidens pursue music and painting when they might earn a dollar a day at useful, productive toil? Such arguments are as familiar to us as the more orthodox doctrine drawn from the curse of Canaan used to be in days gone by. To an attitude thus predisposed, manifestation of higher qualities on the part of the people held in despite is both unwelcome and embarrassing. The justification of oppression is always based on the absence of higher faculties. Phyllis Wheatley and Frederick Douglass were more persuasive and potential anti-slavery arguments than all the flood of eloquence poured forth in behalf of an oppressed race. There was serious hesitation in admitting that the Negro possessed a soul and was entitled to the rites of baptism, on the ground that it was not right to hold a Christian in slavery. There is a sneaking feeling in the breast of humanity that the ennobling circle of kindly sympathy should include all persons and peoples who display aptitude for the higher intellectual and spiritual cult.

Despite traditional theories and centuries of cruel

usage, there have been more or less continual outcroppings of the Negro's suppressed and stunted
soul. Any striking emanation from this dark and
forbidden background was at one time called a freak
of nature not to be calculated in the ordinary course
of events. But when freaks become too frequent
they can no longer be ignored in any rational scheme
of philosophy.

Music is the easiest outlet of the soul. The pent-
up energy within breaks through the aperture of
sound while the slower and more accurate delibera-
tions of the intellect are yet in process of formulation. Plantation melody, that blind, half-conscious
poetry that rose up from " the low ground of sorrow," was the first expression of the imprisoned soul
of an imprisoned race. It was the smothered voice
of a race crying in the wilderness, " with no language
but a cry." These weird, plaintive, lugubrious longings go straight to the heart without the interven-
tions of cumbersome intellectual machinery. They
came from the unsophisticated soul of an humble and
simple-minded black folk and make the strongest appeal to the universal heart. There can be no stronger
argument of the sameness of human sympathy. " As
in the water face answerest to face, so the heart of
man to man." Negro melody has been called the
only autochthonous music of the American Continent. The inner soul of the red man is not preserved
to us in song. The European brought his folk-
thought and folk-song acquired by his ancestors in
the unremembered ages. It was reserved for the
transplanted African to sing a new song racy of the
soil, which had been baptized with his blood and wa-
tered with his tears. This music is the spontaneous
expression of the race soul under new and depress-
ing environment. It is the folk-genius of the Afri-

can, not indeed on his ancestral heath, but in a new though beloved land. Unlike the captive Jew, who, under like circumstances, hung his harp upon the willow tree and sat down by the rivers of Babylon and wept, the transplanted African made a contribution to the repertoire of song which moistens the eye and melts the heart of the world. These songs are not African, but American. The scene, circumstances and aspirations are not adapted to some distant continent, but to their new environment in a land, not of their sojourn, but of their abiding place. Shall they not immortalize the soil from which they sprung? Robert Burns has gathered the superstitions, the sorrows, the sufferings, the joys, the strivings of the lowly life of Scotland and woven them into soulful song, and has thus rendered old Scotia ever dear to human memory. The tourist makes his eager pilgrimage around the world to view " the banks and braes o' bonnie Doon " where the peasant lass poured out her soul in anguish. What halo of glory hovers over that ghostly route traversed that dreary night by the tippled Tam O'Shanter! The glory of a locality rests as much upon the folk-song or folk-story that grows out of and gathers about it as upon the tradition that this or that great man was born there. If the human heart ever turns with passionate yearning to our own Southland, it will not be so much in quest of the deeds and doings of her renowned warriors and statesmen, as to revel in the songs, the sorrows, the sighings, the soul strivings of her humble black folk and to realize the scenes amid which these pathetic melodies took their rise. Which of their musical achievements would the American people not gladly give in exchange for " Steal Away to Jesus " or " Swing Low, Sweet Chariot "? What song yet ascribed to the glory of " Hail Columbia!'" equals in power of pathetic appeal and strength of local endearment the yearnful quest of the slave for his home land, "'Way Down Upon the Suwannee River"? The motif of the world renowned "Dixie," the musical inspiration of the Southern Confederacy, is based upon the yearning of a slave removed from his native Sunny South for the land where he was born. The South is the home of the Negro, not merely because he has aided in the development of its resources by his strong and brawny arm, but also because he has hallowed it by the yearnings of his soul.

There is a dispositon on the part of the more sensitive members of the colored race to affect to feel ashamed of these melodies which solaced and sustained their ancestors under burdens as grievous as any the human race has ever been called upon to bear. They fear to acknowledge a noble influence because it proceeded from a lowly place. All great people glorify their history, and look back upon their early attainment with spiritualized vision. What nation is there that cannot find in its earlier struggles those things which, if interpreted in light of present conditions, would count for humiliation and shame? But through the purifying power of spiritual perspective they are made to reveal a greater degree of glory. However trying and perplexing experiences may be while we are in the midst of them, yet a longer range of vision gives us the assurance that "it will afterwards please us to remember even these things." A race that is ashamed of itself or of its historic humiliation which has been overcome makes a pitiable spectacle in the eyes of the world to which it appeals for sympathy and tolerance. A people who are afraid of their own shadow must forever abide in the shade. These plantation melodies represent the Negro's chief contribution to the purifying influences that soften and solace the human spirit. Can the oyster be ashamed of the pearl, or the toad of the jewel in its head? For the Negro to despise his superior natural qualities because they differ from those of another class would be of the same order of folly as if the female sex, in derogation of its natural endowment, should refuse to sing soprano, because the males excel in baritone.

This music is indeed inimitable. Its racial quality is stamped on every note. The writer remembers the anomalous spectacle of a white principal trying to lead his colored pupils in the rendition of jubilee glees. The requisite melodic, pathetic quality of voice is a natural coefficient which is as inalienable as any other physical characteristic. It rings out from the blood. As we listen to its sad, sighing cadence, we naturally expect to look and see, and say, " These are they who have come up through great tribulation." A white man attempting a plantation melody is as much a racial anomaly as a Negro affecting to feel in his soul the significance of that line of a celebrated hymn in which the singer passionately avows that he will never " blush to speak His name."

Immediately after the war troupes of Negro singers invaded the North and sang the songs whose melodic pathos melted the heart like wax. The Fisk Jubilee singers carried the ministration of this music to the remotest ends of the earth; and kings and emperors have wept before these soul-moving wailings. Many a school in the South owes its endowment to this sweet, sad singing. The plantation melodies possess the quality of endurance. It fulfils Keat's definition, " A thing of beauty is a joy

forever." Whenever and wherever they are faithfully rendered, the people are moved mightily.

Transition from plantation melody to the standard tunes of Watts and Wesley was as easy as the
second step in walking. Indeed, the Negro's gift
for psalmody and his wonderful melodic and har-
monic endowment is the marvel of the musical world.
The wonder is how these people can sing so well
without having learned. To listen to a Negro camp-
meeting in the backwoods of the Carolinas rendering
the good old songs of Zion is almost enough to "rob
the listening soul of sin."

The rise of rag-time music, which for the past few
years has been the rage, marks another stage of
Negro music. The potency of its spell has been all-
pervasive. Half the world has been humming its
tunes. The small boy whistles it on the street; the
Italian grinds it from his music box while the urchins
gambol on the commons; it jingles in our ears from
the slot machine while we wait for the next train or
sip a glass of soda; it has captivated the European
capitals; the ultra dilettante and his alabaster lady
in the gilded palace of wealth glide gracefully over
the tufted fabric to the movement of its catchy,
snatchy airs. The critics may indeed tell us that
music is one thing and rag-time another, but the common people, and the uncommon ones as well, hear it,
not only gladly, but rapturously. Rag-time is essentially Negro in motive, meaning, movement, and
indeed, in composition. It is neither serious nor soul
deep, like its plantation prototype, but is rather the
outcome of a silly, flippant, dilettantism of the " new
issue." The scene is in the city, not the country.
Indeed it might well be called " city airs " in contra-
distinction from " plantation melodies." While this

music portrays faithfully the Negro race in a certain phase of development, and while some of it bites deep into the experiences of human nature, yet it lacks the element of permanence, and seems destined to pass away, like the jingles of the variety stage which tickle the ear only for a season. It is here for the first time that the Negro figures as a composer of music. The words and music of the plantation melodies are attributed to no definite authorship. The " coon songs," a sort of connecting link between the old and the new, were composed mainly by white authors. It is not generally known that such famous songs as " Ben Bolt," " Listen to the Mocking-Bird," and " Rally Round the Flag, Boys " bear the stamp of Negro workmanship, as respects either words or music. But the Negro's chief musical distinction, up to the rise of rag-time, rested upon rendition, rather than upon composition. For the past few years, however, music sheets by Negro authors have been flying from the press as thick as the traditional autumn leaves. There has scarcely been a musical collection, so the critics tell us, during that interval that has not contained songs by Negro authors. Colored troupes in the rôles of Negro authorship or improvisation have crowded the largest theaters in all parts of the land. Several such troupes have undertaken European tours with marked success. There is a group of Negro composers in New York whose works bear the imprint of the best-known publishing houses. Some of them have accumulated fortunes from their composition and performance. Such famous pieces as " All Coons Look Alike to Me," " Under the Bamboo Tree," and " Go 'Way Back and Sit Down," are sung between the oceans and, indeed, around the world. Gus L. Davis, the most famous Negro composer, died a few years ago. He belonged to the era of the " story-song " and did not attempt any piece of purely Negro sentiment. Whenever the world plays or thrums, or hums, or whistles, or sings " The Light-House by the Sea," " The Baggage Coach Ahead," or " The Fatal Wedding," it pays homage to the musical genius of the Negro race.

The Negro race is indeed a highly musical people. The love of music crops out everywhere. The back room of every Negro barbershop is a young conservatory of music. In the ordinary Negro household the piano is as common a piece of furniture as the rocking-chair or center-table. That rosewood piano in a log cabin in Alabama, which Dr. Booker T. Washington's burlesque has made famous, is a most convincing, if somewhat grotesque, illustration of the musical genius of the Negro race. Music satisfies the Negro's longing as nothing else can do. All human faculties strive to express or utter themselves. They do not wait upon any fixed scheme or order of development to satisfy our social philosophy. When the fires of genius burn in the soul it will not await the acquiring of a bank account or the building of a fine mansion before gratifying its cravings. The famished Elijah, under a juniper tree, was the purveyor of God's message to a wicked king. Socrates in poverty and rage pointed out to mankind the path of moral freedom. John the Baptist, clad in leather girdle, and living on the wild fruits of the fields, proclaimed the coming of the kingdom of God. Would it be blasphemy to add, that the Son of Man, while dwelling in the flesh, had not where to lay His head? Our modern philosophy would have advised that these enthusiasts cease their idle ravings, go to work, earn an honest living, and leave the pursuit of truth and spiritual purity to those who had acquired a competency. Is it a part of God's economy that the higher susceptibilities of the soul must wait upon the lower faculties of the body? Should Tanner paint no pictures because his race is ignorant and poor? Should a Dunbar cease to woo the Muses till every Negro learns a trade? The Negro in poverty and rags, in ignorance and unspeakable physical wretchedness, uttered forth those melodies which are sure to lift mankind at least a little higher in the scale of spiritual purity.

There are scattered indications that the Negro possesses ambition and capacity for high-grade classical music. The love of music is not only a natural passion, it is becoming a cultivated taste. The choirs of the best colored churches usually render at least one high-grade selection at each service. Blind Tom and Black Patti are at least individual instances of the highest musical susceptibility. There are numerous colored men and women who have completed courses, both instrumental and vocal, in the best American conservatories, and several have pursued their studies under famous European masters. In almost every center where a goodly number of cultivated colored people are to be found, there is a musical organization devoted to the rendition of the standard works of the great composers.

But music is only one of the forms of art in which the Negro has given encouraging manifestations. Frederick Douglass was among the foremost orators of the anti-slavery crusade, the second great oratorical epoch in the annals of American history. Booker T. Washington, according to some, is the most effective living orator that speaks the English tongue. Phyllis Wheatley, the Black Daughter of the Sun; and Dunbar, the peerless poet of lowly life, wooed the Muse of Song, who did not disdain their suit because their skin was dark. Pictures by Tanner adorn the walls of many a gallery in two hemispheres, one of which is on its way to the Louvre. If we might be permitted to cross the ocean and include those whom the Negro race can claim through some strain of their blood, Pushkin stands as the national poet of Russia, and the Dumas as the leading romancers of France. It is noticeable that the names which the Negroes have contributed to the galaxy of the world's greatness are confined almost wholly to the fine arts. Toussaint L'Ouverture stands almost alone among Negroes of whose fame the world takes account, whose renown rests upon solid deeds.

The Negro's order of development follows that of the human race. The imaginative powers are the first to emerge; exact knowledge and its practical application come at a later stage. The first superlative Negro will rise in the domain of the arts. The poet, the artist and the musician come before the engineer and the administrator. The Negro who is to quicken and inspire his race will not be a master mechanic nor yet a man of profound erudition in the domain of exact knowledge, but a man of vision with powers to portray and project. The epic of the Negro race has not yet been written; its aspirations and strivings still await portrayal. Whenever a Dunbar or a Chestnut breaks upon us with surprising imaginative and pictorial power, his race becomes expectant and begins to ask, " Art thou he that should come, or do we look for another? "

Mr. W. D. Howells, writing in the introduction of Mr. Dunbar's first volume of poems, says: " I said that a race which had come to this effect in any member of it, had attained civilization in him, and

I permitted myself the imaginative prophecy that the hostilities and prejudices which had so long constrained his race were destined to vanish in the arts; that these were to be the final proof that God had made of one blood all nations of men. I accepted them as an evidence of the essential unity of the human race."

THE EARLY STRUGGLE FOR EDUCATION

A FULL knowledge of the education of the Negro cannot be had without making some reference to the earlier educational efforts. It is well known that slavery discouraged the dissemination of literary knowledge among persons of African descent, and, in most cases, this discouragement amounted to a positive prohibition. But despite the rigid regulations of the slave regime there were many kind-hearted slaveholders who taught their slaves to read and write. Many others picked up such knowledge in ways which it is mysterious to comprehend. The fact that book information was withheld from the Negro made him all the more anxious to acquire it. Stolen waters are sweet, and the fact that they are forbidden leads those from whom the privilege is withheld to suspect that they possess mysterious efficacy. Such hungering and thirsting after knowledge amid dark and dismal discouragements is surely a compliment to the intellectual taste of the African. The antebellum struggle of the free colored people and the more ambitious slaves to acquire the use of printed characters is almost incomprehensible in view of the liberal educational provisions of these latter days. The experience of Frederick Douglass was not without many parallels and counterparts. In his autobiography he tells us:

The most interesting feature of my stay here (in Baltimore) was my learning to read and write under somewhat marked disadvantages. In obtaining this knowledge I was compelled to resort to indirections by no means congenial to my nature, and which were really humiliating to my sense of candor and uprightness. My mistress, checked in her benevolent designs toward me, not only ceased instructing me herself but set her face as a flint against my learning to read by any means.

She would rush to me with the utmost fury, and snatch the book or paper from my hand with something of the wrath and consternation which a traitor might be supposed to feel on being discovered in a plot by some dangerous spy. The conviction once thoroughly established in her mind that education and slavery were incompatible with each other, I was most narrowly watched in all my movements. If I remained in a separate room from the family for any considerable length of time, I was sure to be suspected of having a book, and was at once called to give an account of myself. Teaching me the alphabet had been the " inch " given; I was now waiting only for the opportunity to take the " ell." Filled with determination to read at any cost, I hit upon many expedients to attain my desired end. The plan which I mainly adopted, and the one which was most successful, was that of using my white playmates, with whom I met in the streets, as teachers. I used to carry almost constantly a copy of Webster's Spelling Book in my pocket, and when sent on errands, or when playtime was allowed me, I would step aside with my young friends and take a lesson in spelling.

Meanwhile I resolved to add to my educational attainments the art of writing. After this manner I began to learn to write. I was much in the shipyard, and observed that the carpenters after hewing and getting ready a piece of timber to use, wrote on the initials of the name of that part of the ship for which it was intended. When, for instance, a piece of timber was ready for the starboard side, it was marked with a capital *S;* a piece for the larboard side was marked *L;* larboard aft marked *L. A.;* starboard aft *S. A.;* starboard forward *S. F.* I soon learned these letters, and for what they were placed on the timbers. My work now was to keep fire under the steambox, and to watch the shipyard while the carpenters had gone to dinner. This interval gave me a fine opportunity to copy the letters named. I soon astonished myself with the ease in which I made the letters, and the thought was soon present, if I can make four letters, I can make more. With playmates for my teachers, fences and pavement for my copy-books, and chalk for my pen and ink, I learned to write.

This was the university training of the most illustrious American Negro, which could be duplicated in the experience of thousands of his fellow-slaves who remained " mute and inglorious."

A different and less strenuous phase of early educational opportunities may be found in the experience of another distinguished colored American, the late Prof. John Mercer Langston. Mr. Langston thus recounts the early schooling of his brother:

His father (a Virginia white man), manifesting the deepest interest in him, sought by his own efforts and influence to give him such thorough English education, with general information, and mental and moral improvement, so as to make him a useful man. He (at 7 years) was required to appear for his recitations in his father's special apartments the year around at 5 o'clock in the morning.

A second brother was put through the same regime, and John M., though too young for definite training when his father died, had ample provision made for his education.

These citations represent two phases of Negro education before the Civil War. The one gives a picture of the dauntless, self-impelling determination to gain knowledge at any cost; the other, the kind and genial disposition of a father-master, in spite of the rigorous requirements of the law. These instances may be regarded as typical, and might be multiplied by hundreds and thousands. There were also organized efforts for the education of the colored race. Schools were established for the free colored people within the limits of the slave territory. These were mainly in the large cities. A careful and detailed study of such early educational efforts for the several States and cities affords a rich field for interesting and valuable monographic writing. This chapter attempts little more than to present some of the hindrances, embarrassments, personal and economic sacrifices under which the Negro in the slave territory labored during the dark days of slavery, in order to secure what he considered the talismanic power of knowledge.

In Alabama the law of 1832 provided that " any person or persons that shall attempt to teach any free person of color, or slave, to spell, read, or write, shall upon conviction thereof by indictment, be fined in a sum of not less than $250, nor more than $500."

In 1833 the mayor and aldermen of the city of Mobile were authorized by law to grant licenses to such persons as they might deem suitable to instruct for limited periods the free colored creole children within the city and in the counties of Mobile and Baldwin, who were the descendants of colored creoles residing in said city and counties in April, 1803, provided, that said children first receive permission to be taught from the mayor and aldermen and have their names recorded in a book kept for the purpose. This was done, as set forth in the preamble of the law, because there were many colored creoles there whose ancestors, under the treaty between France and the United States in 1803, had the rights and privileges of citizens of the United States secured to them.

Arkansas seems to have had no law in the statute book prohibiting the teaching of persons of African descent, although the law of 1838 forbade any white person or free Negro from being found in the company of slaves or in any unlawful meeting, under severe penalty for each offense. In 1843 all migrations of free Negroes and mulattoes into the State was forbidden.

There was no law expressly forbidding the instruction of slaves or free colored people in the State of Delaware until 1863, when an enactment against all assemblages for the instruction of colored people, and forbidding all meetings except for religious purposes and for the burial of the dead, was made.

While the free colored people were taxed to a certain extent for school purposes, they could not enjoy the privileges of public instruction thus provided, and were left for many years to rely principally upon individual efforts among themselves and friends for the support of a few occasional schools. In 1840 the Friends formed the African School Association in the city of Wilmington, and by its aid two very good schools, male and female, were established in that place.

In 1828 the State of Florida passed an act to provide for the establishment of common schools, but white children only of a specified age were entitled to school privileges.

In Georgia the following law was enacted in 1829:

> If any slave, Negro, or free person of color, or any white person, shall teach any other slave, Negro, or free person of color to read or write, either written or printed characters, the said free person of color or slave shall be punished by fine and whipping, or fine or whipping, at the discretion of the court; and if a white person so offend he, she, or they shall be punished with a fine not exceeding $500 and imprisonment in the common jail, at the discretion of the court.

In 1833 a penalty not exceeding $500 was provided for the employment of any slave or free person of color in setting up type or other labor about a printing-office requiring a knowledge of reading or writing. The code remained in force until swept away by events of the Civil War.

In 1833 the city of Savannah adopted an ordinance that if any person shall teach or cause to be taught any slave or free person of color to read or write within the city, or who shall keep a school for that purpose, he or she shall be fined in a sum not exceeding $100 for each and every such offense; and if the offender be a slave or free person of color, he or she may also be whipped not exceeding thirty-nine lashes.

Notwithstanding this severe enactment, there were, nevertheless, several schools for colored children clandestinely kept in Augusta and Savannah. The poor whites would often teach Negro children clandestinely. If an officer of the law came round the children were hastily dispatched to the fictitious duty of "picking chips." The most noted Negro school was opened in 1818 or 1819 by a colored man from Santo Domingo. Up to 1829 this school was taught openly. The law of that year made concealment and secrecy a necessity.

In Kentucky the school system was established in 1830. In this provision the property of colored people was included in the basis of taxation, but they were excluded from school privileges.

Louisiana, in 1830, provided that whoever should write, publish, or describe anything having a tendency to produce discontent among the free population or insubordination among the slaves, should upon conviction be imprisoned at hard labor for life or suffer death, at the discretion of the court. It was also provided that all persons who should teach or permit or cause to be taught any slave to read or write should be imprisoned not less than one month or more than twelve.

In 1847 a system of public schools was established for the education of white youth, and one mill on the dollar upon the ad valorem amount of the general list of taxable property might be levied for its support. Prior to the Civil War the only schools for colored youth in Louisiana were a few private ones in the city of New Orleans among the creoles.

St. Francis Academy for colored girls was founded

in connection with the Oblate Sisters, in Baltimore, Md., and received the sanction of the Holy See October 2, 1831. There were many colored Catholic refugees who came to Baltimore from Santo Domingo. The colored women who formed the original society which founded the convent and seminary were from Santo Domingo. The Sisters of Providence is the name of a religious society of colored women who renounced the world to consecrate themselves to the Christian education of colored girls. This school is still in successful operation. A colored man by the name of Nelson Wells left by will to trustees $7,000, the income of which was to be applied to the education of free colored children. The Nelson Wells school continued from 1835 to the close of the Civil War.

Dr. Bokkelen, State superintendent of education, recommended in 1864 the establishment of colored schools on the same basis as those of the whites, and states in his recommendation:

· I am informed that the amount of school tax paid annually by these [colored] people to educate the white people in the city of Baltimore for many years has been more than $500. The rule of fair play would require that this be refunded unless the State at once provided schools under this title.

By an act of January, 1833, the legislature of Mississippi provided that the meeting of slaves and mulattoes above the number of five at any place or public resort or meeting-house in the night or at any schoolhouse for teaching reading or writing in the day or night was to be considered an unlawful assembly. In 1846 an act was passed establishing a system of public schools from all escheats and all fines, forfeitures, and amercement from licenses to hawkers and all income from school lands. These schools were for the education of white youths.

The legislature of Missouri in 1847 provided that no person should teach any schools for Negroes or mulattoes.

In North Carolina until 1835 public opinion permitted the colored residents to maintain schools for the education of their children. These were taught sometimes by white persons, but frequently by colored teachers. After this period colored children could only be educated by confining their teaching within the circle of their own family or by going out of the limits of their own State, in which event they were prohibited by law from returning home. The public system of North Carolina declared that no descendant of Negro ancestors to the fourth generation, inclusive, should enjoy the benefits thereof.

In 1740, while yet a British colony, South Carolina took the lead in directly legislating against the education of the colored race:

Whereas the having of slaves taught to write, or suffering them to be employed in writing, may be attended with inconvenience, be it enacted, That all and any person or persons whatsoever, who shall hereafter teach or cause any slave or slaves to be taught, or shall use or employ any slave as scribe in any manner of writing whatever, hereafter taught to write, every such person or persons shall for every such offense forfeit the sum of £100 current money.

In 1800 free colored people were included in this provision. In 1834 it was provided:

If any person shall hereafter teach any slave to read or write, or shall aid or assist in teaching any slave to read or write, or cause or procure any slave to be taught to read or write, such person, if a free white person, upon conviction thereof, shall, for each and every offense against this act, be fined not exceeding $100 and (suffer) imprisonment not more than six months; or if a free person of color, shall be whipped not exceeding 50 lashes. . . . And if any free person of color or slave shall keep any school or other place of instruction for teaching any slave or free person of color to read or write, such free person of color shall be liable to the same fine, imprisonment, and corporeal punishment.

And yet there were colored schools in Charleston from 1744 to the close of the Civil War.

In 1838 Tennessee provided a system of public schools for the education of white children between the ages of 6 and 16, but the colored children never enjoyed any of its benefits, although the free colored people contributed their due share to the public fund.

Texas never expressly forbade the instruction of Negroes, although the harsh and severe restrictions placed upon the race made a provision scarcely necessary.

In 1831 the general assembly of Virginia enacted, among others, the following provisions:

That all meetings of free Negroes or mulattoes of any schoolhouse, church, meeting-house, or other place for teaching them reading or writing, either in the day or night, under whatsoever pretext, shall be deemed an unlawful assembly. . . . If any white person or persons assemble with free Negroes or mulattoes at any schoolhouse, church, meeting-house, or other place for the purpose of instructing such free Negroes or mulattoes to read or write, such person or persons shall, on conviction thereof, be fined in a sum not exceeding $50, and, moreover, may be imprisoned, at the discretion of a jury, not exceeding two months.

It is known, however, that schools for the colored children were established and maintained in such cities as Petersburg, Norfolk, and Richmond.

The early educational efforts of the colored people of the District of Columbia have been studied with more fulness than those of any other Southern community. He who presents the movement in Baltimore, Richmond, Louisiana, Charleston, and other Southern centers with as much detail and accuracy will render no inconsiderable service to the history of education.

There does not seem to have been any express law forbidding the education of colored people in the District of Columbia. In 1807 the first schoolhouse for the use of colored pupils was erected by three colored men,—George Bell, Nicholas Franklin, and Moses Liverpool,—not one of whom knew a letter of the alphabet. They had been former slaves in Virginia, and, like others of their condition, had an exalted notion of literary knowledge. A white teacher was secured. From this time to the opening of the new regime, brought on by the Civil War, there was a tolerably adequate number of schools, supported mainly by the colored people themselves, but not without assistance from Northern philanthropy. But that these schools did not always have plain and smooth sailing may be gathered from the fact that in 1835, on account of an alleged indiscreet utterance of a colored resident, colored schools were attacked by a mob, some of them burned, and property destroyed, while the most conspicuous Negro teacher, Mr. John F. Cook, was compelled to flee for his life. This outbreak is known as the " Snow Riot."

Many of the best-known names in the District were both products of and factors in these early schools, the most noted of whom, perhaps, is Mr. John F. Cook, who subsequently became a tax collector of the District of Columbia. For substance, dignity and influence he stands as one of the conspicuous names of the National Capital, regardless of race distinction. His brother, George F. T. Cook, who was both a pupil and a teacher in the antebellum schools, subsequently became superintendent of the colored public schools of Washington and Georgetown, which position he held for thirty years.

This survey has been limited to the Southern or slave States. In the free States of the North the Negro had a more picturesque and exciting educational experience. The Northern States did not expressly forbid the education of colored persons, but the hostility to such movements is attested by many a local outbreak.

It was amid such dangers and difficulties that the Negro began his educational career. It must not be for a moment supposed, however, that the laws above referred to were rigidly enforced. It is known that pious and generous slaveholders quite generally taught their favorite slaves to read, regardless of the inexorable provisions of law. Quite a goodly number also learned the art of letters somewhat after the furtive method of Frederick Douglass; in the cities, schools for Negroes were conducted in avoidance, connivance, or defiance of ordinances and enactments.

In 1865 there was to be found in every Southern community a goodly sprinkling of colored men and women who had previously learned how to read and write.

The censuses of 1850 and 1860 give the number of free colored people attending school in the several States. These figures, for obvious reasons, represent only a small fraction of the Negroes, free and slave, who were openly or furtively gaining the elements of literary knowledge. The decline in avowed school attendance between 1850 and 1860 is due to the growing intensity of feeling which culminated during that decade.

FREE NEGROES ATTENDING SCHOOL

STATE	1850	1860	STATE	1850	1860
Delaware	187	250	Texas...........	20	11
Maryland	1,616	1,355	Arkansas........	11	5
District of Columbia		467	Tennessee	70	92
		678	Kentucky	288	205
Virginia.........	64	41	Missouri	40	155
North Carolina ..	217	133			
South Carolina ..	80	365	Slave States	4,414	3,661
Georgia.........	1	7	Free States	28,213	22,800
Florida..........	66	9			
Alabama	68	114	Total,	32,627	26,461
Mississippi......		2			
Louisiana	1,219	275			

It will be noticed that most of the enactments against the education of the Negro were made subsequently to 1830. The Nat Turner insurrection and the opening up of the anti-slavery campaign in the North had a decidedly reactionary effect in the slave territory.

A people who have made such sacrifice and run such risks for the sake of knowledge, who of their own scanty means were ever willing to support schools for the education of their children, although their property had been taxed for the support of an educational system from which they were excluded, surely deserve a larger and fuller draught of that knowledge of which the regime of slavery permitted them to gain only a foretaste. The Civil War wiped out all of these restrictions, and at its close the Freedmen's Bureau, religious and benevolent associations, and the reconstructed governments of the former slave States threw wide open the gate of knowledge.

The avidity and zeal with which the erstwhile sup-

pressed population seized upon the new opportunity
furnish the most interesting chapter in the history
of American education.   Educational opportunities
were thus thrown open to a people who desired and
needed them above all, and who had shown by long
and persistent endeavor that they were fully worthy
and deserving of them.

A BRIEF FOR THE HIGHER EDUCATION
OF THE NEGRO

RIDICULE and contempt have characterized the habitual attitude of the American mind toward the Negro's higher strivings. The African was brought to this country for the purpose of performing manual and menial labor. His bodily powers alone were required to accomplish this industrial mission. No more account was taken of his higher suscepti-bilities than of the mental and moral faculties of the lower animals. As the late Mr. Price used to say, the white man saw in the Negro's mind only what was apparent in his face, "darkness there, and nothing more." His usefulness in the world is still measured by physical faculties rather than by quali-ties of mind and soul. The merciless proposition of Carlyle, that the Negro is useful to God's creation only as a servant, still finds wide acceptance. It is so natural to base a theory upon a long-established practice that one no longer wonders at the preva-lence of this belief. The Negro has sustained servile relation to the Caucasian for so long a time that it is as easy as it is agreeable to Caucasian pride to conclude that servitude is his ordained place in so-ciety. When it was first proposed to furnish means for the higher development of this race, some, who assumed the wisdom of their day and generation, en-tertained the proposition with a sneer; others, with a smile.

MANIFESTATIONS OF HIGHER QUALITIES

As the higher susceptibilities of the Negro were not wanted, their existence was at one time denied.

The eternal inferiority of the race was assumed as a part of the cosmic order of things. History, literature, science, speculative conjecture, and even Holy Writ were ransacked for evidence and argument to support the ruling dogma. While the slaveholder had proved beyond all possibility of doubt the incapacity of the Negro for knowledge, yet he, prudently enough, passed laws forbidding the attempt. His guilty conscience caused him to make assurance doubly sure by re-enacting the laws of the Almighty.

For three hundred years the Negro by his marvelous assimilative power and by striking individual emanations has been constantly manifesting the higher possibilities of his nature, until now whoever assumes to doubt his susceptibility for better things needs himself to be pitied for his incapacity to grasp the truth. The same Carlyle who regards the Negro as an " amiable blockhead," and amenable only to the white man's " beneficent whip," also declares: " That one man should die ignorant who had capacity for knowledge, this I call a tragedy, were it to happen forty times in a minute." When it is known that the Negro has capacity for knowledge and virtue there can be no further justification for shutting him out from the higher cravings of his nature.

IS THE HIGHER EDUCATION OF THE NEGRO WORTH WHILE AS A PRACTICAL PHILANTHROPY?

The education of the Negro is not of itself a thing apart, but is an integral factor of the general pedagogic equation. Race psychology has not yet been formulated. No reputable authority has pointed out just wherein the two races differ in any evident mental feature. The mind of the Negro is of the same nature as that of the white man and needs the same nurture. The general poverty of the Negro, however, and his inability to formulate and direct his own scheme of culture, render the question not so much one of abstract pedagogics, as of practical philanthropy. The philanthropist is supremely indifferent as to whether an individual, white or black, should study Kant or Quaternious, except in so far as the resulting development reacts beneficially upon the common welfare. Does the higher education of the few capable Negroes possess sufficient advantage to the race at large to justify its continuance by a wise and discriminating philanthropy? The great missionary societies, representing the philanthropic arms of the Congregational, Presbyterian, Methodist and Baptist denominations after forty years of arduous, earnest endeavor and the expenditure of many millions of dollars in this field, answer this question emphatically in the affirmative. An ounce of opinion from such sources should be worth a ton of speculation from those who reach their conclusions by a process of " pure reasoning."

THE FUNCTION OF EDUCATION TO A BACKWARD RACE

The African was snatched from the wilds of savagery and thrust into the midst of a mighty civilization. He thus escaped the gradual progress of evolution. Education must accomplish more for a backward race than for a people who are in the forefront of progress. It must not only lead to the unfoldment of faculties but also equip for a life from which the recipient is separated by many centuries of development. The African chieftain who would make a pilgrimage from the jungle to Boston might accomplish the first part of his journey by the original modes of transportation—in the primitive dugout or on the backs of his slaves; but he would complete it upon the steamship, the railway, the electric car and the automobile. How swift the transformation and yet how suggestive of centuries of toil, struggle and mental endeavor. It required the human race thousands of years to bridge the chasm between savagery and civilization, which must now be crossed by a school curriculum of a few years' duration. In a settled state of society the chief function of education is to enable the individual to live the life already attained by his race, but the educated Negro must be a pioneer, a progressive force in the uplifting of his race, and that, too, notwithstanding the fact that he belongs to a backward breed that has never taken the initiative in the progressive movements of the world.

THE HIGHER TRAINING OF CHOICE YOUTH

The first great need of the Negro is that the choice youth of the race should assimilate the principles of culture and hand them down to the masses below. This is the only gateway through which a new people may enter into modern civilization. Herein lies the history of culture. The select minds of the backward race or nation must receive the new cult and adapt it to the peculiar needs of their own people. Japan looms up as the most progressive of the non-Aryan races. The wonderful progress of these Oriental Yankees is due in a large measure to their wise plan of procedure. They send their picked youth to the great centers of western knowledge; but before this culture is applied to their own needs it must first be sifted through the sieve of their native comprehension. The graduates of the schools and colleges for the Negro races are forming centers of civilizing influence in all parts of the land, and we confidently believe that these grains of leaven will ultimately leaven the whole lump.

SELF-RELIANT MANHOOD

Another great need of the race, which the schools must in a large measure supply, is self-reliant manhood. Slavery made the Negro as dependent upon the intelligence and foresight of his master as a soldier upon the will of his commander. He had no need to take thought as to what he should eat or drink or wherewithal he should be clothed. Knowledge necessarily awakens self-consciousness of power.

When a child learns the multiplication table he gets a clear notion of intellectual dignity. Here he gains an acquisition which is his permanent, personal possession, and which can never be taken from him. It does not depend upon external authority; he could reproduce it if all the visible forms of the universe were effaced. It is said that the possession of personal property is the greatest stimulus to self-respect. When one can read his title clear to earthly possessions it awakens a consciousness of the dignity of his own manhood. And so when one has digested and assimilated the principles of knowledge he can file his declaration of intellectual independence. He can adopt the language of Montaigne, "Truth and reason are common to every one, and are no more 'his who spake them first than his who speaks them after; 'tis no more according to Plato than according to me, since he and I equally see and understand them."

Primary principles have no ethnic quality. We

hear much in this day and time of the white man's civilization. We had just as well speak of the white man's multiplication table. Civilization is the common possession of all who assimilate and apply its principles. England can utilize no secret art or invention that is not equally available to Japan. We reward ingenuity with a patent right for a period of years upon the process that has been invented; but when an idea has been published to the world it is no more the exclusive property of the author than gold, after it has been put in circulation, can be claimed by the miner who first dug it from its hiding-place in the earth. No race or nation can preëmpt civilization any more than it can monopolize the atmosphere which surrounds the earth, or the waters which hold it in their liquid embrace.

I have often noticed a young man accommodate his companion with a light from his cigar. After the spark has once been communicated, the beneficiary stands upon an equal footing with the benefactor. In both cases the fire must be continued by drawing fresh supplies of oxygen from the atmosphere. From whatever source a nation may derive the light of civilization, it must be perpetuated by the exercise of the nation's own faculties. Self-reliant manhood is the ultimate basis of American citizenship.

TRAINING FOR LEADERSHIP

The work of the educated colored man is largely that of leadership. He requires, therefore, all the discipline, judgment and mental equipment that long preparation can afford. The more ignorant and backward the masses the more skilled and sagacious should the leaders be. If a beneficial and kindly contact between the races is denied on the lower plane of flesh and blood, it must be sought in the upper region of mental and moral kinship. Knowledge and virtue know no ethnic exclusiveness. If indeed races are irreconcilable, their best individual exponents are not. All dignified negotiation must be conducted on the high plane of individual equality.

> " For east is east, and west is west, and never the twain shall meet,
> Till earth and sky stand presently at God's great judgment seat;
> But there is neither east nor west, border nor breed nor birth,
> When two strong men stand face to face, though they come from the ends of the earth."

Irreconcilables become reconciled only after each has manifested the best possibilities of a common nature. The higher education tends to develop superior individuals who may be expected to exercise controlling influence over the multitude. The individual is the proof, the promise and the salvation of the race. The undeveloped races which, in modern times, have faded before the breath of civilization have probably perished because of their failure to produce commanding leaders to guide them wisely under the stress and strain which an encroaching civilization imposed. A single red Indian with the capacity and spirit of Booker T. Washington might have solved the red man's problems and averted his pending doom.

THE MORAL IMPOTENCY OF ELEMENTARY AND ME-CHANICAL KNOWLEDGE

Again, the higher education should be encouraged because of the moral impotency of all the modes of education which do not touch and stir the human spirit. It is folly to suppose that the moral nature of the child is improved because it has been taught to read and write and cast up accounts, or to practice a handicraft. Tracing the letters of the alphabet with a pen has no bearing on the Golden Rule. The spelling of words by sounds and syllables does not lead to observance of the Ten Commandments. Drill in the multiplication table does not fascinate the learner with the Sermon on the Mount. Rules in grammar, dates in history, sums in arithmetic, and points in geography do not strengthen the grasp on moral truth. The ability to saw a line or hit a nail aplomb with a hammer does not create a zeal for righteousness and truth. It is only when the pupil comes to feel the vitalizing power of knowledge that it begins to react upon the life and to fructify in character. This is especially true of a backward race whose acquisitive power outruns its apperceptive faculty.

THE SOCIAL SEPARATION OF THE RACES

The Negro has now reached a critical stage in his career. The point of attachment between the races which slavery made possible has been destroyed. The relation is daily becoming less intimate and friendly, and more business-like and formal. It thus becomes all the more imperative that the race should gain for itself the primary principles of knowledge and culture.

The social separation of the races in America renders it imperative that the professional classes among the Negroes should be recruited from their own ranks. Under ordinary circumstances, professional places are filled by the most favored class in the community. In a Latin or Catholic country, where the fiction of " social equality " does not exist, there is felt no necessity for Negro priest, teacher, or physician to administer to his own race. But in America this is conceded to be a social necessity. Such being the case, the Negro leader, to use a familiar term, requires all the professional equipment of his white confrere, and special knowledge of the needs and circumstances of his race in addition. The teacher of the Negro child, the preacher to a Negro congregation, or the physician to Negro patients certainly requires as much professional skill as those who administer to the corresponding needs of the white race. Nor are the requirements of the situation one whit diminished because the bestower is of the same race as the recipient. The Negro has the same professional needs as his white confrere and can be qualified for his function only by courses of training of like extent and thoroughness. By no other means can he be qualified to enlighten the ignorant, restrain the vicious, care for the sick and afflicted; administer solace to weary souls, or plead in litigation the cause of the injured.

THE PROFESSIONAL NEEDS OF THE CITY NEGRO

According to the census of 1900, there were 72 cities in the United States with a population of more than 5,000 persons of color, averaging 15,000 each, and aggregating 1,000,000 in all. The professional needs of this urban population for teachers, preachers, lawyers and physicians call for 5,000 well-equipped men and women, not one of whom would be qualified for his function by the three R's or a handicraft.

THE EFFECT OF HIGHER EDUCATION UPON THE RURAL MASSES

The supreme concern of philanthropy is the welfare of the unawakened rural masses. To this end there is need of a goodly sprinkling of well educated men and women to give wise guidance, direction and control. Let no one deceive himself that the country Negro can be uplifted except through the influence of higher contact. It is impossible to inaugurate and conduct a manual training or industrial school without men of sound academic as well as technical knowledge. The torch which is to lighten the darksome places of the South must be kindled at the centers of light.

THE IMPORTANCE OF CULTIVATED TASTE

Rational enjoyment, through moderation, is perhaps as good a definition as can be given of culture. The reaction of culture on conduct is a well-known principle of practical ethics. The Negro race is characterized by boisterousness of manner and extravagant forms of taste. As if to correct such deficiencies, his higher education, hitherto, has largely been concerned with Greek and Latin literature, the norms of modern culture. It is just here that our educational critics are liable to become excited. The spectacle of a Negro wearing eye-glasses and declaiming in classic phrases about the "lofty walls of Rome," and the "wrath of Achilles" upsets their critical calmness and composure. We have so often listened to the grotesque incongruity of a Greek chorus and a greasy cabin and the relative value of a rosewood piano and a patch of early rose potatoes that if we did not join in the smile in order to encourage the humor, we should do so out of sheer weariness. And yet we cannot escape the conviction that one of the Negro's chief needs is a higher form of intellectual and esthetic taste.

THE RELATIVE CLAIMS OF INDUSTRIAL AND HIGHER EDUCATION

Whenever the higher education of the Negro is broached, industrial training is always suggested as a counter-irritant. Partisans of rival claims align themselves in hostile array and will not so much as respect a flag of truce. These one-eyed enthusiasts lack binocular vision. The futile discussion as to whether industrial or higher education is of greater importance to the Negro is suggestive of a subject of great renown in rural debating societies: which is of greater importance to man, air or water. We had as well attempt to decide whether the base or altitude is the more important element of a triangle. The two forms of training should be considered on the basis of their relative, not rival, claims.

THE HIGHER EDUCATION STIMULATES INDUSTRIAL ACTIVITY

Indeed, one of the strongest claims for the higher education of the Negro is that it will stimulate the dormant industrial activities of the race. The surest way to incite a people to meet the material demands of life is to teach them that life is more than meat. The unimaginative laborer pursues the routine rounds of his task, spurred on only by the immediate necessities of life and the taskmaster's stern command.

To him, it is only time and the hour that run through the whole day. The Negro lacks enlightened imagination. He needs prospect and vista. He does not make provision because he lacks prevision. Under slavery he toiled as the ass, dependent upon the daily allowance from his master's crib. To him the prayer, Give us this day our daily bread, has a material rather than a spiritual meaning. If you would perpetuate the industrial incapacity of the Negro, then confine him to the low grounds of drudgery and toil and prevent him from casting his eyes unto the hills whence come inspiration and promise. The man with the hoe is of all men most miserable unless, forsooth, he has a hope. But if imbued with hope and sustained by an ideal, he can consecrate the hoe as well as any other instrument of service, as a means of fulfilling the promise within him. When a seed is sown in the ground it first sends its roots into the soil before the blades can rise out of it. But is it not actuated by the plant-consciousness to seek the light of heaven? For what is the purpose of sending its roots below, if it be not in order to bear fruit above? The pilgrim fathers in following the inspiration of a lofty ideal developed the resources of a continent. Any people who attempt to reach the sky on a pedestal of bricks and mortar will end in confusion and bewilderment as did the builders of the Tower of Babel on the plains of Shinar in the days of Eld. It requires range of vision to stimulate the industrial activities of the people. The most effective prayer that can be uttered for the Negro is, " Lord, open thou his eyes." He cannot see beyond the momentary gratification of appetite and passion. He does not look before and after. Such stimulating influence can be brought to bear upon the race only through the inspiration of the higher culture.

MEN OF HIGHER TRAINING THE LEADERS OF INDUSTRIAL EDUCATION

It requires men of sound knowledge to conceive and execute plans for the industrial education of the masses. The great apostles of industrial education for the Negro have been of academic training, or of its cultural equivalent. The work of Hampton and Tuskegee is carried on by men and women of a high degree of mental cultivation.

DR. BOOKER T. WASHINGTON AN EXAMPLE OF HIGHER CULTURE

Dr. Booker T. Washington (note the title) is the most influential Negro that the race under freedom has produced. He is the great apostle of industrial training. His great success is but the legitimate outcome of his earnestness and enthusiasm. And yet there is no more striking illustration of the necessity of wise, judicious and cultivated leadership as a means of stimulating the dormant activity of the masses than he who hails from Tuskegee. His success is due wholly to his intellectual and moral faculties. His personal opportunities of association and contact have been equivalent to a liberal education. Several of America's greatest institutions of learning have fittingly recognized his moral and intellectual worth by decorating him with their highest literary honors. Mr. Washington possesses an enlightened mind to discover the needs of the masses, executive tact to put his plans in effective operation, and persuasive ability to convince others as to the expediency of his policies. He possesses no trade or handicraft; if so, he has never let the American people into the secret. Nor can it easily be seen what pos-

sible benefit such trade or handicraft would be to
him in the work which has fallen to his lot. Tuskegee has been built on intellect and oratory. If Mr.
Washington had been born with palsied hands, but
endowed with the same intellectual gifts and powers
of persuasive speech, Tuskegee would not have suffered one iota by reason of his manual affliction.
But, on the other hand, had he come into the world
with a sluggish brain and a heavy tongue, whatever
cunning and skill his hands might have acquired, he
never could have developed the institution which has
made him justly famous throughout the civilized
world.

THE DEFICIENCY OF THE SLAVE MECHANIC

Slavery taught the Negro to work, but at the
same time to despise those who worked. To them all
show of respectability was attached to those whom
circumstances placed above the necessity of toil. It
requires intellectual conception of the object and
the end of labor to overcome this mischievous notion.
The Negro mechanics produced under the old slave
regime are rapidly passing away because they did
not possess the power of self-perpetuation. They
were not rooted and grounded in rational principles
of the mechanical arts. The hand could not transmit its cunning because the mind was not trained.
They were given the knack without the knowledge.

MONEY SPENT FOR THE HIGHER EDUCATION OF THE NEGRO NOT WASTED

The charge has recently been made that money
spent on the higher education of the Negro has been
wasted. Does this charge come from the South?

When we consider that it was through Northern philanthropy that a third of its population received their first impulse toward better things; that these higher institutions prepared the 30,000 Negro teachers whose services are utilized in the public schools; that the men and women who were the beneficiaries of this philanthropy are doing all in their power to control, guide and restrain the South's ignorant and vicious masses, thus lightening the public burden and lifting the general life to a higher level; that these persons are almost without exception earnest advocates of peace, harmony and good-will between the races; to say nothing of the fact that these vast philanthropic contributions have passed through the trade channels of Southern merchants, it would seem that the charge is strangely incompatible with that high-minded disposition and chivalrous spirit which the South is so zealous to maintain. Does this charge come from the North? It might not be impertinent to propound a few propositions for their consideration. Is it possible to specify a like sum of money spent upon any other backward race that has produced greater results than the amount spent upon the Southern Negro? Is it the American Indian, upon whom four centuries of missionary effort has produced no more progress than is made by a painted ship on a painted sea? Is it the Hawaiian, who will soon be civilized off the face of the earth? Is it the Chinese, upon whom the chief effect of Christian philanthropy is to incite them to breathe out slaughter against the stranger within their gates? It is incumbent upon him who claims that this money has been wasted to point out where, in all the range of benevolent activity, the contributions of philanthropy have been more profitably spent.

It is true that forty or fifty millions of dollars

have been thus spent, but when we consider the magnitude of the task to which it was applied, we find that it would not average one dollar a year for each Negro child to be educated. Why should we marvel, then, that the entire mass of ignorance and corruption has not put on enlightenment and purity?

NOT MERE THEORIZERS

We often hear that the advocates of higher education are mere theorists without definite, tangible plans and propositions. There has recently sprung into prominence a class of educational philosophers who deny the value of stored-up knowledge. We are informed that only such information as will be honored at the corner grocery or is convertible on demand into cash equivalent is of practical value, while all else is an educational delusion and a snare. The truth is, that all knowledge which clarifies the vision, refines the feelings, broadens the conception of truth and duty and ennobles the manhood is of the highest and most valuable form of practicability. An institution which sends into the world a physician to heal the sick, a lawyer to plead the cause of the injured, a teacher to enlighten the minds of the ignorant, or a preacher to break the bread of life to hungry souls, is rendering just as practical service to the race as those schools which prepare men to build houses and plant potatoes.

NEED FOR THE NEGRO COLLEGE

It is sometimes claimed that the few capable Negroes can find opportunity for higher training in the institutions of the North. It is by no means certain as to what extent these institutions would admit colored students. The Northern college is not apt to inspire the colored pupil with the enthusiasm and fixed purpose for the work which Providence has assigned him. It is the spirit, not the letter that maketh alive. The white college does not contemplate the special needs of the Negro race. American ideals could not be fostered in the white youth of our land by sending them to Oxford or Berlin for tuition. No more can the Negro gain racial inspiration from Harvard or Yale. And yet they need the benefit of contact and comparison, and the zeal for knowledge and truth which these great institutions impart. The Negro college and the Northern institutions will serve to preserve a balance between undue elation for want of sober comparison, and barren culture, for lack of inspirational contact with the masses.

DOES THE HIGHER EDUCATION LEAD AWAY FROM THE RACE?

It is often charged that the higher education lifts the Negro above the needs of his race. The thousands of graduates of Negro schools and colleges all over the land are a living refutation of this charge. After the mind has been stored with knowledge it is transmitted to the place where the need is greatest and the call is loudest, and transmuted into whatever mode of energy may be necessary to accomplish the imposed task.

The issues involved in the race question are as intricate in their relations and far-reaching in their consequences as any that have ever taxed human wisdom for solution. No one can be too learned or too profound in whose hands are entrusted the temporal and eternal destiny of a human soul. Even if the educated Negro desired to flee from his race, he soon learns by bitter experience that he will be thrown back upon himself by the expulsive power of prejudice. He soon learns that the Newtonian formula has a social application: "The force of attraction varies directly as the mass."

ROOSEVELT AND THE NEGRO

THE late Senator Ingalls, in one of his luminous
flashes, defined politics as "the metaphysics of
force." This definition fits with philosophic fineness
the nature of Theodore Roosevelt, who is its most
strenuous exemplar. In effective political dynamics
and intensity of accelerative energy, he easily sur-
passes all the present-day rulers of the earth. He
has no reserved physical or psychical potencies. All
the energies of his nature are in the active voice and
present tense. With him pure reasoning is a burden, and disquisitional niceties a waste of while and
a weariness of flesh. His one superlative passion is
how to bring things to pass. His mind works with
the celerity of feminine intuition. He reaches conclusions and settles issues with a swiftness and self-
satisfying certainty that startles the more cautious
statesmen who rely upon the slower processes of reason and deliberation. He has diagnosed the case,
prescribed the remedy, and cured, or killed, the
patient before the ordinary physician has finished
feeling the pulse. After the deed is done, he leaves
to the college professor or the senile moralist discussion of the moral quality of the method employed.
If he has not a Jesuitical disregard of means, he at
least considers them as but subsidiary processes,
which must not too seriously embarrass the righteous
end in view. He is the greatest living preacher of
righteousness; but it is always righteousness as it
is in Roosevelt. He holds to his conception of public

duty with the tenacity of infallible assurance. If others are too stubborn to accept or too dull to appreciate his more enlightened point of view, the worse is the perversity, or the more the pity. He never reaches either intellectual or moral sublimity, but is transcendent only in action. His deeds are never dull. Even in dealing with the commonplaces of life he infuses into them the energizing spirit of his own nature. He dramatizes the Ten Commandments and vitalizes time-worn moral maxims with a spirit and power as if they were fresh pronouncements to arouse the energies of a lethargic world. A man almost or wholly without Anglo-Saxon blood, he is the ideal embodiment of the Anglo-Saxon spirit which glorifies beyond all things else the power of doing things.

> " The Celt is in his heart and hand,
>   The Gaul is in his brain and nerve."

He is absolutely self-centered, and believes that he was sent into the world to set things right. The world has accepted him at his own appraisement, as it is prone to do with all ardent natures, especially if they be serious and incessant in the advocacy of their high pretensions. He accomplishes his sovereign purposes while his fellow-citizens stand amazedly at gaze, as an astronomer when a new luminary flashes suddenly upon his vision and pursues its uncomputed orbit across the skies.

HIS EARLY CAREER

He begins his public career by defying James G. Blaine, the magnetic statesman, who, like Agamemnon, was a born king of men. He leads a little hand-

ful of rough and ready dare-devils up a little hill in
a little skirmish, and is covered with the military
glamour and glory of a great hero in a great conflict. Our party captains, fearing the exorbitancy
of his foreshadowed power, force him into the Vice-
Presidential office as a sure political quietus, but it
proved to be merely an instance of the folly of men
trying to defeat a career marked out by destiny. The
assassin's bullet takes off McKinley, the beloved, and
installs Roosevelt, the strenuous. His high place but
affords a vantage ground for the exercise of his
strenuousness and power. By the word of his might,
he commands two powerful nations engaged in Ti-
tanic struggle to stay their strife and sue for peace,
and forthwith they obey him. He commands peace
or war, according to the dictates of his high conception of righteousness. With one bold Roosevel-
tian stroke he acquires a canal connecting the mighty
waters which had washed separate shores since recorded time, a consummation which American statesmanship had sought for half a century in vain. He
regulates railroads, throttles trusts, defies labor
cliques, and holds in leash both the millionaire and
the mob. He makes even the wrath of Tillman to
praise him, and the remainder of his wrath he holds
in contempt. The universality of his sway was never
more strikingly illustrated than by the grotesque
spectacle of the last session of Congress, where the
spectator might look and see Roosevelt's mighty
hosts advancing against the stronghold of plutocracy, with Tillman leading on! There is no question of human interest whose magnitude or minuteness
is beyond his strenuous handling. He gives the
American women salutary advice as to their domestic
function and duty; with an off-hand stroke of the
pen seeks to reform English orthography, which has

been slowly modifying from Chaucer to Mark Twain; sets up as expert detective of nature fakirs; while Americans, of however high reputation and standing, who persist in seeing things under other than his own angle of vision, may regard themselves as lucky indeed if they escape being relegated to his famous " Index Prævaricatorum."

THE WEAK AND HELPLESS

When one considers what manner of man is this whom the strong and mighty hold in awe, the man who gives the word and the nation obeys, he who speaks and it is done, he might feel disposed to ask who is the despised Negro that he should be mindful of him, or that he should bestow upon him one moment of his august consideration and regard! There is little room for the weak and helpless in a strenuous philosophy which glorifies the valiant man. What hope has the feeble and the heavy laden in a dispensation whose gospel relegates the hindermost to the mercy of his satanic captor? Roosevelt has never been the champion of manhood rights. But rather, like Lyman Abbott, he believes in manhood first and rights afterward. He has little of the humanitarian sentimentalism that would stoop to the infirmities of the weak. His motto is " all men up " who can get up and stand up. But if some men allow themselves to be pushed down, the overthrowers rather than the overthrown command his higher respect because they manifest the greater degree of power. Had he been born at an earlier season he doubtless would have opposed the reconstruction scheme as he now opposes independence for the Philippine Islands. His very nature revolts at the idea of clothing weakness with authority.

ROOSEVELT NOT BAPTIZED WITH THE FIRE OF OUR CIVIL WAR

He is the first commanding statesman of his party who was not baptized with the spirit of the Civil War. The political and civil equality of all men was burned into the soul as the outcome of that great struggle. Orthodoxy in this doctrine was at one time the one determinative test of patriotism, the only passport to public favor and power. But now we have a new Pharaoh who knew not Joseph the black. With the new issue have come new issues. Tax and tariff, trade and transportation, plutocracy and trusts, expansion and subjugation, now monopolize public attention. The issues of life to-day are material rather than moral, and are placed on a hard, unsentimental metallic basis. The dollar is the highest common divisor of values, in terms of which we measure all forms of excellence—yea, even human rights. Indeed, whoever is so archaic in this material day as to insist on the political doctrine of a generation ago is apt to be waived aside as a doctrinaire enthusiast, or perhaps as a moral mollycoddle. Roosevelt embodies the new spirit rather than the old, which he espouses with a moral enthusiasm and a preachment of a type of righteousness which well befits the new faith.

ALTERNATION OF GOOD AND ILL WILL

Roosevelt's relations with the Negro have been marked by an almost whimsical alternation of good and bad impressions. At one time he elicits his highest praise, only at the next turn to evoke his bitterest curses. He is a man of instantaneous impulse and promptitude of action, and is unhampered by the

tedium of logical coherence or consistency of procedure. He follows the latest impulse. The Negro is
by no means the only alternate beneficiary and victim
of his impulsive caprice. The Southern whites have
also experienced like vicissitudes. No President has
been so bitterly abused or so highly extolled by the
white South as its half-son who claims a national
poise by reason of the balance of his blood. The
people who but yesterday were heaping upon him
maledictions which exhaust the lexicon of malignity,
are now proclaiming him their hearts' idol and chief
delight. The praise and blame which he receives at
the hands of the white South and the black race are
at the same time antithetical and complementary.
Like the illumined and bedarkened portions of the
moon's surface, the one increases at the expense of
the other. In dealing with the delicate questions
complicated by race antagonisms he has not as yet
found a policy that is satisfying to all—a statesmanlike consummation devoutly to be wished. And
so whites and blacks alike have experienced, with
fluctuating humor, the variable phases of the amplitude of his impulse.

> "But through the shift of mood and mood
>   Mine ancient humor saves him whole,
>   The cynic devil in his blood
>   That makes him mock his hurrying soul."

AS CIVIL SERVICE COMMISSIONER

Theodore Roosevelt entered upon his public ministry as an ardent advocate of administrative purity.
He believed in righteous methods applied to public
business. It was as Civil Service Commissioner that
he first came in practical contact with the race issue.
He served as Commissioner under the second admin-

istration of Grover Cleveland, who himself was a consistent disciple of administrative reform. It was the boast of many of the supporters of the new administration that they would take the departments at Washington out of mourning by removing all the darksome embellishments in the shape of colored employees. But Grover Cleveland was made of the same sort of stern, dogged integrity as his doughty young Commissioner. Mr. Roosevelt strenuously insisted that all applicants should be treated according to their degree of fitness on the established scale of merit, to the utter disregard of such extraneous issues as race, color or political alignment. It was due in large part to the courageous insistence of this intrepid Republican official under a Democratic administration, backed up by the stubborn honesty of his chief, that black applicants for clerical positions were not blackballed by a party which had posed as their traditional political adversary. It cannot be claimed that Commissioner Roosevelt assumed this attitude out of any special regard for the brother in black, or rather the brother in colors, but to preserve the integrity of his principles. It is a very imperfect philosophy which breaks down at the color line. That scheme of political or moral ethics which awaits answer to the query, " Of what complexion is he? " before applying its beneficence cannot be entertained by a noble nature or a broadly enlightened mind. There is nothing in Roosevelt's strenuous philosophy that would cause him to propound this query or await its answer. If the Negro can drink of the cup of which the white man drinks and be baptized with the baptism with which he is baptized withal, he holds that he should share with him the glory, honor, and power of his kingdom. If his faith in the Negro is small it is only because he has not been impressed with sufficiently numerous examples of strenuosity and success to guarantee it as a race characteristic.

AS ROUGH RIDER

Roosevelt's second point of contact with the Negro race was during the Spanish War. In that famous charge up San Juan Hill—or was it Kettle Hill?—the courage and intrepidity of the Negro troops saved Colonel Roosevelt and his Rough Riders from utter destruction. Had it not been for their courageous intervention he would have been cut off in the flower of his youth, and his dazzling career lost to the American people. Gratitude is not characteristic of a self-centered nature. When one is overburdened with a sense of his ordained primacy, he naturally looks upon lesser men as being put into the world as auxiliaries to his higher mission. While the whole world was extolling the prowess of the Negro soldier, it was reserved for the chief beneficiary of that prowess to sound the sole discordant note. In a notable magazine article, where our present-day warriors are wont to fight their battles with an ingenuity and courage rarely equalled on the tented field, Colonel Roosevelt either discredited their valor or damned them with such faint praise as to dim the luster of their fame. This ungenerous criticism dumbfounded the Negro race. Disparagement of the Negro soldier, as subsequent developments have clearly shown, touches the pride and arouses the resentment of this race as nothing else can do. The Negro's loyalty and patriotism, as exemplified in all the nation's wars, is perhaps the chief tie of endearment that binds him to the heart of the American people. If that tie becomes tenuous his hold upon

the nation's affection would be precarious indeed.
For a time there was no more unpopular man in
America throughout Afro-Americandom. But election time was approaching. Political exigencies
made him the available candidate for the governor-
ship of the Empire State of New York. The chief
factor in this availability was the military glamour
that gathered about him because of San Juan Hill,
where the colored troops fought so nobly. The results at this election depended upon the colored vote,
whose resentment he had aroused. Candidate Roosevelt so mollified and qualified the strictures of Colonel Roosevelt as to take away much of the keenness
of the sting. By the use of such blandishments as
the politician knows well how to apply to salve the
sores of an aggrieved class during the unrest of a
heated campaign, the injury was forgiven, or at
least held in abeyance. Under the rallying cry of
the Grand Old Party the Negro vote came to the
rescue and supported him almost to a man. The
slender margin of his victory showed that his success
was due to that support. Had the Negro persisted
in a spiteful spirit and sought vengeance at the polls
his political career doubtless would have been cut
short and the pent-up energies of his nature must
have sought outlet through a different channel. It
was thus that the Negro saved his political life at the
ballot-box as he had saved his physical life on the
battlefield.

AS GOVERNOR OF NEW YORK

During his brief service as Governor he appointed
one or two colored men to unimportant positions and
entertained a colored artist at the gubernatorial
mansion. He accepted an invitation to deliver the

dedicatory address at the unveiling of the Frederick Douglass monument at Rochester. Perusal of this address enables one to sympathize with an official who feels forced to perform a ceremony in which he has little spirit or zest, in order to accommodate a constituency whom it is desirable to keep in good humor. On the whole his administration as Governor preserved the general attitude of his party toward its black allies without any notable departure either to their benefit or disadvantage.

As candidate for Vice-President and for President he not only secured the black man's loyal support, but commanded his enthusiastic, yea, rapturous applause.

THE APPOINTMENT OF CRUM

Toward the latter part of McKinley's administration there were mutterings of disquiet and unrest among the Afro-American contingent. After the unfortunate outcome of the Lake City horror, it was reported that the President had abandoned the policy of appointing colored men to Federal offices in the South. It was also whispered that he was giving aid and encouragement to the propaganda of the Lily Whites, a breed of political exotics which neither toils nor spins, but delights to array itself in all the spoils and splendor of office. An open revolt was narrowly averted during the campaign of 1900. When Theodore Roosevelt became President the Negro's hopes revived. Here was a man of granitic character whose courageous righteousness on all national questions admitted of no variableness nor shadow of turning. The test was not long in coming, and Roosevelt stood it unfalteringly. Dr. William D. Crum, a most highly capable and respected

citizen of Charleston, South Carolina, became his
party's choice for collector of that ancient and honorable port. His name was sent to the Senate for
confirmation. The whole white South became en-
raged and lashed itself into fury. Was this a re-
opening of the issue at Charleston supposed to have
been settled at Lake City? Political agitation, especially when tinged with race antagonism, never
obeys the formulas of logic. It booted nothing to
point out that colored men had held throughout the
South the highest Federal places since the days of
Grant. It was also shown that both at Savannah
and Wilmington, more important ports environing
Charleston on the south and on the north, colored
men sat at the receipt of customs.

All sorts of direful predictions filled the air. The
ear of the nation tingled with the choice of blood-
shed, race war, Negro domination, Anglo-Saxon superiority, and like rhetorical fustian which such an
occasion is calculated to evoke. But Roosevelt stood
by his guns as he always does while the firing continues. The sleepy old city by the sea had not had
so much national attention focused upon it since the
firing upon Fort Sumter. The Republican leaders
became frightened. Some were disposed to balk,
others to dodge. It was Roosevelt who applied the
whip and inspirited his party to stand by its great
traditions. In the midst of this raging controversy
he took occasion to announce to the world that he
would not shut the door of hope upon any class of
American citizens. The principle was established.
Crum was confirmed. The door of hope still stands
ajar; albeit few there be who enter thereat. The
swarthy collector now sits calmly at his window over-
looking Fort Sumter, straining his eyes for sight of
an occasional ship in quest of unlading or clearance

at his port. The citizens are again tracing their favorite phantoms. The good old city has sunken into its traditional ways, reveling in the glory of by-gone days, dreaming of things of yore in the shadow of Calhoun's Monument, and basking in the soft, silvery moonlight over the Battery. No more heed is taken of the racial personality of the dignified and leisurely collector than of the cut of his coat or the color of his necktie.

THE INDIANOLA POST OFFICE

At Indianola where an irascible community defied the national authority because of the unfashionable color of a Federal official, the President upheld the national dignity and prestige with a firm and unflinching hand.

THE BOOKER WASHINGTON DINNER

A simple act of civility on the part of the President toward an eminent colored American called down upon his head the fires of wrath of his white brethren in the South. Dr. Booker T. Washington, the consulting statesman for the Negro race, was invited to dinner at the White House. There is, perhaps, no other person in America of like standing and relation to public questions who has not received such semi-official courtesy. But immediately a mighty storm arose. Had the President suddenly turned traitor and flagrantly violated our most sacred religious or moral code he could not have been more bitterly or blatantly denounced. That two gentlemen of world-wide reputation and of congenial temperament should occasionally sit together at meat might naturally be expected anywhere outside of the

Brahmin caste. Mr. Washington is our only domestic ambassador.

He has been picked out and set up as the representative of an overshadowed nation surrounded by
an overshadowing one. An ambassador usually has
immediate access to the presence of the chief ruler to
whom he is accredited without the intermeddling of
official understrappers. Nice courtesies and high
civilities usually accompany diplomatic procedure.
Should the representative from Corea or Hayti or
Turkey be invited to dine alone with the President
at the White House the act would hardly be construed into one of social intimacy, but it would be
regarded merely as a convenient opportunity to consult over some weighty matters of state. Indeed,
only a few days after the famous Washington dinner
a red Indian chief who had not passed beyond the
blanket and feather stage of civilization was received
by the President and the incident only excited curious pleasantry. Mr. Washington has mingled in
close pleasant personal touch with princes and po-
tentates of the Old World and with merchant princes
and money barons of the New. He is entirely familiar with high social favors. The colored race has
not the slightest concern with whom Mr. Washington, in his personal capacity, may or may not be
invited to dine. A man's dinner list is his private
affair. It is the prerogative of every citizen to
extend, accept, or decline such invitation, according
to the dictates of his own taste and pleasure. But
to affirm as a principle that the man who is looked
upon as the chiefest among ten millions, in his am-
bassadorial capacity, is not eligible to the established
modes of courtesy, at the high court of the nation,
cannot be accepted with satisfaction by any manly
man of the blood thus held in despite.

These acts on the part of the President evoked the highest plaudits from the colored race. It was felt that his views were broad, based upon the fundamental principle of our institutions which accord to all classes of citizens the same official consideration and courtesy. Indeed, these laudations became so loud and fulsome that they must have proved embarrassing to one who did not pose as the special champion of an unpopular class.

POLICIES NOT SUSTAINED

But it must be said that these evidences of friendship and good will have not been systematic and sustained, nor followed up to their logical conclusion. Roosevelt never surrenders, but often seems to evacuate his stronghold as soon as he has demonstrated the enemy's inability to capture it. In the final estimate of history, if his reputation falls short of superlative greatness, it will be because he lacks consecutiveness and persistence of purpose and policy. He is not permanently wedded to any one question as the dominant note of his career. He suddenly takes up a measure, settles it and drops it, and goes in quest of issues new. And so in dealing with the Negro. He has established the principle, but has desisted at the point of practical operation. Crum was made collector of Charleston in face of a frowning South, but he makes no more such appointments against local opposition. He closed the post office at Indianola, but it was shortly reopened in substantial harmony with the contentions of its white patrons. He preserved a dignified and becoming silence while the storm of wrath raged over the Booker Washington dinner, but no more do he and the famous Tuskegeean break pleasant bread and shake

the friendly glass while conferring over weighty matters of the nether state.

The tentative policies which President Roosevelt
has pursued concerning the political welfare of the
race have not been calculated to command their cor-
dial co-operation and cheerful acquiescence. These
may be considered under three distinct heads.

1. His scheme of selecting referees with whom to
consult on political dealings in the South is something new under the political sun. While he has
sought diligently to find men of the highest standing
and character to serve in this consultive capacity, yet
his selections have usually been of the Democratic
persuasion, and sometimes of strong anti-Negro bias.
According to the universal method of American politics, the administration is controlled in its local matters by the leaders of the organization of the same
party faith. When an administration discards its
own party supporters and seeks advice from its political adversaries it may not expect the approval
of the regular workers who have borne the brunt and
burden of battle. This feeling is by no means confined to the Negro race, but is shared in or perhaps
it would be more accurate to say is directed by the
white manipulators of the shattered Republican
fragments in the South.

BOOKER WASHINGTON AS SPOKESMAN

2. Dr. Booker T. Washington has been chosen
as referee at large and as the sole spokesman for the
entire Negro race. His selection was not due to his

political activity or experience, for the whole tenor
of his teaching has been to persuade his race to place
less proportional stress on politics and to concentrate its energies upon things economic and material.
But by reason of his general prominence and the
world-wide esteem he was put in command of political
forces, to the relegation of war-scarred veterans who
had borne the heat and burden of the day. Othello
naturally objects to his loss of occupation. Most
of them have yielded, but only after they learned
that the only road to official favor was the straight
and narrow path that leads to Tuskegee. No Negro,
whether in Vermont or Texas, whatever has been his
service to the party, can expect to receive consideration at the hands of the President unless he gets the
approval of the great educator. It should, in all
fairness, be said that this position was not of Mr.
Washington's own seeking. It has on more than one
occasion caused him serious embarrassment. It
might seem that active participation in politics would
impair his usefulness along other lines to which he
has devoted the chief energies of his life. It is needless to say, as some are wont to aver, that Mr. Washington's function as adviser to the President does not
make him a practical political participant. The pro-
curement of office and the manipulations incident
thereto are the chief concern of the typical politician. Mr. Washington was impressed into this service on the demand of the President, which no patriotic citizen feels inclined to refuse. Indeed, there is
no prominent Negro who would not have accepted
the assignment upon the slightest intimation that he
might be the Presidential choice. That Mr. Washington has filled the assignment with an eye single
to the best interest of his race is wholly aside from
the merits of the question. Mr. Roosevelt would

readily assent to the proposition that the political
boss is an undesirable person. And yet he has set up
Mr. Washington as the boss of ten millions, and
commanded the rest to obey him on penalty of political disfavor. He has put at his disposal the means
by which all bosses retain their influence—the persuasive power of public patronage. For where the
patronage is, there the subserviency of the politician
will be also. This policy is not calculated to teach
the Negro the needed lesson in self-government and
manly political activity.

Should succeeding administrations follow Mr.
Roosevelt's example in this regard, the Negro would
remain in perpetual thraldom to an intermediary boss
set up at the whim or caprice of whoever happens
to be President. We cannot hope that every administration will be as fortunate in its selection as Mr.
Roosevelt has been. Contemplation of the continuance of such conditions is repugnant to every principle of manly American politics.

FEDERAL OFFICES FOR NORTHERN NEGROES

3. Strangely enough, one of the most significant
moves of the President affecting the political life of
the Negro has almost or wholly escaped attention.
He has shifted the center of gravity from the South
to the North. Hitherto the important Federal places
accorded the race have gone to persons below the
Mason and Dixon line. This recognized the race as
a factor in local Republican organizations and gave
some prestige at national conventions. It also recognized the potential political rights of the Negro
which neither suppression nor temporary nullifica-
tion can take away. To withhold recognition because
suppression has rendered non-effective the exercise

of political power seems to be equivalent to an abandonment of the principles for which the Republican party has stood from the days of Grant until now. The Minister to Hayti, the Register of the Treasury, the Fourth Auditor of the Treasury, the most conspicuous positions given to the race, are filled by Negroes from the North. Such appointments have not been made solely on the basis of the local weight and influence, but as recognition and satisfaction of the claims of the entire race. But one commanding national position is now held by a Southern Negro, and that is the recordership of deeds for the District of Columbia, a purely local office which has widespread fame as being the conceded allotment to the Negro, whether Democrats or Republicans are triumphant. The favorites of political fortune have come from the North and from the South, from the East and from the West, and ensconced themselves in this snug office, while the voteless sons of the District have been ignored. Dame Rumor has it, or had it, that among the first acts of the present administration was the shifting of the colored collector of the port of Wilmington, N. C., to the District of Columbia to relieve embarrassment to the Lily White propaganda, which he at that time is said to have encouraged. Judge Peter C. Pritchard, who was then the administration's intermediary in Southern politics, could write an interesting inside account of this transaction. It would seem from present tendency that there are to be no more new Negro appointees in the South, but merely a continuance in office of those officials against whom local Democratic protest is not too loud and boisterous. It requires little power of prevision to foresee the outcome of this policy. In a few years there will not be a Negro Federal official south of the Mason and Dixon line.

This would prove to be a blow to the race, for which the appointment of Northern Negroes were but a poor compensation. When the Southern Negro has been eliminated from the political equation with the connivance and implied sanction of the party of Grant and Sumner, it will not be long before his Northern brother will begin to feel its baleful effect. With a rare political sagacity the Northern Negro feels that in order to preserve his own liberties he must insist upon the rights of his brethren in the South. Shifting the stress of political emphasis from the region where the Negro is, to the section where he is not, is like placing the center of gravity outside the basis of support. The result must be unstable political equilibrium. But here again the President is displaying his characteristic disposition which glorifies the effective component of force, and takes little heed of power, reserved or suppressed, which fails of effective expression. The Negro vote in the North is a practical present political dynamic. In the South it is an inert potentiality, whose unfoldment, like faith, is the substance of things hoped for, the evidence of things not seen. The President deals with the real and the tangible rather than the remote and the contingent. While this policy may seem to answer the immediate demands of political exigencies, it will prove disastrous to the Negro political outlook and vista.

THE BROWNSVILLE AFFAIR

The chief irritating issue between the President and the Negro race is the outcome of a most deplorable incident. The Negro soldier has ever been an object of detestation to the Southern whites. The soldierly spirit is incompatible with the status to which the black man is assigned in their political and social scheme. Every Southern State has disbanded its colored militia. This feeling was accentuated by the Spanish War, where Negro and Southern white troops were placed on a footing of soldierly equality, and where the black troops gained the higher meed of glory. Occasional friction between local authorities and Negro troops passing through the South to and from the front but added fuel to the flame.

In face of this feeling a Negro battalion was quartered in an obscure town on the remote frontier of Texas. The air about Brownsville became tense with trouble. Citizens goaded soldiers to the point of acute irritation. One dark night some shooting was done in the streets, resulting in the death of a barkeeper and the wounding of an officer of the law. The alarm was sounded that the Negro soldiers had " shot up the town." Race passion was stirred to the utmost. Brownsville would have been drenched in blood had it not been for the firm attitude of the gallant commander of the fort. The local grand jury could not find sufficient regular evidence for indictment of the hated troops quartered among them. Word was flashed to the commander-in-chief at Washington, who forthwith proceeds to deal with the matter out of hand. The army inspector was dispatched to the scene to investigate and report. Unfortunately the inspector was a man of Southern birth and bias. The distress cry of the city through the undercurrent of communication made its subconscious appeal with Masonic secrecy and force. Every thoughtful student knows that where race passion is aroused the judicial temperament takes flight. Suspicion or even suggestion of wrongdoing on the part of the Negro if reiterated with loud outcry and demand for blood is assumed to be confirmation strong as holy writ. Instantaneously every white man aligns himself on the side of his race. Where racial instinct is appealed to the laws of evidence have little weight. "Lynch the brutes!" was on the lips of every citizen, and the execution was stayed only by the too fearful aspect of Uncle Sam's bayonets. In the midst of this inflammable state of things a son of Georgia, as inspector-general, repaired to Brownsville. Instantly he assumed the feeling of the community. The investigator acted the rôle of prosecutor with preconceived conviction of guilt. He accepted the representation of the citizens of Brownsville and propounded a few shrewdly calculated questions to the suspected soldiers, whose answers were designed to confirm their guilt. No opportunity was afforded them to prove their innocence. Assuming the existence of a criminal conspiracy, he demanded of the non-commissioned officers the names of their guilty companions. Compliance with this request would inevitably have been self-incriminatory, convicting the respondent of murder if personally involved, or of guilty knowledge if a non-participant. Following the method of the mob in dealing with a black culprit, he declared them guilty, and graciously offered them the opportunity to confess. Affirming their innocence, they refused to confess; and declaring their ignorance, they declined to inform on their fellows. The inspector hastened to Washington and reported to the President that some fifteen or twenty men out of a total of one hundred and sixty-seven had shot up the town, murdered and maimed its citizens, while the rest had guilty knowledge of the deed, but were disposed to shield their companions in crime. The city of Brownsville had worked out the case with such cir-

cumstantial confirmation of detail as to deceive even
the commanding major, who reluctantly assented to
the findings of the inspector-general. On fuller investigation, however, Colonel Penrose changed this
opinion and now stoutly affirms his belief in the innocence of his men.

When this report was presented to President
Roosevelt he was bound to accept in good faith the
findings of the inspector-general, the regularly authorized agent for such service, and especially so
when concurred in by the chief officers of the command.

A flood of righteous indignation welled up within
him at this outrage upon the national arm. He would
teach the wrongdoers a lesson which would never be
forgotten. The color of the offenders, he stoutly
avers, neither mitigated nor magnified the character
of the offense in his mind. The discipline of the
army must be upheld. It is easy to believe that the
President's conduct at this stage was not based upon
consideration of color. He is himself of a military
mold of mind. In military matters, as elsewhere, he
is a law unto himself and has little reverence for
those above, around, or beneath him. He shatters a
military idol with as little hesitancy as he would
reprimand a common soldier. Did he not criticise
and discredit the sagacity of his own commanding
general with a little round robin? The man who
spoke disparagingly of the troops who saved his life
on the battlefield, who unceremoniously reprimanded
General Miles, the gallant head of the army and
hero of many battles; who imputed cowardice to Ad-
miral Schley, our only naval hero who has triumphed
with modern guns over modern armor, might naturally be supposed to act vigorously in case of reported wrongdoers at Brownsville.

Basing his action on General Garlington's report, the President with ruthless hand, though righteous purpose, ignored all forms and precedents of military, judicial, or executive procedure, and proceeded to mete out drastic punishment. Although there was no pretense at determination of individual guilt, and although not more than ten per cent. of the battalion could possibly have participated in the outrage, the whole number were dismissed without honor, and in the hot indignation of his wrath he imposed upon them serious civil disability by executive fiat. The disqualifying feature of his order was flagrantly *ultra vires* and void by virtue of its own nullity. It was afterwards rescinded, but its original issuance stands as a memorial of the state of mind actuating the President at the time.

This order of the President violates every principle of our jurisprudence. It assumed that the men were guilty and imposed upon them the onus of proving their innocence; it condemned them without even the formality of a trial; it imposed punishment without proof of individual culpableness; by it one hundred and fifty probably innocent men were made to suffer in order that fifteen possibly guilty ones might not escape.

The President must have foreseen or forefelt the tumult which the issuance of this order was calculated to excite, for with prudent political sagacity he held it up till the day after the election, in which the Negro vote might prove a determining factor, and especially in the congressional district where the political fate of his son-in-law was involved. In the meantime he had betaken himself to the high seas, planning to return, it would seem, after the clouds had rolled by.

But instead of rolling by to accommodate the return of the President, the clouds continued to gather in density and ominousness. The whole Negro race was dazed. Theodore Roosevelt had for the second time struck at the Negro soldier, the pride and idol of the race. Protest, indignation, cries of outrage flew thick and fast from the Negro press, pulpit, and platform. The great papers of the country with practical unanimity condemned the order as one of unusual and unnecessary severity. Those versed in constitutional lore declared that the President had set a precedent which might prove dangerous to the principle of American liberty. It was reserved for Senator Tillman to describe the act as executive lynching, a description which characterizes the deed with his wonted picturesque aptness of language. It possesses the essential characteristics of mob vengeance. It inflicts punishment on demand of the rabble rather than by judicial process. It furnishes victims to appease popular vengeance without nice regard to the identity of the perpetrator. The punishment of the possibly innocent effectually destroys the evidence by which the guilty might subsequently be apprehended. The Secretary of War with political forethought sought to have the order suspended until further investigation, but to no avail. What was written was written. " The moving finger writes and having writ Moves on; nor all your piety nor wit Shall lure it back again Nor all your tears blot out a line of it."

From a racial point of view it was doubly unfortunate that the President should have selected the weak and helpless Negro, the increasing object of the nation's contumely and despite, upon whom to make this drastic departure from the usual procedure. The disciplinary value of the example would doubtless have been more effective had he applied it in the first instance to the white troops guilty of the offense charged against the colored troops in Ohio some months previous. Coming, too, as it did, swiftly upon the heels of the Atlanta riot, it added the color of justification to that awful slaughter. Indeed, John Temple Graves, the justifier of this atrocious murder of innocent men, employs the same line of justificatory argument as that used to defend the President's position. But the most unjust and unkindest cut of all occurs when the President, acridly assuming a defensive attitude, holds the race up to the world, by executive decree, as fostering a criminal fellowship.

ANNUAL MESSAGE

In the meantime, the session of Congress was approaching. In his annual message the President undertook to discuss the subject of lynching. In this document he imputed to the colored race a lecherous tendency which is not justified by the infrequent occurrence of clearly proved cases of assault. He placed upon the whole race the responsibility of restraining and controlling the wild passion of the dastardly few. In his eagerness to effect the wished-for consummation he overlooked the absurdity of imposing upon a race studiously deprived of governmental power and authority, without the means of inflicting punishment, the obligation of reaching, correcting, and coercing the criminally disposed. This vicarious burden is imposed upon no other class of citizens. The alleged infirmities of the Negro race are thus set forth and embalmed in an official document and held up to the gaze of all the world. However holy and righteous may have been the President's intentions, this message is calculated to do the

Negro more harm than any other state paper ever issued from the White House. Construed as it was in connection with the Brownsville order and the recent Atlanta barbarities, this message seemed to accentuate the Negro's rapidly culminating ills.

With the opening of Congress the Brownsville order assumed the character of political discussion. It threatened to split in twain the triumphant Republican party. The President's closest personal and political friends felt forced to uphold his contentions, though not without apology. The Southern Democrats, with a single and grotesquely singular exception, reversed the tenor of their teachings and traditions and upheld the President in the unwarranted exercise of executive power. The aroused passion of race has twisted their immemorial political doctrine. Then came Senator Foraker, like a gallant knight of old, and stepped into the arena as the champion of the helpless and overborne. The voice of ten million Americans, unheard and unheeded in the conduct of the nation's affairs, found expression in this eloquent and fearless Ohioan. And yet not so much he proclaimed because the victims were black, but because the method employed was violative of the principles of American jurisprudence and liberty. He assumed neither the innocence nor guilt of the accused, but planted himself firmly on the bed-rock principle of the law, that a full and fair trial should precede conviction and punishment. The country and the Senate sided with Mr. Foraker, although by the nice amenities of legislative verbiage they refrained from wounding the Presidential pride. An inquiry by the Senate was ordered. In the meantime the President had dispatched a law officer to Brownsville in quest of confirmatory evidence. He found what he was sent for.

By a prudential intuition these government agents seem to divine the conclusion of the Presidential mind. His method was of the same *ex parte* character as that of the army inspector, and of course the foregone conclusion was confirmed. The President became incensed at the persistent attitude of the colored race, and in several special messages reiterated his inuendoes with redoubled vim and emphasis. Senator Foraker became the principal object of his wrath. It was rumored that at a social function, where secrecy was imposed upon all present, a personal colloquy between the two was sharp and bitter. All of this served to make Senator Foraker the hero and idol of the Negro heart. Foraker gained what Roosevelt lost. The Ohio Senator is the only commanding statesman of our day who has risked his public career on an issue involving the Negro's cause. Whatever may be the immediate outcome of the issue, he has, and will have, his reward, for no one who devotes his powers to the defense of the helpless will fail to receive the highest meed of praise when the rancor and hate of the conflict have passed away.

FORAKER, THE NEGROES' CHAMPION

Under the guidance of Senator Foraker the Senate inquiry has now proceeded for several months. At the instance of the President several eminent Republican Senators reluctantly consented to reinforce the Democrats in upholding his hand. The accused soldiers have been given a hearing. Their straightforward, manly, unwavering testimony in their own behalf has raised in the public mind a reasonable doubt of their guilt. That one hundred and sixty-seven men, ignorant and unlettered, unskilled in the art of double-tongued dialectics, should unite and persist in one straightforward tale and suffer loss of livelihood and honor without one confessing or informing voice would be the most remarkable psychological phenomenon in the history of criminal procedure.

FAR-SIGHTEDNESS AND MYOPIA

On the other hand the citizens of Brownsville have given the most positive and circumstantial evidence of guilt. These far-sighted witnesses have testified under oath that they saw these men in the act and distinguished their uniform, color, and visage at a distance of a hundred yards on a dark night, when the trained eyesight of army officers could not recognize a brother officer ten feet away. The weight of this testimony is weakened by the prepossessions of the witness as well as by its inherent incredibility. Aroused race passion is as heedless of fact as it is of reason and logic. It blunts the physical as well as the moral sense. For any white citizen of Brownsville to say one word contradictory of the popular prejudice means permanent banishment or sure and sudden death. The wealthiest man of the town was assassinated because he had the temerity to question the accuracy of certain of this testimony. Had these Springfield rifles in the hands of men who have never failed to use them when ordered by their commanders proved less dissuasive from violence, and had half a dozen Negro soldiers been lynched on the broadest street of Brownsville in broad daylight, neither the army inspector, nor the President's law officer, nor the Senate committee could have found a single citizen who was able to see such happenings under the bright sunlight of a Texas sky. These same citizens with far-sighted vision in the gloom of night would have developed suddenly cases of myopia that could not distinguish objects of their own handling in open day. The rule works both ways. A witness who will not see that which he does not want to see can easily compound for the failure by seeing things which do not exist in obedience to the demand of prejudice or passion.

The Senate Committee, after prolonged and exhaustive inquiry, brought in a majority report upholding the President's contention as to the guilt of the accused soldiers, with a strong dissentient minority report under the leadership of Senator Foraker. The majority findings were made possible by the solid vote of the Southern members of the committee, whose attitude, it is not unjust to say, had no relation to the judicial merits of the case under inquiry. The minority party often assumes the privilege of casting their vote so as to produce the greatest political embarrassment to the responsible majority. That the vote of these Southern Senators was prompted by racial and political motives and was wholly void of ethical or judicial weight, is seen from the fact that they voted at one time with Foraker to embarrass the administration and at another time, on the same measure, they voted with the administration to embarrass Foraker.

Before the report of the committee could be presented to the Senate, President Roosevelt, by one of his surprising strategic strokes, proclaimed his " vindication," and proposed, through the unsearchable depth of administrative mercy, that the accused might be restored to the service if they could convince him of their innocence. These dismissed and dishonored soldiers might be remanded, not for trial, but for reconsideration of sentence, if they could prove their innocence in the estimation of the man who had served as their judge and executioner and had de-nounced them in the utmost vehemence of language as murderers and criminal conspirators. Senator Foraker aptly characterized this recommendation as " the most remarkable proposition ever submitted to a civilized legislature."

As the matter now stands before the bar of public opinion, this black battalion is at least entitled to a Scotch verdict—" not proven." There is all but a universal concurrence in this verdict except among those whose racial sentiment renders them incapable of considering the case with judicial calmness and poise. But whatever may finally be proved as to the guilt or innocence of some or all of these men, they have not received a " square deal " at the hands of its author, who borrowed the phrase from the gaming table and consecrated it to a higher and worthier ideal.

This affair has shaken the prestige of the President as has no other occurrence in his public career. It gives him no end of keen concern. There is every reason to believe that he could wish the deed undone. He has sought to conciliate the Negro with the blan-dishment of office, but to no avail. With the double view of disconcerting Foraker and reconciling the colored brother, at the psychological moment, when the Ohio Senator was booked to make a strategic move in the Brownsville affair, announcement was made of the intention to appoint a colored citizen to the leading Federal office in the Senator's own State and home city. But as this move seemed to embarrass the President's own friends, including his son-in-law, as much as it did the offending Senator, it was abandoned. But not to be outdone, on the day of the evening that Senator Foraker was announced to sound the keynote of his position in a speech to his constituents, the Associated Press announced to the country that Ralph W. Tyler, a worthy colored citizen of Ohio, had been appointed Auditor of the Treasury Department at Washington. But this conspicuous appointment had not the slightest effect upon racial sentiment, except to intensify it against the President. A nice young man got a nice fat office without changing the attitude of a single Negro in or out of Ohio. The whole race is wounded and sore. There is no division of sentiment. Never before has there been such unanimity. The balm of office cannot heal it. Even the colored members of the President's official household can only preserve a prudent and salutary silence.

When Senator Foraker found that he was unable to get through Congress a simple measure of justice to the dismissed soldiers against the united opposition of the South and the President's personal supporters in his own party, by a skillful parliamentary move, he had the whole issue deferred until after the pending presidential election. A considerable fraction of the Negro voters in the North and West will undoubtedly desert the Republican party on account of the stubborn attitude of the President. This may result in the defeat of his party and of the policies which bear his personal brand. So great a matter the Brownsville fire kindleth.

THE NEGRO'S JUST GRIEVANCE

There has recently appeared a cartoon by a clever Negro artist representing the " Black Man's Burden." It is in the form of a cross, not a crown of thorns, but a cross of skulls. At the top of the vertical upright is the head of Roosevelt; Hoke

Smith and Tom Watson are arranged underneath; on
the left of the crosspiece are Thomas Dixon and
John Temple Graves; on the right, Tillman and Vardaman.   An athletic Negro with broken body is
bowed beneath this awful load.   Theodore Roosevelt,
America's most passionate civil patriot, whose every
impulse beats in sympathetic resonance with the welfare and betterment of the nation, who had stood
firmly by the Negro at Charleston and Indianola,
and who had proclaimed to the race the gospel of a
" square deal " and an open door, is placed as chief
among those who breathe out hatred and slaughter
against the Negro with every vital breath.   It is the
law of human passion that friendship which lapses
or seems to lapse begets the bitterest hate.   The
good deeds are forgotten; the hurtful act rankles
in the soul.   A deliberate and candid judgment would
declare this attitude unjust; but it would be equally
uncandid to deny that it is real.

President Roosevelt is easily the most popular man
in America.   The whites who join issue with him on
the Brownsville incident regard it as a thing apart.
With the Negro it overshadows all else.   With a
consenting nod he could have been re-elected President
almost by acclamation.   Not only so, but he is easily
the foremost man of all the world to-day.   Had the
Peace Congress while sitting at The Hague ushered
in Tennyson's prophesied " Parliament of man, the
Federation of the world," Roosevelt, by unanimous
consent of the participating nations, would have been
chosen speaker of this world-controlling body.   And
yet he has so wounded his colored fellow-citizens that
to-day they stand apart from this world acclaim.
As he treads the dizzy highway of universal fame,
he must feel a certain sad, unsatisfied something
prompting him to become reconciled to his black
brother who may justly have aught against him.